Cowardice

Francesco Scaramuzza, Dante's Inferno, Canto III (1865).
Photograph by Marco Beck Peccoz. Collezione Perizzi, Parma, Italy

Cowardice

A BRIEF HISTORY

Chris Walsh

PRINCETON UNIVERSITY PRESS

PRINCETON AND OXFORD

Copyright © 2014 by Princeton University Press
Published by Princeton University Press, 41 William Street, Princeton, New Jersey 08540
In the United Kingdom: Princeton University Press, 6 Oxford Street, Woodstock,
Oxfordshire OX20 1TW

press.princeton.edu

Jacket art: Still from *Paths of Glory* © 1957 Harris Kubrick Pictures Corp. All rights reserved.
Courtesy of MGM Media Licensing.

Library of Congress Cataloging-in-Publication Data

Walsh, Chris, 1966–
Cowardice : a brief history / Chris Walsh.
    pages cm
  Includes bibliographical references and index.
ISBN 978-0-691-13863-3 (hardback)
1. Fear—History.   2. Cowardice—History.   3. Courage—History.   4. Emotions—
History.   I. Title.
BF575.F2W25 2014
152.4'6—dc23
2014005479

British Library Cataloging-in-Publication Data is available

This book has been composed in Sabon Next

Printed on acid-free paper. ∞

Printed in the United States of America

10 9 8 7 6 5 4 3 2 1

It is with inexpressible Concern that the General upon his first Arrival in the army, should find an Officer sentenced by a General Court-Martial to be cashier'd for Cowardice. A Crime of all others, the most infamous in a Soldier, the most injurious to an Army, and the last to be forgiven; inasmuch as it may, and often does happen, that the Cowardice of a single Officer may prove the Distruction of the whole Army. . . .

—GEORGE WASHINGTON, GENERAL ORDERS, JULY 7, 1775

Where there is a choice between cowardice and violence,
I would advise violence.

—MAHATMA GANDHI, "THE DOCTRINE OF THE SWORD"

It is thus that mutual cowardice keeps us in peace. Were one-half of mankind brave, and one-half cowards, the brave would be always beating the cowards. Were all brave, they would lead a very uneasy life; all would be continually fighting: but being all cowards, we go on very well.

—SAMUEL JOHNSON, *THE LIFE OF SAMUEL JOHNSON*

Let us not speak of them, but look, and pass on.

—DANTE, *INFERNO*

CONTENTS

INTRODUCTION

Before any of us knew who they were or why they had done it or what they might do next, one thing seemed certain: the Boston Marathon bombers were cowards. Overlooking the expressway leading into the city, an electronic billboard flashed the message the day after the bombing, complete with a hashtag: #COWARDS. It felt good to see and say this, a bitter and righteous rebuke to those who would terrorize us. The billboard came courtesy of the International Brotherhood of Electrical Workers, Local 103, and everyone from president Barack Obama to governor Deval Patrick to the management of the Boston Red Sox echoed the sentiment. Something similar had happened a dozen years earlier, when president George W. Bush and many others called the perpetrators of the 9/11 attacks cowardly.

Calling terrorists "cowards" felt good for a few reasons. First, the word satisfies the need to lay offenders low with the nastiest term of abuse, and without resorting to obscenity. There is nothing worse than a terrorist, goes the rough logic, and, as long tradition has it, there is nothing worse than a coward. The cowardly begin the book of Revelation's list (21:8) of those damned to burn forever in a lake of fire, and they are the most despicable souls in Dante's *Inferno*. The Scottish philosopher Adam Smith and the Danish philosopher Søren Kierkegaard held that no one

International Brotherhood of Electrical Workers Local 103

was more contemptible than the coward, an idea that figures as a kind of refrain in the surrealist Russian novelist Mikhail Bulgakov's *The Master and Margarita*.[1] Samuel Johnson asserted that cowardice is "always considered as a topic of unlimited and licentious censure, on which all the virulence of reproach may be lawfully exerted," and it is not hard to find—in just about any age or place—evidence to support that assertion.[2] Here is how Urban dictionary.com defines *coward*:

1. One who is not brave
2. One who fears many things
3. The most insulting word known to man

Calling the 9/11 and Boston Marathon terrorists "cowards" also felt good for the perhaps childish reason that the terrorists had used the term first. In his 1996 fatwa calling for holy war, Osama bin Laden said that American withdrawals from Vietnam and then Beirut had shown that, if attacked, the United States would abandon its commitments in the most cowardly way. The "most disgraceful case," he said, came in Somalia in 1993. After seventeen American soldiers were killed and one pilot's body was dragged through the streets of Mogadishu, U.S. forces withdrew. This was truly cowardly, in bin Laden's view—but then so was Muslim inaction against American military presence in Muslim countries. To remove the stain of this cowardice, he said, righteous Muslims were obliged to attack Americans wherever they were: "Terrorizing you [Americans], while you are carrying arms on our land, is a legitimate and morally demanded duty. . . . The coward is the one who lets you walk, while carrying arms, freely on his land and provides you with peace and security." Not attacking the Americans would be cowardly, and because the Americans had shown themselves to be cowardly, bin Laden reasoned, there was reason to hope that attacking them would bring triumph.[3]

Finally, calling the terrorists "cowards" was comforting. Three days after the Boston Marathon bombing, when the suspects were identified and came out of hiding, armed and dangerous, my family heard the sirens and helicopters. The suspects lived a mile away from us, and that night they killed a Massachusetts Institute of Technology police officer just down the road, then hijacked a car and engaged in a deadly firefight with the police. It was a scary time, but as we followed the orders to "shelter in place"—a phrase we'd never heard before—it was reassuring to think of the suspects as cowardly. If they were cowardly then they were scared too—vulnerable, weak. And thinking them weak somehow made another new phrase—"Boston Strong"—seem more convincingly true.

It felt good to call the terrorists "cowards," but whether it was accurate to do so was another matter. Applying the label to the 9/11 attackers provoked objections from an ideologically diverse group of commentators, from William Safire to Susan Sontag.[4] Dinesh D'Souza raised his objection on Bill Maher's TV talk show *Politically Incorrect*. Strictly speaking, the terrorists were not cowards but "warriors," he said. Maher agreed, claiming that Americans "have been the cowards, lobbing cruise missiles from two thousand miles away. That's cowardly. Staying in the airplane when it hits the building—say what you want about it—it's not cowardly."[5] This conversation was broadcast less than a week after the attacks—not a time for speaking strictly. Raw-nerved viewers were outraged, sponsors balked, and soon *Politically Incorrect* went off the air.

The episode provoked considerable debate about freedom of speech and patriotism. Much less discussed was the question central to the controversy: What is cowardice? The *New York Times* made short work of the matter. Noting that linguists agreed that *cowards* was not the right word for the 9/11 terrorists, the newspaper cited *Webster's New World College Dictionary*'s definition of the word *coward*: "a person who lacks courage, especially one who is shamefully unable to control fear and so shrinks from danger or trouble."[6] The importance of fear to the idea is reflected in the root of the word, the Latin *cauda*, meaning "tail." The cowardly creature "turns tail" to escape danger, or "puts its tail between its legs" in fear and submission. The cowardly lion of the film *The Wizard of Oz* (1939) dramatizes the coward's tail problem in comical fashion when he tries to run even from the wizard, who is supposed to give him courage. "I'd be too scared to ask him for it!" says the lion, fiddling anxiously with his tail, wiping tears away with its brushy tip. Dorothy and the scarecrow stop him from fleeing:

DOROTHY Come on.

LION (*absently tugs at his tail with his paws and gives a wail of fear*) Ow-oo!

SCARECROW (*as they turn*) What happened?

LION (*bawling*) Somebody pulled my tail!

SCARECROW You did it yourself![7]

Yet simply having a tail is not regrettable. A tail helps one maintain balance; it can signal danger to one's mates. Fear itself should *not* be feared but valued as a natural, adaptive response to danger. It is *excessive* fear that makes the coward. Before passing *cauda* on to English, the Old French added the usually pejorative suffix *-ard*.

That cowardice manages to pull its own tail frustrates the effort to come to a clear schematic understanding of it. Aristotle says that the coward is both excessively fearful and deficient in confidence; the reckless person has the opposite problem (not enough fear, too much confidence); the courageous person observes the mean in situations that inspire fear or confidence. It is tempting to visualize the vice–virtue–vice continuum as in this table.

recklessness	courage	cowardice
too little fear	fear/confidence	too much fear
too much confidence	properly proportioned	too little confidence

But, blurring the left end of the table, Aristotle also observed that reckless men are usually in fact cowards; they pretend to courage, ardently hoping for danger to come—only to shrink when it does.[8] On the right side of the table, the Earl of Rochester's eighteenth-century observation that "all men would be cowards if they durst" turns cowards into the envy of the brave.[9] Yes—giving in to one's fears can sometimes be said to require real daring. Suicide, the ultimate act of cowardice in the opinion of some, is in the opinion of others the ultimate act of courage.[10]

Kinds of cowardice can conflict, too. The Roman general Fabius Maximus was mocked for his strategy of keeping to the hills, near enough to Hannibal to threaten him, but never engaging him directly. When Fabius's friends advised him to take the fight to the enemy, he said, "In that case, surely, I should be a greater coward than I am now held to be, if through fear of abusive jests I should abandon my fixed plans."[11] Excessive fear of being or seeming cowardly can lead to cowardice.

Both Aristotle and the dictionary underemphasize the fact that, unless one's responsibilities require one to face danger, avoiding it may not be cowardly but instead prudent. Military codes such as the one articulated in the American *Manual for Courts-Martial* remedy this vagueness by defining cowardly conduct as the "refusal or abandonment of a performance of *duty* before or in the presence of the enemy as a result of fear."[12] The emphasis here is my own: the term *duty* specifies a standard against which we can judge alleged cowardice. The coward fails to do something he is supposed to do.

Duties can themselves conflict, of course. One might be called to duty as a patriot to take up arms to defend one's country, and also as a pacifist to refuse to do so, for example; and what to one person is a sacred duty—to engage in civil disobedience, say—is to another a crime. But the idea of duty can help us detach cowardice from courage. Some philosophers have argued that the terms occupy "different ethical matrices," that while a courageous act is by definition "supererogatory"—done beyond the call of duty—cowardice must be understood *within* the context of a corresponding duty.[13] The U.S. military follows this thinking in its definition of cowardice and in stipulating that the Medal of Honor should be given only to someone who has "distinguished himself conspicuously by gallantry and intrepidity at the risk of his life above and beyond the call of duty."[14]

Keeping cowardice in mind also helps us understand the common tendency to label the "mere" fulfillment of certain duties as courageous. We seem to do so when we refrain from calling those who do not perform such duties cowardly.[15] Consider, for example, the actions of the New York City firefighters and police who went into the World Trade Center on 9/11. Because we do not call the firefighters and police who left the World Trade Center cowards, we can call those who remained inside courageous. Their performance of their duty was, if not technically supererogatory, nonetheless extraordinary.

Still, speaking strictly about these matters has always been very difficult. In Plato's *Laches*, after discussing the many and sometimes contradictory ways men can be courageous or cowardly, Socrates says, "Then what are cowardice and courage? This is what I want to find out." But the protracted conversation about courage that follows proves inconclusive—"Then we have not discovered," Socrates says toward the end of the dialog, "what courage is"— and cowardice is not even mentioned again.[16] Paradoxes abound in discussing both the virtue and the vice, and the vice may be all the more difficult because the attribution of cowardice often results from the perceived lack of some other quality (courage, as the dictionary says, or a sense of duty, honor, or shame). Surely William Ian Miller is right when he asserts that the idea of cowardice may be so various in its manifestations, and in the judgments they provoke, "that a unitary concept can never be sufficiently refined to get the moral call right."[17]

But it is possible to settle on a working definition: A coward is someone who, because of excessive fear, fails to do what he is supposed to do. As we dig into military examples as well as artistic and philosophical explorations of cowardice, this definition will be challenged in just about every way. We will see a form of cowardice characterized by too little fear. We will see duty deemed absurd. We will occasionally see cowards to whom we cannot refer with the masculine pronoun. Like a good coward, though, this baseline formula will give way and live to fight another day, and it will help us see how the idea of cowardice has endured—even as it has lost currency.

Canfield Design

That the idea has lost currency is shown dramatically by a Google Ngram graph that depicts the declining use of the word *cowardice* as a percentage of all words appearing in books in the Google corpus in English between 1800 and 2008 in figure 0.2. The downward slope of *coward* is less steep, falling by half instead of 80 percent, suggesting that the insult—#COWARDS, as the billboard read—endures more strongly than discussion of the idea behind it.[18] Many nearby terms have fallen into almost complete disuse. The 1864 edition of Noah Webster's dictionary offered an elaborate taxonomy that sounds, to twenty-first-century ears, antediluvian: "*Coward* denotes literally one who slinks back like a terrified beast with tail between the legs. A *craven* is literally one who begs off, or shrinks at the approach of danger. A *poltroon* is a mean-spirited coward. *Dastard* has become one of the strongest terms of reproach in our language."[19] The Google Ngram graphs for *craven*, *poltroon*, and *dastard* slope down toward nothing, and the latter two terms today seem cartoonishly archaic.

As the graph shows, mentions of *cowardice* have risen over the last decade, and the uptick for the term *coward* is sharper still. My suspicion is that these increases come from instances of the kind we saw after 9/11 and the Boston Marathon bombings. This is a time-honored way of speaking—linguist H. W. Fowler lamented in 1926 that "the identification of coward & bully has gone so far in the popular consciousness that persons and acts in which no trace of fear is to be found are often called *coward(ly)* merely because advantage has been taken of superior strength or position"[20]—and if enough people misuse a term for long enough, the misusage becomes usage. But a shift in usage suggests that it is not only the currency of cowardice in the sense of circulation that has fallen; the value of that currency has also been debased.

Good riddance, one might say. Cowardice is not the worst thing; reflexive contempt for it is. Too often, conduct is wrongly judged cowardly when it is really prudent or even courageous. Such misjudgment has done terrible damage, most obviously in the undeserved punishment of those men (it is almost always men) who have suffered, even unto death, for their alleged cowardice. Less obvious but far more pervasive harm has been caused by those who fear being judged cowardly and so behave recklessly. Were it not for such fear, history would be a much less bloody affair.

"Cowardice," which in this skeptical view needs quotation marks around it, is an instrument that the powerful use to get the less powerful to do awful things to others and to themselves. [21] The powerful are subject to the force of this instrument too. The fear of being or of seeming "cowardly" has led to savage acts and terrible blunders. Witness the tyrannically sure sense of cowardice that helped the 9/11 terrorists steer their way to slaughter. They were sure that Americans were cowardly and that to turn from battle against them would be cowardly too. The U.S. government's response reflected a similar feeling: the terrorist acts were cowardly, and such cowardice meant that the terrorists and their associates (the people and even the countries who "harbored" them) could be subdued if they were attacked—and it would be cowardly not to attack.

Opponents of the cowardly label can argue that the logic of cowardice is brutal and barbaric. When it comes to judging alleged cowards, those who are "unable to control fear and so shrink from danger or trouble," as the dictionary puts it, should not be judged morally but instead helped therapeutically. By definition, they are "unable"—*they cannot help it*. Cowardice is a misunderstood condition of some kind, often an understandably adverse reaction to trauma. The coward in this light is a victim being crushed by authority, the state, and his peers. The very idea of cowardice is one of his victimizers.

Yet proponents of the contempt for cowardice can say that just because the idea has caused harm does not mean we should throw it out altogether. It asserts the importance of duty, the efficacy of will, and the power—the very existence—of human agency. Properly understood, the idea of cowardice posits a moral self to be held responsible for its choices, and helps clarify and enforce moral thinking. The coward casts a shadow that throws heroes into relief, giving them substance and credibility. In a report describing a battle in which his unit had performed well, Confederate lieutenant general William J. Hardee observed that it would be "unjust to my brave and enduring soldiers, who stood by their colors to the end, if I did not mention that many straggled from their ranks or fell back without orders."[22] Without the possibility of cowardice, courage becomes a hollow notion, a booster's term.

Cowardice, in fact, seems to overshadow courage in soldiers' minds. As combat theorist S.L.A. Marshall noted after World War II, "Whenever one surveys the forces of the battlefield, it is to see that fear is general among men, but to observe further that men are commonly loath that their fear will be expressed in specific acts which their comrades will recognize as cowardice. The majority are unwilling to take extraordinary risks and do not aspire to a hero's role, but they are equally unwilling that they should be considered the least worthy among those present."[23] The wish to avoid the imputation of cowardice has led many to do their duty to the larger group, even the most awful duty of killing and being killed. In his study of the motivation of American Civil War soldiers, James M. McPherson notes that in their letters home men "wrote much about cowardice because they worried they might be guilty of it, and they desperately wanted to avoid the shame of being known as a coward—and that is what gave them courage."[24]

In a similar vein Horace follows his famous testament to patriotic courage—"dulce et decorum est pro patria mori" (it is sweet

and proper to die for one's country)—with far less famous but no
less important lines:

> *mors et fugacem persequitur virum*
> *nec parcit imbellis iuventae*
> *poplitibus timidove tergo*

> [death hunts down also the man who runs away
> and has no mercy on the hamstrings of the unwarlike youth
> and his cowardly back][25]

The ancient Roman poet operates on the same principle as the
Union and Confederate soldiers do: the shame of cowardice reinforces the call for sacrifice.

Exactly, says the other side in this debate: that is the problem.
Shaming people into sacrifice has caused uncountable horrors.

This debate never ends, and it is joined both in individual cases
of alleged cowardice (should we condemn—or sympathize with—
the accused?) and in broader debates about peoples and policies.
Sometimes the debate occurs within us, in our ambivalence when
we struggle to make a judgment about someone's (sometimes our
own) conduct in the face of fear.

Thoughtfully considering cowardice requires not only navigat-
ing between the two sides in this debate, but also steering around
"cowardly" figures such as terrorists, who are often joined in the
public mind by serial killers, rapists, pedophiles, and other preda-
tory criminals. Calling such figures cowardly exploits the contempt
we feel about cowardice, but it is also, as we have seen, of doubtful
accuracy. The more significant problem this usage presents is that it

makes cowardice seem a rare and monstrous thing. #COWARDS: the flashing billboard applies to them, but not to us.

Sensational villains distract us from thinking about the idea in a way that is both more quotidian and more profound, a cowardice more common but also less commonly contemplated. The classic depiction of those guilty of this sort of cowardice occurs very early in Dante's *Inferno*. Just past the sign that says to abandon all hope, just after he passes through the gate of hell, Dante hears a noise so terrible it makes him weep. In languages familiar and strange, from voices whispering and shrill, hoarse and anguished, come lamentations and rages, cries and sighs, whimpers and screams; there is also the sound of slapping—an awful, woeful din. Dante learns from his guide Virgil that these are the abject wretches who lived with neither disgrace nor praise. Paradise won't have any such shades tainting its beauty, and the Inferno is barred lest the condemned have someone to glory over. (This is what makes them the most despicable—in the root sense of being-looked-down-upon—souls in the *Inferno*.) So there the numberless cowards are, not across the Acheron in hell proper, but in the anteroom, hell's squalid lobby, where they are doomed to wait for all eternity.[26]

The terms Dante uses for these souls have been variously translated as "neutrals," "trimmers," "opportunists," and "nonparticipants," as well as "cowards." The last is the best catchall word, for their sin is cowardice in its most basic form: the fearful failure in the duty to *live*.[27] In contrast to those who perpetrated spectacular, evil acts, these souls were cowardly because of what they did not do or say—even because of what they failed to see, or know, or be. Between the spectacular criminals and the tepid, timid neutrals lies the paradigmatic candidate for the examination of cowardice: the soldier. Aristotle said that the fear of death in battle brings out the truest courage, because battle's dangers are greater and more noble than any others.[28] Millennia after Aristotle, war is still extraordinarily representative in our imaginations. William Ian Miller asserts that a book about courage that did not pay attention to war would be "hollow at its core."[29] The same can be said for a book about cowardice. Even though the relevance of cowardice to combat has increasingly been called into question, the cowardly soldier remains the poster boy, so to speak, for cowardice.

Stories of cowardice can be extraordinarily rich in conflict and drama, yet, aptly enough, they have been honored mostly with evasion. It may be the most common and profound human failing, but cowardice remains strikingly underreported and underanalyzed. A Spanish proverb observes, "De los cobardes no se ha escrito nada" (Of cowards, nothing is written). In his long career as a military historian, Max Hastings has noted, "No US or British regimental war diary that I have ever seen explicitly admits that soldiers fled in panic, as of course they sometimes do."[30] The details of the cases of 306 soldiers executed by British authorities for cowardice and desertion in World War I were kept a state secret for over seventy years.[31] During the recent campaign for pardons for these men, J. Douglas Harvey, an activist in the campaign as well as a memoirist and World War II veteran, wrote that the topic of cowardice is one "that has largely been ignored in the annals of British military history. In fact, to unearth evidence pointing in that direction takes considerable effort and would in the end prove inconclusive, for so many of the pertinent records have vanished or been deliberately destroyed. Cowardice and its reasons will probably always remain a deeply obscured subject."[32] The world does not allow cowards any fame, Dante's guide Virgil tells him, and even Virgil himself, giving the tour of sin that is the *Inferno*, does not want to discuss the numberless cowards who dwell just inside hell's gate. "Let us not speak of them," he tells Dante.[33]

Cowardice seems complicit in its obscurity. Kierkegaard, who may have made more of the subject than any other philosopher, noted how it is not "noisy and alarming, but quiet" and that "there must be something wrong with cowardliness, since it is so detested, so averse to being mentioned, that its name has completely disappeared from use."[34] After war, when victors write history, as they proverbially do, they focus on their bravery and triumphs. If cowardice enters the narrative, it generally does so in the distance, a feature of the vanquished enemy. When war is on, cowardice on one's own side does not get much attention, except perhaps to note its absence. In the middle of World War II, a German magazine noted that, thanks to the political education of its citizens, "cowards have been abolished. For the cases of cowardly conduct are so vanishingly rare that as exceptional phenomena they can be dealt with with exceptional severity."[35] Two years later, in December 1944, a front page article in the *New York Times* noted that "not a single American soldier in France has been executed for cowardice . . . or any other military offense for which death is mandatory." It was "a record believed to be unparalleled in modern war. . . ."[36] A little over a month later, U.S. Army private Eddie Slovik was executed for desertion in Saint Marie-aux-Mines, France, the only American executed for a military crime since the Civil War. The *Times* did not mention Slovik's case until 1954, when a book about it was published.

Being paired with that most dramatic and attractive virtue, courage, helps cowardice hide. Usually vice gets more press than virtue. Pride draws our attention more than humility; lust is obviously sexier than chastity. But courage almost always steals the show from cowardice.[37] In Siegfried Sassoon's "The Hero," a 1916 poem about a woman learning of the death of her son in the Great War, the officer who delivers the news tells "some gallant lies" and leaves the mother feeling proud of her "brave" and "glorious" son. But the officer leaves thinking

> how "Jack," cold-footed, useless swine,
> Had panicked down the trench that night the mine
> Went up at Wicked Corner; how he'd tried
> To get sent home, and how, at last, he died,
> Blown to small bits. And no one seemed to care
> Except that lonely woman with white hair.[38]

Thus does courage cover for and cover over cowardice.

Cowardice is also at a disadvantage against its opposing vice, rashness. One might think they should be equally reviled but, as Johnson pointed out, rashness is "never mentioned without some kind of veneration."[39] Apparently it is better to act, even rashly, than to risk being thought cowardly. In ancient Rome, generals were never tried for "tactical stupidity," but they were sometimes tried for cowardice.[40] In the run-up to the Spanish-American War, one U.S. congressman noted, "I have no sympathy with those rash, intemperate spirits who would provoke war simply for the sake of fighting, and yet I would rather follow them, and suffer all the miseries and misfortunes their heedlessness would bring than follow those other contemptible and mercenary creatures who are crying out for 'peace at any price.'" These remarks met with great applause.[41]

Why such an imbalance in our disregard for these vices? Johnson reasons that rashness is less reviled, and sometimes even venerated, because it can be seen to represent an excess of courage, and because such excess can be checked. A deficiency, such as that of the coward, is much harder to remedy. Johnson also observes that rashness and cowardice pose equal threats to "any publick or private interest."[42] This may not always be so, however, for while the enemy will likely stop the rash soldier eventually, the cowardly soldier can continue indefinitely, seeking his own safety and sowing panic as he goes, the miles of his flight, and the extent of his damage, checked only by the strength of his legs.

Narratively speaking, cowardice typically must content itself to serve as footnote or footman, fit sometimes to begin a story but rarely to feature in it. Henry Morford's 1864 novel *The Coward: A Novel of Society and the Field in 1863* begins as the young Philadelphia lawyer Carlton Brand chooses not to fight for the Union at the Battle of Gettysburg, even though it is the Confederacy's great attempt to gain a foothold in the North and in his very own state. He confesses to his sister something he had believed about himself all along: he is a coward. But the bulk of the novel depicts Brand performing an amazing variety of brave feats. Every episode of the 1960s television Western *Branded* opened with the scene of a man being stripped of his insignia, having his sword broken, and being expelled from the Union Army as punishment for cowardice. The rest of the hour depicted this same man's acts of courage.[43]

The scarcity of primary source material is easier to understand than the lack of scholarly work on the subject. Every other species of human baseness, it seems, has rated a monograph; the seven deadly sins have been dissected. Yet no one has devoted a scholarly book or even a substantial article to cowardice in and of itself. Some fifteen years ago, having already written a book about humiliation and then one about disgust, William Ian Miller set out to complete a trilogy of studies of human lowliness with a book about cowardice. He found that he could not do it. His intended subject "gave way," he wrote; "that's what cowardice always does."[44] The book Miller wound up publishing makes many subtle and important points about cowardice, but it is titled *The Mystery of Courage*. A gap in scholarship and general intellectual discourse endures.

Yet although no scholarly book has been devoted to the subject, and although historical records are not plentiful, cowardice has not escaped notice altogether. Military leaders have always grappled with the challenge of preventing and punishing it. Since ancient times, philosophical contemplation of courage has often included the contemplation of cowardice as well; something similar can be said about the explorations of courage in the work of poets, playwrights, novelists, and filmmakers. Rich if comparatively brief traditions in anthropology, sociology, literary studies, cultural studies, and gender studies have examined how moral codes are conceived and applied. Psychologists and neurologists have examined how human beings experience and react to fear and trauma.[45] The campaign for posthumous pardons that occasioned the activist Harvey's observation that many records about cowardice have disappeared or been destroyed resulted in the release, twenty-five years before their status as state secrets was to expire, of the records of the soldiers executed by the British.[46] Records of American court-martial cases involving cowardice are also available.[47] And though Virgil does not want to speak of them, he does tell Dante to look at the souls he sees in the anteroom, and when Dante presses him about why they are weeping and wailing so, Virgil relents a little, saying, "I will tell thee very briefly."[48]

A variety of touchstone texts and historic figures and episodes illuminate the American conception of cowardice that is the primary though not exclusive focus of these pages. Samuel Davies's 1758 sermon *The Curse of Cowardice* and Morford's *The Coward* announce their unusual preoccupation in their titles. Cowardice also figures centrally in Stephen Crane's 1895 novel *The Red Badge of Courage: An Episode of the Civil War*,[49] and in James Jones's *The Thin Red Line* (1962), a novel Jones said he wrote in order to show that "bravery" and "cowardice" have no "human reference any more."[50] William Bradford Huie wrote two books that focused on the topic—the nonfiction work *The Execution of Private Slovik* (1954) and the novel *The Americanization of Emily* (1959)—both of which were turned into films (in 1974 and 1964, respectively). There seems to be no such thing as a famous coward, but figures such as Eddie Slovik did achieve a kind of prominence, and men such as Theodore Roosevelt and George S. Patton had famously severe attitudes toward the cowardly. There are even a few heroes in these pages, brave men driven in part by the terrible stigma of cowardice. John Callender, for example, was court-martialed for cowardice at Bunker Hill but afterward fought with great distinction for the Continental Army. Sergeant Georg-Andreas Pogany was briefly infamous when he was accused of cowardice early in the 2003 invasion of Iraq; since that time he has become a relentless advocate for military veterans—a courageous soldier in what William James called the moral equivalent of war.

Ranging widely through such sources and sometimes revisiting them from different angles, while also striving to follow Virgil's example in being brief, this book traces the diminishing significance and enduring power of cowardice on and beyond the battlefield. Chapter 1 surveys how the idea of cowardice has figured in American history, presenting a profile that, from a certain point of view, has not changed in 250 years. What Samuel Davies called a curse in 1758 retains its power to insult and provoke today. Investigating the deep roots in human history and prehistory that help explain this persistent power, chapter 2 considers also why we are so conflicted about cowardice, as well as why human culture addresses this conflict most centrally in its judgment of the conduct of men at war. Chapters 3 through 5 trace the movement suggested by the graph of diminishing mentions of the word. Focusing on duty, fear, and moral agency in turn, these chapters explore how the meaning and utility of the idea of cowardice has, especially in the past century and especially in its archetypal, military setting, faded in significance.

This development is not inexorable or universal—we will see many cases of resistance to it—but it does suggest the possibility that, without its archetypal frame of reference, the idea of cowardice has also become less significant in our everyday, civilian lives. Has a semantic shift impoverished our ethical vocabulary? This is a question that informs this book and a vision—those abject souls flailing and wailing in the *Inferno*—that haunts it throughout, but that comes into focus in chapter 6, which explores cowardice beyond the battlefield, in the lives of criminals and all-too-law-abiding citizens, in philosophy and religion and love, in society and in ourselves.

This is not the most pleasant topic—maybe another reason it has been avoided. To look at what cowards have done, and what has been done to them, can be disturbing. And the topic provokes hard questions. Were bin Laden and his followers cowardly, as many Americans thought, or was he right about American cowardice? Does withdrawal from Iraq and Afghanistan prove his point about American cowardice, a repetition of the pattern established in Somalia, Beirut, or Vietnam? Can this pattern be traced back further, to a history of fickle American foreign policy, a lack of steadfastness characteristic of a commercial democracy largely isolated from the rest of the world, as Alexis de Tocqueville observed long ago?[51] Is the American obsession with security itself cowardly? Far from the literal or figurative battles of geopolitics, cowardice can have an uncomfortably personal relevance. In allowing fear and self-concern to win out over the call of duty, the coward presents a sometimes disgusting case of moral failure; and contemplating others' cowardice can push us to contemplate our own.

To face such unpleasantness requires courage, one might think. In the *Laches* Socrates urged his companions to persevere in their inquiry, "so that courage itself won't make fun of us for not searching for it courageously."[52] But since Socrates died for his philosophy, applying his pronouncement to the present inquiry seems altogether too grand. It may be less grand and therefore more useful to think that cowardice would make fun of us for being cowardly in searching for it. Used well, the idea can function as a goad, humbly helpful in a way that courage is not. When Dante wavers before passing through the gate of hell, Virgil does not "encourage" him; he does not, that is, try to give him courage in any direct way. Rather, he rebukes him:

Your soul has been assailed by cowardice,
which often weighs so heavily on a man—

distracting him from honorable trials—
as phantoms frighten beasts when shadows fall.[53]

This scolding steels Dante to go on.

Our worship of heroes who brave fear and go beyond the call of duty distracts us from the importance of those who simply (not easily) fulfill their duty in the face of fear—those, that is, who avoid cowardice. If it is a dangerous idea, as we shall see again and again, it is also a bracing one. More abstractly, pondering cowardice illuminates (from underneath, as it were) our moral world. What we think about cowardice reveals a great deal about our conceptions of human nature and responsibility, about what we think an individual person can and should have to endure, and how much one owes to others, to community or cause. Cowardice and cowards have something to teach us. Let us speak of them.

Chapter 1

PROFILES IN COWARDICE

A Shadow History of the Home of the Brave

A brief survey of how the idea of cowardice has figured throughout U.S. history, uniting and dividing Americans, spurring brave
feats and reckless mistakes, might begin in 1758, during what was
for the British side one of the darkest hours of the French and Indian War. In North America the conflict had begun in May 1754,
when a twenty-three-year-old major named George Washington bungled an attempt to stop the French from building Fort
Duquesne at the strategic fork of the Monongohela and Ohio Riv-
ers. Washington and his men built a sorry stockade downriver that
they called, all too aptly, Fort Necessity. In July, French troops over-
whelmed Washington and his men there. Over the next four years,
the British had few victories and many defeats. Leaders and forts
fell, and hundreds of colonists were killed or kidnapped.[1] Yet the
army repeatedly faltered in its effort to raise troops or other forms
of support from among colonial subjects. Recruiting soldiers was
an immense challenge—as difficult as raising the dead, Washington lamented.[2]

By 1758, changes in leadership in Virginia and in Great Britain brought an increase in political and material support for the

military effort. Hopes were high that the war would turn in British favor. But then, hopes had been high before. In April, conscription was ended and pay was increased, but still Virginia was having trouble raising men. Morale among such troops that were raised was low. As the Reverend Samuel Davies prepared to deliver a sermon in Hanover, Virginia *"to raise a Company for Captain Samuel Meredith,"* he faced circumstances that would challenge the best recruiter.[3]

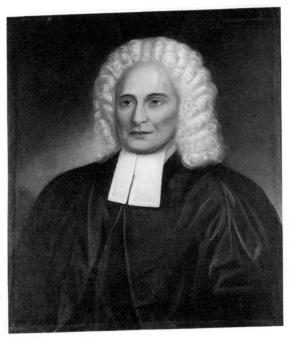

Princeton University Library

Davies was precisely that.[4] He was a tall "New Light" Presbyterian who spoke with the fire of a true believer, and he had the fragile but intense aspect of someone who was often very ill. A well-educated man who would in 1759 become president of the College of New Jersey (later Princeton University), a post he would hold until his death in 1761, he was able to speak in strong and vivid terms calculated to appeal to his much less well-educated listeners.[5] As a dissenter from the Anglican Church, he would not be suspected of being a toady of the Crown. In short, Davies was in the ideal position and had the ideal style to recruit successfully.

Yet witnesses to Davies's wartime sermons remembered the "gloom and dejection" on the faces of his auditors.[6] On May 8, 1758, they must have been deeply skeptical too. Why should *they* fight, and why fight now? Why should *they* leave their farms and families and face the rigors of military life? Virginia did have a claim on much of the contested territory, but it was only a few elites who would profit from defending that claim. Men of lower status—men who would do most of the actual fighting—could not see how they would benefit.[7] As we shall see in later chapters, either danger or authority might have compelled the men in his audience to act, but both seemed remote. Many in Hanover were, furthermore, not English settlers from eastern Virginia but Scotch-Irish and Germans from colonies to the north.[8]

Such was the situation as Davies stood on the muster grounds of Hanover, Virginia, and delivered a recruiting sermon he called *The Curse of Cowardice*. Warning Virginians that danger was at hand, even if they could not see it, Davies asserted that cowardice was "now as execrable as ever" it had been in the scripture he quoted.[9] Playing on his audience's fear of being cowardly seems to have proved successful. The company for which he was recruiting filled beyond capacity, and he was asked to speak again later that day at a local tavern.[10] (The sermon was also widely circulated as a pamphlet, and was reprinted at least four times.[11]) By June 5, these men were in the military, and in late November, just before their term of service was to end, the French realized that their erstwhile

The CURSE *of* COWARDICE:

A

SERMON

PREACHED

To the MILITIA of

HANOVER COUNTY,

IN

VIRGINIA,

AT

A General MUSTER, MAY 8, 1758.

With a View to raise a COMPANY for
Captain *SAMUEL MEREDITH.*

✢✢✢✢✢✢✢✢✢✢✢✢✢✢✢✢✢✢✢✢✢✢✢✢✢✢✢✢✢✢✢

By SAMUEL DAVIES, *A. M.*

✢✢✢✢✢✢✢✢✢✢✢✢✢✢✢✢✢✢✢✢✢✢✢✢✢✢✢✢✢✢✢

Printed for J. BUCKLAND, in *Pater-noster Row*; J.
WARD, in *Cornhill*; and T. FIELD, in *Cheapside.*
MDCCLVIII.

Indian allies would not come to their aid and burned Fort Duquesne to the ground. Before the end of 1758 the British were building a settlement just upstream and calling it Pittsburgh.[12]

If the British authorities are to be believed, however, colonial soldiers such as those recruited by Davies should not get much credit for this or any other victory in the French and Indian War. British military leaders in North America considered the American colonists to be generally cowardly; King George and other leaders back in England held similar views. When these colonists started to rebel, this belief led British rulers to think that the rebels could be defeated with a small force.[13]

The colonists had a similar view of the British. In Boston in 1770, as they hurled snowballs and taunts of "Damned rascally scoundrel lobster son of a bitch," crowds called British soldiers cowards and dared them to fire. They fired, killing five men in an incident that would become known as the Boston Massacre.[14] A few years later, independence-minded polemicists called those who remained loyal to the Crown or advocated neutrality cowardly.[15] In 1777, one Massachusetts minister exhorted his congregation to "gird on the sword of the Lord and of Gideon, and determine to conquer or die! . . . Do not let us hear of any of you who behave like cowards."[16]

But of course some men did behave like cowards. The problem came up for the Continental Army as soon as it was formed out of a motley of colonial militias in 1775. One of Washington's first official acts upon taking over the Army was to approve the court-martial for cowardice of John Callender, who had not acquitted himself well at Bunker Hill. When general Israel Putnam found him pulling two cannons away from the battle, Callender told him that his men had fallen back and that he was retreating. Putnam asked him on whose authority, and Callender said his own. He also claimed that he was out of cartridges. Finding that Callender did indeed have cartridges, Putnam drew his pistol and ordered him to return with the cannons to the Bunker Hill lines. Callender reluctantly did, only to abandon his artillery soon thereafter, and disappear. He was found guilty of cowardice and "dismissed from all further service in the Continental Army as an officer."[17] Looking back on this episode several weeks later, Washington noted, "I have made a pretty good Slam among such kind of officers as the Massachusetts Government [a]bound in since I came to this Camp, having broke [Callender and two other officers] for Cowardly beh[avior in] the action on Bunker's Hill."[18]

Callender's story does not end there, though, for he voluntarily remained with his unit and, as Samuel Swett's early nineteenth-century account put it, "desperately exposed himself in every action." At the Battle of Long Island in 1776, he fought so fiercely that he won the admiration of a British officer who kept his men from killing him, an incident commemorated in a centennial sketch that appeared in *Harper's* magazine in 1876. Callender was held prisoner for more than a year until he was exchanged. Upon his release, Washington gave him "his hand and his cordial thanks," expunged his court-martial, and reinstated his officership. Swett presents Callender as a "glorious instance of the buoyancy of genuine heroism and the redeeming efficacy of 'the mind conscious of rectitude.'"[19] His story presented an enduring object lesson in the bracing utility of the shame of cowardice.

When late 1776 brought a winter of defeat and doubt to the independence forces, the coward remained a favored bogeyman in Revolutionary era rhetoric. "These are the times that try men's souls," Tom Paine wrote to begin *The Crisis*, and then he introduced a theme he wove throughout this document: "The summer

Howard Gotlieb Archival Research Center, Boston University

soldier and the sunshine patriot will, in this crisis, shrink from the service of their country." In the dark hours of this war, as in the previous one, the "curse" of cowardice loomed: "The heart that feels not now is dead," Paine wrote; "the blood of his children will curse his cowardice, who shrinks back at a time when a little might have saved the whole. . . ."[20] Stamping as cowardly those who failed to fight the British was an integral part of forming a new nation under the banner of courage.

A similar pattern obtained in the War of 1812. The United States had a variety of motives—on the one hand resentment about the British blockade of Europe, about the impressment of men on

American ships into the Royal Navy, and about the provision of weapons and other material support to Native American enemies; on the other a desire to annex Canada—but the idea of cowardice played its part. As the *Washington National Intelligencer* argued, "The final step ought to be taken, and that step is WAR. . . . Any further discussion, any new attempt at negotiation, would be as fruitless as it would be dishonorable." Delay was cowardly, as was the objection that "we are not prepared for war, and ought therefore not to declare it. This is an idle objection, which can have weight with the timid and pusillanimous only." The *Intelligencer's* statement was published on April 14, 1812. War was officially declared in June.

In 1814, watching the Americans repel a British attempt to take Baltimore, Francis Scott Key wrote "Defence of Fort McHenry," which in its third stanza disparages the British forces as mercenary or conscripted: "No refuge could save the hireling and slave / From the terror of flight, or the gloom of the grave." The cowardice implied in the text of what would come to be known as the "Star-Spangled Banner" formed a fitting contrast to buttress the celebration of the "home of the brave."

A few decades later, the fear or shame of cowardice helped propel the United States into war with itself. As early as the 1840s abolitionists were touting disunion as "preferable to immoral compromises and cowardly submission."[21] During the Kansas crisis of 1856, a New York paper lamented "the bullying of the slaveocracy, . . . impudently taunting the entire north with cowardice."[22] On the proslavery side in that same year, the *Montgomery Advertiser* exhorted its readers to confront Northerners' insulting criticism of slavery in a manly way, not "shrink from it like cowards."[23]

The rhetoric of cowardice grew more heated as war approached. Southerners who were against secession had good reason to worry that their appeals for prudence and dialog would be called cowardice.[24] In December 1860, the Georgian Henry Jackson said that secessionists must "cow" the hesitating "cowards" among them, "[f]or if we retreat an inch, the cowardly . . . will take to their heels. . . ."[25] Northerners who were willing to compromise with the slaveholding states could also be subject to the charge of cowardice. Frederick Douglass even went so far as to credit Southerners for their misguided bravery and to excoriate Northerners as "miserable cowards, insensible alike to the requirements of self-respect or duty. Was ever a people so terribly frightened as are we . . . at this moment?"[26] As Abraham Lincoln was campaigning for the presidency he was deeply wary of "men who would like to frighten me, or, at least, fix upon me the character of timidity and cowardice."[27] It was around this time that Lincoln first grew a beard.

After war began, it was not ideology or a desire for glory that made men attack a fortification or hold their position when under assault. "The force that compelled them," as Bell Wiley put it, "above all else, was the thought of family and friends and the unwillingness to be branded cowards"[28]—an unwillingness, as have seen in the introduction, that was the subject of many of their letters home. When soldiers measured themselves in battle, they were quicker to damn themselves as cowardly than to praise themselves as courageous, and the damnation seemed to have a staying power that the praise lacked. While a belief in their courage could be undone by one cowardly act, shame about cowardice was not so easily dispelled.[29]

The sectional conflict was welcomed by some who thought it would help cure cowardly inclinations on their own side. In a note of consolation to the mother of Robert Gould Shaw, after her wealthy and refined son had died leading the Fifty-Fourth

Massachusetts Volunteer Infantry into battle, Henry Ward Beecher wrote, "Our young men seemed ignoble; the faith of old heroic times had died ... but the trumpet of this war sounded the call and O! how joyful has been the sight of such unexpected nobleness in our young men!"[30] Southern whites considered war a way to "put aside luxuries and idleness," as Bertram Wyatt-Brown put it, "vices that weakened resolve."[31]

At the beginning of the war the prevailing belief that the enemy was cowardly made some on each side eager to do battle and confident of victory.[32] The Confederates thought business and prosperity made the Yankees soft, and the Yankees thought the Confederates weak dandies who made their slaves do all the hard labor.[33] The experience of actual battle fairly quickly disabused many soldiers of the belief in the enemy's cowardice.[34] When it turned out that both sides generally put up a good fight, it was hard to label either cowardly. The first battle of Bull Run, though, with the Federals panicking and rushing off the field, seemed to confirm to some on both sides that the Northerners were more cowardly than the Southerners, and it has been argued that Confederate soldiers felt for the duration of the war that the average Yankee lacked the character to be a real soldier—a feeling that contributed to Southern soldiers' belief in their invincibility.[35]

The military justice system reinforced the prevailing belief that nothing was more shameful than cowardice. Of the nearly one hundred thousand Union general court-martial cases on file at the National Archives, cowardice was the ninth most common charge, with roughly five hundred cases.[36] And other offenses, such as desertion (by far the most common charge), shameful abandonment of post, and self-mutilation often carried with them the implication of cowardice. As we shall see, soldiers convicted of such crimes were often humiliated and imprisoned, sometimes physically branded or even executed.

Since most Confederate court-martial records have been lost, it is impossible to compare the official military attitudes and practices regarding cowardice in the North and the South. Some Civil War scholars emphasize how similar the general and military populations and their mores were;[37] clearly both sides had strong feelings about cowardice. But the Confederate attitudes seem to have been more extreme. In 1861, having been jokingly accused of cowardice by some of his comrades-in-arms, one Alabama recruit, Charles P. Robinson, replied that he "would show them how a Roman could die," and then stabbed himself in either side of the neck and bled to death.[38] In 1865 a Confederate seaman named Marion Stevens twice tried to kill himself, the second time—with a pistol to his head—successfully. As the Richmond *Daily Dispatch* reported, "It is believed that the act was committed in consequence of deep mortification existing in the mind of the deceased at being, some time since, reduced from a lieutenant's position to a private in the ranks on the charge of cowardice."[39]

Even more than their white counterparts, black Union soldiers worried about being thought cowardly. The popular belief among whites was that, while blacks were capable of reckless aggression— savagery, that is—they would falter in the face of sustained danger.[40] And so they often went to battle with such enthusiasm that no one could ever charge them of cowardice.[41] There were cases in which black soldiers were so charged, but a far more common problem for officers of "colored troops" was holding their men back.[42]

The fear of the shame of cowardice that helped drive the States to war with themselves also helped prolong their war. The South might have surrendered earlier if some had not thought that doing so would be cowardly.[43] As the *Richmond Whig* put it in February 1865, "To talk now of any other arbitrament than that of the sword is to betray cowardice or treachery."[44] And the aftermath of the Civil War might have been very different if a certain actor from the South had not thought himself guilty of cowardice. "For four years," John Wilkes Booth wrote to his mother in late 1864, "I have lived (I may say) a slave in the north . . . not daring to express my thoughts or sentiments, even in my own home, constantly hearing every principle, dear to my heart, denounced as treasonable, and knowing the vile and savage acts committed on my countrymen, their wives & helpless children, that I have cursed my willful idleness, and begun to deem myself a coward and despise my own existence." Booth needed to assassinate Lincoln to redeem himself.[45]

April 9, 1865, when general Robert E. Lee surrendered the Army of Northern Virginia, is the usual date given for the end of the Civil War, but Confederate president Jefferson Davis remained at large and held out hope of continuing hostilities. He was apprehended by Union forces while wearing his wife's shawl, an episode that provoked delighted scorn in the North. Perhaps the war felt more truly over when the enemy leader was captured a coward.

The relative peace of the remaining decades of the nineteenth century did not dispel worries about cowardice. On the contrary, it seemed to foster them, lamented one female commentator in 1894. "Idleness and luxury have made men flabby," she wrote, "and the man at the head of affairs [Grover Cleveland was president at the time] is beginning to ask seriously if a great war might not help them pull themselves together."[46] After the sinking of the *Maine* in 1898, president William McKinley's reluctance to act against Spain

JEFFERSON DAVIS AS AN UNPROTECTED FEMALE!

Howard Gotlieb Archival Research Center, Boston University

was depicted by some Americans as cowardly. No one was more strident in his criticism than Theodore Roosevelt, who declared that McKinley "had no more backbone than a chocolate éclair." War soon followed.[47]

Roosevelt had similar things to say about president Woodrow Wilson, seventeen years later, in his 1915 book *America and the World War*. After German atrocities in Belgium and elsewhere, Roosevelt saw fit to remind Americans who advocated neutrality that "Dante reserved a special place of infamy in the inferno for those base angels who dared side neither with evil nor with good." Wilson was the leader of a "cult of cowardice," Roosevelt wrote, and he had many followers.[48] As he wrote to his son Archibald Bulloch Roosevelt that same year, "Every soft creature, every coward and weakling, every man who can't look more than six inches ahead, every man whose god is money, or pleasure, or ease, and every man who has not got in him both the sterner virtues and the power of seeking after an ideal, is enthusiastically in favor of Wilson."[49] Roosevelt was not alone in accusing advocates of neutrality or pacifism of cowardice. In 1917, prowar Harvard students mocked members of the Harvard Union for Neutrality by hanging posters in yellow ink asserting that "THE HARVARD UNION FOR AMERICAN NINCOMPOOPS BELIEVES" among other things that "This country should invite the Kaiser to annex it" and that "It is unladylike to stand up for our rights."[50]

Wilson for his part said that he would "not be rushed into war, no matter if every damned congressman and senator stands up on his hind legs and proclaims me a coward." Eventually, though, he did ask the Senate to declare war, and the shame of cowardice figured (along with massive conscription) in efforts to drum up troops. A 1917 recruiting poster depicted a man in a suit with bow tie standing inside, one hand grasping his lapel, the other in his pants pocket. He looks distractedly outside, where a giant flag billows and doughboys march shouldering guns. "ENLIST," the poster reads; "On Which Side of the Window are YOU?" Alexis de Tocqueville had remarked that Americans generally did not adhere to martial, aristocratic ideas of courage, preferring to honor a more commercial version—"the courage," for example, "that renders one almost insensitive to the sudden reversal of a painfully acquired fortune and immediately prompts new efforts to construct

Library of Congress, Prints and Photographs Division

a new one."[51] But there were limits to the possibilities for valor, or avoiding disgrace, in commerce. When war was on, it was time to close shop.

The shame of cowardice had driven the enemy too, as the German novelist Erich Maria Remarque depicted in *All Quiet on the Western Front* (1928). At the beginning of the Great War, "even one's parents were ready with the word 'coward,'" Remarque writes; "no one had the vaguest idea what we were in for."[52] What they were in for would make people less ready with that word—or so Remarque hoped. Indeed, the cataclysm of the Great War provoked many writers to explode what the English soldier-poet Wilfred Owen called "the old lie" put forth by Horace "that it is sweet and just to die for your country"—and that it is bitter and shameful not to be willing to die so. In Ernest Hemingway's *A Farewell to Arms*, Frederic Henry, an American who had (like Hemingway) volunteered to serve in the Italian military's ambulance corps, famously laments, "Abstract words such as glory, honor, courage, or hallow were obscene"; if such is the case, then infamy, dishonor, and cowardice must be obscene, too, at best irrelevant, a matter for jest. Henry feels guilty about deserting, and his lover Catherine Barkley consoles him by saying, "It's only the Italian Army."[53]

Despite these writers' efforts, the "old lie" that celebrated the glory of war did not die with the Great War. Antiwar advocates in the run-up to World War II were reviled like their predecessors had been. As early as 1935, one speaker at a meeting of the Foreign Policy Association noted those who favored isolationist policies were "turn[ing] the American Eagle into a turtle."[54] Neville Chamberlain's policy of appeasement in the late 1930s was championed by many at the time as prudent, but in retrospect "appeasement" became a byword for cowardly capitulation. And cowardice was, as always, a concern during the war as well, most famously in 1943 when general George S. Patton called two soldiers who said they were suffering from battle fatigue "cowards" and, for good measure, slapped them. But Patton was convinced that America's enemies in Europe were more cowardly. Addressing his troops in Tunisia before they embarked to do battle in Sicily, he wrote, "When we land, we will meet German and Italian soldiers whom it is our honor and privilege to attack and destroy. Many of you have in your veins German and Italian blood, but remember that these ancestors of yours so loved freedom that they gave up home and country to cross the ocean in search of liberty. The ancestors of the people we shall kill lacked the courage to make such a sacrifice and continued as slaves."[55]

Certainly cowardice was a prominent—if often implicit—subtext of the Cold War. Campaigning for vice president on a ticket with Dwight D. Eisenhower in 1952, Richard Nixon referred to Democratic presidential nominee Adlai Stevenson as "Adlai the Appeaser," holder of a "PhD from Dean Acheson's cowardly college of Communist containment."[56] When Lyndon Baines Johnson became president, worry over cowardice helped shape his decision to keep American troops in Vietnam. Withdrawal would not only ruin American credibility and invite Soviet and Chinese aggression; it would make him an "unmanly man," he said. He worried that his nemesis Robert Kennedy would lead a campaign against him, and it would pivot on the idea that Johnson was cowardly, an unworthy heir to John F. Kennedy. Being seen as cowardly wasn't just a personal problem; it had huge geopolitical implications, Johnson believed. "If I left that war and let the Communists take over South Vietnam," he said in retrospect, "then I would be seen as a coward and my nation would be seen as an appeaser and we would both find it impossible to accomplish anything for anybody anywhere on the entire globe."[57]

Johnson thought that had it been braver in the run-up to both world wars, the United States could have avoided getting involved in either. As he put it, "Cowardice has gotten us into more wars than response has." He made this statement at a meeting of the National Security Council on February 6, 1965, to justify his fateful decision to escalate American military involvement in Vietnam.[58] Around this time Johnson was having a recurring dream that offers a glimpse of a primal scene, the tribe moving against the individual who has failed it out of fear: "Every night when I fell asleep I would see myself tied to the ground in the middle of a long open space. In the distance, I could hear the voices of thousands of people. They were all shouting at me and running toward me: 'Coward! Traitor! Weakling!' They kept coming closer. They began throwing stones. At exactly that moment I would generally wake up . . . terribly shaken."[59] Whether these thousands thought him a coward for not being more militarily aggressive in Vietnam or for not withdrawing, Johnson did not make clear.

The idea of cowardice preoccupied not just the Texan in the White House who thought of himself as a brave cowboy, but Americans in the military and in the streets as well. In denying private Melvin Myers's appeal of his conviction for cowardice in 1967, the appeals court asserted the gravity and shamefulness of the soldier's crime: "We well recognize that the offense of which appellant stands convicted is a most serious one; to brand an individual as a coward in battle has consequences which will persist long after the more temporal aspects of punishment have been completed." Myers's sentence of imprisonment, loss of pay, and a bad conduct discharge stood.[60] When in New York City men burned their draft cards in protest against the war, they were confronted by a crowd who tried to extinguish the fires with water. The Ad Hoc Committee of Veterans for Peace in Vietnam held up a banner, but there was also a sign that read, "THANKS PINKOS QUEERS COWARDS DRAFT DODGERS MAO TSE TUNG & HO CHI MINH"—and, in slightly smaller caps: "WE SUPPORT OUR BOYS IN VIETNAM."[61]

High Museum of Art, Atlanta

In 1975, America did withdraw from Vietnam—and, in the ensuing years, as Osama bin Laden would note in 1996, America withdrew from Beirut and Somalia as well. And then came 9/11 with its controversy over whether the term *coward* should be applied to the terrorists. The controversy quickly faded, but the term did not disappear as a rhetorical weapon. In early 2002, as part of a campaign of psychological warfare conducted during the invasion of Afghanistan, the American military dropped leaflets featuring

U.S. Department of Defense

a doctored picture of bin Laden, beardless and turbanless, a winsome smile beneath a neatly trimmed mustache, and sporting a snazzy business suit. The same connection of cowardice and commerce made by the "On Which Side of the Window are YOU" poster was this time being directed not at potential recruits but at an enemy of America. "Usama bin Laden, the murderer and coward, has abandoned you" read the message in Pashtun. The Department of Defense produced an English-language version for American consumption. Bin Laden returned the volley less than a year later, noting that the Americans "depend on massive air strikes so as to conceal their most prominent point of weakness, which is the fear, cowardliness, and the absence of combat spirit among US soldiers."[62]

Worries about appearing cowardly have certainly figured in U.S.-Iraq relations over the past twenty-five years. A history of such worries might begin with a 1990 secret cable from the American Embassy in Baghdad that reported on a meeting between the U.S. Ambassador to Iraq and Saddam Hussein. Hussein noted that "IF IRAQ IS PUBLICLY HUMILIATED BY THE USG, IT WILL HAVE NO CHOICE BUT TO 'RESPOND,' HOWEVER ILLOGICAL AND SELF DESTRUCTIVE THAT WOULD PROVE.... HE CANNOT ALLOW HIMSELF TO BE PERCEIVED AS CAVING IN TO SUPERPOWER BULLYING."[63] Much illogical and self-destructive behavior followed. During the American debate over the 2003 invasion of Iraq, proponents of the war cast critics of it as "abject pacifists."[64] Leaflets dropped over Iraq noted that "Saddam is a coward,"[65] an idea confirmed in the view of many when he was found hiding in a "spider hole" ("Cowardly Lyin' Saddam: Bush Whacks Scaredy Rat for Crawling in Hole," was the headline in the *New York Post*).[66] Rumors that Osama bin

Daily Express (London)

Laden "used his wife as a human shield" when Navy Seals closed in on him proved unfounded, but it was not surprising to see the story allege that he had died a coward.

Critics of military action wielded cowardice as a rhetorical weapon, too. At the end of George W. Bush's second term, one commentator noted that his "most toxic legacy" was his "hide-under-the-bed-and-shoot ethos," his "cowardice, masquerading as he-man toughness"—shades of Aristotle's reckless cowardice—which "led him to do unforgivable things" such as invade Iraq and torture prisoners. Democrats who went along for fear of being labeled cowardly were cowardly too, in this view, as were the American people as a whole for the extreme measures they would accept to achieve an unachievable "total security."[67]

And yet the desire for such security is understandable when one sees how the shame of cowardice continues to animate the rhetoric of violent jihad. Bin Laden's own spin on the rhetoric of cowardice did not die with him. One radical Islamist asked, are Muslim Americans "proud of associating themselves with a nation that continues to maim and kill the ummah [Muslim peoples] around the world both directly and indirectly? Are they proud of paying taxes that are converted into bullets and missiles that penetrate the bodies and homes of the downtrodden Palestinian Muslims? Or are they proud of being American because being one welcomes cowardice and hiding one's head under the sand while the real problems exasperate throughout the Muslim lands?"[68] Such is the rough English of *Inspire* magazine, an online publication of al-Qaeda's Yemen affiliate, which also featured an article titled "Make a Bomb in the Kitchen of Your Mom," and which was among the favored reading of Tamerlan Tsarnaev, the older of the two Boston Marathon bombers.[69]

Chapter 2

OF ARMS AND MEN

Why is contempt for cowardice so stubborn and powerful that it could figure so forcefully and diversely in American history? At first glance, fleeing from danger even when duty dictates that you should not seems like a good survival strategy. After Henry Fleming runs from battle in Stephen Crane's *The Red Badge of Courage*, he throws a pinecone at a squirrel and watches it flee "with chattering fear." "The youth felt triumphant at this exhibition," Crane writes. "There was the law, he said. Nature had given him a sign. The squirrel, immediately upon recognizing danger, had taken to his legs without ado. He did not stand stolidly baring his furry belly to the missile, and die with an upward glance at the sympathetic heavens. On the contrary, he had fled as fast as his legs could carry him; and he was but an ordinary squirrel, too—doubtless no philosopher of his race. The youth wended, feeling that Nature was of his mind."[1]

Fleming might further have wondered if, having had the good sense to follow the natural instinct to preserve itself and flee to safety, the cowardly creature would then reproduce more cowardly creatures, while, as Charles Darwin put it in *The Descent of Man*, those "who freely risked their lives for others, would on an average perish in larger numbers."[2] Over time, nature would make cowardice universal.[3] In the case of human beings, everyone would behave like the Buid and the Semai, two peoples of southeast Asia who have so thoroughly adopted a policy of fleeing from fear that they do not even have a word to condemn the behavior. The Buid, a mountain-dwelling people of the Philippines, have many words for "fear, fleeing and leaving others behind," but none are pejorative, for they see such feeling and conduct as the only sensible response to danger.[4] The Semai, who live in heavily forested valleys in Malaysia, may be the most fearful—in the sense of being full of fear—people on earth. They seldom show joy, anger, or grief; they do not even laugh with much gusto. But fear they show with great energy and regularity. According to Clayton Robarchek, an anthropologist who has studied them closely, the Semai fear "virtually everything," even dragonflies and butterflies. Because torrential rains fall almost daily, the Semai must grow accustomed to these storms and wait them out patiently and calmly—or so one would assume. In fact, every storm makes them frantically fearful, often to the point of "abject terror." They are known to abandon grandmothers in collapsed shelters, or to flee their houses for the woods, where falling trees pose greater danger.[5] Neither people have contempt for cowardice, or even a notion of cowardice.

But the fact that the Buid and Semai form such a tiny portion of the world's population suggests that giving in to fear is not the best strategy for survival. For that matter, the squirrel's "chattering fear" had more to it than Henry Fleming knew. A squirrel may not bare its belly to a pinecone missile, but if it senses a predator, it may call out to alert its fellows, even though doing so draws dangerous attention to itself.[6] The squirrel acts not out of the evolutionary imperative to preserve itself but out of a different and sometimes contrary imperative to preserve the group. A group with many such squirrels would likely have an advantage over groups that did not. The commonness of such behaviors across the animal kingdom has led researchers to conclude that many creatures are hardwired to do things that benefit others, even if it means risk to themselves, and that group selection fosters this phenomenon.[7] As Darwin wrote about human beings, "A tribe including many members who . . . were always ready to aid one another, and to sacrifice themselves for the common good, would be victorious over most other tribes and this would be natural selection."[8]

This view can make one wonder how the Semai and Buid have survived at all, why cowardice has not vanished from the earth, why all human beings are not brave warriors, the way we picture Spartans or Vikings. But natural selection does not paint in such broad strokes. Thinking of a uniformly brave tribe oversimplifies matters in two ways. First, what might loosely be called cowardly genes can survive within populations that are extreme in their contempt for cowardice because, characteristically, cowardice hides; that is, the person inclined to cowardice does not engage in cowardly conduct for fear of punishment—being beaten or executed or deprived of a mating opportunity—and so he survives and reproduces, passing his cowardly genes on.[9]

The second reason uniform bravery will not hold is that cowardice can sometimes be advantageous to the tribe. Even in primitive life forms—the galling aphid clone, for example—we see how the presence of both types confers an evolutionary edge. Researchers have noted that under certain circumstances "brave soldier" aphids that sacrifice themselves when their colony is attacked get eaten in disproportionately high numbers, and the "cowardly aphids" who flee the colony rather than defend it ultimately help save it. As the researchers

observe, the cowardly aphids seem to be practicing the proverbial wisdom that it is sometimes better to run away so that one
can "live to fight another day."[10] Together, the brave and cowardly
aphids also affirm another bit of clichéd wisdom, that "it takes all
kinds." Under some circumstances, bravery helps the colony or
clan; at other times, fleeing best serves group survival. A mixture of
more and less cautious predispositions enables the group to contend with a range of environmental circumstances. The evolutionary process that leads to such a mixture on the genetic level has
been called *balanced* or *balancing selection*. The balance should not
be imagined as a stable one. The scales can swing wildly depending on conditions. And such selection does not homogenize populations; it diversifies them, and that, coupled with the unending
diversities of circumstance, makes the judgment of conduct and
character a challenge—not for aphids, obviously, but for human
beings.[11]

It may be, as the evolutionary psychologist Jonathan Haidt has
argued, that evolution instills in us unconscious emotions that
animate our "moral intuitions."[12] But the evolutionary legacy is so
complicated and conflicted that it does little to explain our moral
intuitions about cowardice—except perhaps to indicate why they
can be so powerful, and so conflicted and complicated. The judgments we finally make, whatever the moral intuition, are a product
not of nature but culture. The Buid and the Semai are members of
the same species as Spartans and Vikings, after all, so their different attitudes about cowardice can only be explained by looking at
the particulars of their histories and societies. Evolutionary theory
does point us to where we should focus our inquiry—on what
might be called the primal theater of cowardice—war, where the
stigma of cowardice asserts the power of tribe or country, and

where fear makes the individual keenly aware of his separateness, of his body that would preserve itself. As it happens, the bodies typically involved in war, in all their strength and frailty, are male bodies, caught in a conflict, as E. O. Wilson observes, "between honor, virtue, and duty, the products of group selection, on one side, and selfishness, cowardice, and hypocrisy, the products of individual selection, on the other side."[13] As we shall see, even those who wish to criticize or invert the meaning of cowardice find that they have to engage with it in its primal territory, the field of battle, which the archetypical coward flees, if he can.

Not just the idea of cowardice but indeed morality itself may be tied to war, according to primatologist Frans de Waal, among others, for there is nothing like the prospect of combat to escalate group pressure on individuals to put the common good above their own interest.[14] One reason cowardice is so powerfully condemned is that, in failing to put the common good above his own interest, the coward can *destroy* the group. On assuming leadership of the Continental Army, general George Washington's first communiqué after arriving in the field noted "with inexpressible concern" that cowardice was a "Crime of all others, the most infamous in a Soldier, the most injurious to an Army, and the last to be forgiven; inasmuch as it may, and often does happen, that the Cowardice of a single Officer may prove the Distruction of the whole Army."[15]

Cowardice can have a devastating delayed effect, too, once word gets out about it. When the monster Grendel takes to ravaging his people, Beowulf single-handedly defeats him and then his mother. In his old age he faces one last foe, the dragon. This time Beowulf asks for help and some elite warriors join him, but when danger mounts they abandon him. Only the worthy Wiglaf remains by his side. He helps Beowulf slay the dragon, but Beowulf dies. Wiglaf rebukes the cowards afterward, telling them that now their

> whole nation,
> will be dispossessed, once princes from beyond
> get tidings of how you turned and fled
> and disgraced yourselves.

All of Beowulf's courageous deeds, done to protect the clan, will be undone by the cowards' cowardice. At Beowulf's funeral a woman wails

> a wild litany
> of nightmare and lament: her nation invaded,
> enemies on the rampage, bodies in piles, slavery and abasement.[16]

Here the echo of cowardice amplifies defeat into something closer to annihilation.

The relationship between war and cowardice is reciprocal; they beget each other in various ways. It is not coincidental that the Buid and Semai, those people who have no idea of cowardice, are remarkably unwarlike. If, following De Waal, we can say that war in a sense gave us cowardice as an important moral category, it can also be said that cowardice can give us war. The enemy's belief that you are cowardly tempts him to aggression—this is Wiglaf's argument. Correspondingly, the fear of being thought cowardly can cause preemptive violence.

The deep connection between cowardice and violence obtains not just among epic heroes or men steeped in a military ethos. It is said that the Buddha prohibited men from deserting the military, even to join a monastery.[17] In 1920, while insisting that he thought "non-violence is infinitely superior to violence, forgiveness is more manly than punishment," Mahatma Gandhi also wrote, "where there is a choice only between cowardice and violence, I would advise violence.... Hence it was that I took part in the Boer War, the so-called Zulu Rebellion, and [World War I].... I would rather have India resort to arms in order to defend her honor than that she should in a cowardly manner become or remain a helpless witness to her dishonor."[18] Martin Luther King followed Gandhi in this as in many other respects, declaring cowardice the "one evil worse than violence."[19]

Such statements show how general the abhorrence of cowardice is, how directly it is tied to the violence of war and to the larger code of conduct that goes under the name of honor—a consideration as likely to cause war as conflict over land, resources, or power.[20] I will here reduce the substantial volume of writing about the subject by saying that honor pertains, in a phrase, to place (in the sense of standing or rank) and face.[21] A failure to protect one's place—by letting an insult stand, for instance, or failing to defend one's father or avenge some injury done to one's kin—means a loss of face. Losing face out of fear is cowardice, and under a code of honor to be called a coward can be the greatest insult of all, the source of the greatest shame. During the Civil War an officer who exhorted his troops, "Charge, you cowards, charge!" so offended two soldiers that they charged not the enemy but their officer.[22]

Much has been made of the difference between shame and guilt—perhaps too much[23]—but cowardice does seem to bring out the often-observed distinction that while guilt attaches to an act or acts, shame "pertains to the whole self." While guilt can be hidden, shame is inherently caught up with exposure.[24] After he flees the battlefield, Henry Fleming feels that he will bear a "sore badge of his dishonor through life. With his heart continually assuring him that he was despicable, he could not exist without making it, through his actions, apparent to all men." But when he comes back to his company and realizes that no one had seen his flight, he decides that he is not a coward after all: "He had performed his mistakes in the dark, so he was still a man."[25]

Recent research may explain Fleming's thinking. Cowardice is a violation of "indirect reciprocity," in which we do our duty to others and expect that others will do theirs, even if it will not directly benefit us. People are especially inclined to engage in such reciprocity when they think they are being observed, when their reputation is at stake. Evolutionary modeling suggests that "natural selection favors cooperation when observability is sufficiently high."[26] The negative corollary would be that when observability is not high, cooperation—doing one's duty—is not so favored, and failing in that duty is not a big deal. Because no one witnessed his cowardice, Henry Fleming is still a man; in fact it is as if the act of cowardice never happened, and therefore was not cowardice.

The Coward's Carlton Brand is not as lucky as Henry Fleming. He had been a respected lawyer and sometime prosecutor in Philadelphia, but after word gets out about his self-confessed cowardice, he believes,

To-morrow my name may be a scoff and a by-word in the mouth of every man who knows me. I cannot and will not meet this shame, which . . . will be blown abroad by the breath of thousands of personal acquaintances, and perhaps made the subject of jest in the public newspapers. Think how those who have hated and perhaps feared me—criminals whom I have brought to justice ... will gloat over the knowledge that I can trouble them no more—that I have fallen lower, in the public eye, than they have ever been! I am going away, where no man who has ever looked upon my face and known it, can look upon it again![27]

Shame like Carlton's constitutes a powerful deterrent to cowardice. It escalates social pressure so effectively that society need do little work, so deeply has the individual absorbed its moral code. In the world of honor that this novel depicts, social and moral feeling become coterminous, indistinguishable, and they manifest themselves overtly in the physical world.[28] Brand feels the accusation "in his very name."[29]

The shame of cowardice can go well beyond the self to affect one's kin—living, dead, and yet to be born. A Union soldier wrote to his wife of a captain's cowardice, "what a stigma for men to transmit to their posterity—your father a coward."[30] A 1915 British recruiting poster showed a man haunted by the prospect of his daughter asking him, "Daddy, what did _YOU_ do in the Great War?" The stigma could be delivered by one's ancestors, too, as when Tecumseh—in an 1811 speech advocating violent resistance to white encroachment—said, "Accursed be the race that has seized on our country and made women of our warriors. Our fathers, from their tombs, reproach us as slaves and cowards. I hear them now in the wailing winds."[31] Even the afterlife did not absolve the coward; a Northerner who fought for the Confederacy pronounced cowardice "the one sin which may not be pardoned either in this world or the next."[32]

Men do not exempt even their own sons from the shame of cowardice; indeed, the fear of cowardice by association may lead fathers to intensify the shame. Witness Carlton Brand's father,

Daddy, what did **YOU** do in the Great War?

Library of Congress

a veteran wounded in the War of 1812, who in Morford's novel proclaims,

> *My* son a coward! a miserable poltroon to be pointed at, spat upon, and whipped! *My* blood made a shame in the land, by the one whom I trusted to honor it! . . . God's blackest and deepest curse 'light upon the coward! shame, sorrow, and quick death! He shall have neither house, home nor family from this moment. I disown this bastard of my blood! I devote him to ruin and perdition![33]

In failing to protect his country, the son forfeits his father's protection of him. The emphasis—the italics are in the original—suggests that the closer you are to the coward, the greater the need to distance yourself from him. The father of the coward must show that he has not been infected—as must his brothers-in-arms. This is one reason for the common practice of having the coward's unit administer his punishment.

Collection of the New-York Historical Society

Punishment is also necessary because some people are shameless. Such people, Bertram Wyatt-Brown notes, "fail to fulfill a core expectation of the culture of honor, that one's exterior and interior are congruent, that when someone violates the code, the first step toward redemption is showing that he thinks badly of himself."[34] Shaming punishments seek to ensure that the inner moral failing is exposed. Part of the sentence of many Union soldiers found guilty of cowardice was to have accounts of their misdeeds published in their hometown newspapers. An 1862 sketch shows Union private Patrick Cronin of Company E of the Twenty-Fifth Massachusetts Volunteers being drummed out of service wearing a placard that reads COWARD—a common punishment. His head is shaved and the soldiers in front of him have their guns pointed backward, probably to ensure that Cronin proceed slowly on his shameful exit from the military; his running days are over. Five other New England soldiers who fled battle in 1863 were found guilty of cowardice and made to stand on barrels wearing wooden signs on their backs. One read "I shirked"; the next, "I skedaddled"; then came "So did I," "I did too," and "Ditto." The men had to rotate themselves so everyone could see.[35]

In the heat of combat, the most immediate enforcer of shame is one's fellow soldiers. The power of "mutual surveillance" makes the soldier feel the fear of cowardice weighing on him.[36] It presses him forward. Vietnam veteran Tim O'Brien describes this phenomenon in his account of the heaviest of the things men carry to war:

> They carried the common secret of cowardice barely restrained, the instinct to run or freeze or hide, and in many respects this was the heaviest burden of all, for it could never be put down, it required perfect balance and perfect posture. . . . They carried the soldier's greatest fear, which was the fear of blushing. Men killed, and died, because they were embarrassed not to. It was what had brought them to the war in the first place, nothing positive, no dreams of glory or honor, just to avoid the blush of dishonor. They died so as not to die of embarrassment. . . . It was not courage, exactly; the object was not valor. Rather, they were too frightened to be cowards.[37]

Eugene Sledge wrote of himself and other young marines in World War II that "the only thing that we seemed to be truly concerned about was that we might be too afraid to do our jobs under fire.

An apprehension nagged at each of us that he might appear to be 'yellow' if he were afraid."[38] And so they did their jobs under fire.

Women, too, can level the charge of cowardice vehemently and effectively. A third of the forty "Sayings of Spartan Women" collected by Plutarch assert the terrible shame of (male) cowardice and the importance of never fleeing in battle.[39] Elizabeth Fries Ellet's 1856 book, *Women of the American Revolution*, describes how two women came upon some men retreating from battle and demanded their guns, saying that they would fight in their stead. Ellet writes, "The most cowardly of men must have been moved at such a taunt" and reports that the men went back into battle, accompanied by the women.[40] In A.E.W. Mason's 1902 novel *The Four Feathers*, Harry Feversham receives with dismay but relative equanimity the insulting gift of white feathers from three of his fellow officers, the men he has decided not to accompany to war in the Sudan. When his fiancée gives him a fourth feather, however, he suffers greatly, and resolves to redeem himself—by going off to war.[41] How many white feathers got handed out in England during World War I has been the subject of some debate, but the ones that did virtually all came from women. "The women were the worst," one English veteran remembered.[42]

Morford's *The Coward* demonstrates with considerable melodrama the special force of a woman thinking a man cowardly. Margaret Hayley is engaged to marry Carlton Brand, but when she overhears his confession of cowardice she breaks off the engagement. "I cannot and will not marry a man," she declares, "to whom I cannot look up and say: This man has the courage and the will to protect me in every peril!" The book details Brand's many extraordinary feats of bravery in his attempt to win Hayley back: He wins a fistfight and saves a woman from an irate pet bear, rescues a boy from drowning in a deep mountain pool, and rescues a hiker from falling down a cliff. None of these feats is enough to satisfy Margaret Hayley, however, for in her eyes there is something deeply and irredeemably damning about cowardice in war. "The man who knows his duty to his country and dares not do it," she says to Carlton, "through sheer bodily fear, could not be trusted in any relation." (But there is hope for Brand, Hayley says. If he were to strike "but one blow, to prove that he was no coward to fly before the enemies of his country,—I would go barefoot round the world to find him, be his servant, his slave, if he would not forget the past and make me his wife."[43]) One sees a similar sentiment in a World War I poster addressed "To the YOUNG WOMEN OF LONDON": "If your young man neglects his duty to his King and Country, the time may come when he will *NEGLECT YOU.*"

The perception of cowardice at times seems to function as an antiaphrodisiac. A Revolutionary War poem narrated by a chorus of single women exhorted men to "Go act the hero, every danger face, / *Love hates a coward's impotent embrace.*"[44] German slang for *coward—schlapschwanz* ("limp-tail," or "limp-dick")—bespeaks impotence, as does, in the view of Leo Braudy, the Latin root of the English word; *cauda*, as we have seen, means tail, as does *penis,* and putting one's penis/tail between one's legs is much easier if it's limp.[45] Another figure of the emasculating effect of cowardice is the stub left to the court-martialed soldier who has had his sword broken—an image, as has been noted, that appeared at the beginning of every episode of the television show *Branded,* with the rest of the episode depicting, metaphorically speaking, a restoration of the sword to its full length.[46]

Women can also wield the charge of cowardice powerfully in their role as mothers. In one Spartan saying, a mother greets her

TO THE
YOUNG WOMEN
OF LONDON

Is your "Best Boy" wearing Khaki? If not don't **YOU THINK** he should be?

If he does not think that you and your country are worth fighting for—do you think he is **WORTHY** of you?

Don't pity the girl who is alone—her young man is probably a soldier—fighting for her and her country— and for **YOU.**

If your young man neglects his duty to his King and Country, the time may come when he will **NEGLECT YOU.**

Think it over—then ask him to

JOIN THE ARMY TO-DAY

Imperial War Museums

sons who fled combat by asking, "Where have you come now in your cowardly flight, vile varlets? Do you intend to slink in here whence you came forth?"[47] When Henry Fleming takes leave of his mother as he goes off to war, she upsets him by not declaring like a Spartan mother that a son should come back from combat "with his shield or on it," but she does tell him, "yeh must never do no shirking, child, on my account. If so be a time comes when yeh have to be kilt or do a mean thing, why, Henry, don't think of anything 'cept what's right, because there's many a woman has to bear up 'ginst sech things these times, and the Lord'll take keer of us all."[48]

If it's true that women are particularly effective at making the charge of cowardice, it's also true that they are particularly effective at questioning or undermining the power of the charge. A subplot of Morford's *The Coward* reverses the Margaret Hayley–Carlton Brand cowardice dynamic by depicting a woman who sharply criticizes the notion of cowardice. Schoolteacher Kitty Hood criticizes her beau Dick Compton for preferring "standing up to be shot at, to remaining here with me. . . . I say that if you thought half as much of me as you did of public opinion and making a show of your fine new clothes, you would not stir one step."[49]

Dick goes off to war anyway. The episode echoes that classic instance in the *Iliad* of the female critique of the warrior's code—and of the critique's frequent futility: Andromache on the tower, telling her husband Hector not to leave the city walls and make an orphan of his son and a widow of her. Hector replies that his

> shame before the Trojans and their wives
> With their long robes trailing, would be too terrible
> If I hung back from battle like a coward.[50]

He goes down to do battle on the plains of Ilion, where he dies at the hands of Achilles.

Gendered thinking pervades the language and punishments associated with the accusation of cowardice, from Michel de Montaigne in "Of the Punishment of Cowardice" citing as an ancient innovation the Greek practice of replacing the death sentence for cowards with the requirement that for three days they dress as women,[51] to this statement in the massive study of World War II fighting men led by Samuel Stouffer, the results of which were published in 1949 in the two volumes of *The American Soldier: Combat and Its Aftermath*:

> A code as universal as "being a man" is very likely to have been deeply internalized, so the fear of failure in the role, as by showing cowardice in battle, could bring not only fear of social censure on this point as such, but also more central and strongly established fears related to sex-typing. To fail to measure up as a soldier in courage and endurance was to risk the charge of not being a man. ("Whatsa matter, bud—got lace in your drawers?" "Christ, he's acting like an old maid.") If one were not socially defined as a man, there was a strong likelihood of being branded a "woman," a dangerous threat to the contemporary male personality.[52]

This is tricky territory, given the underlying misogyny that makes it such an insult to call men womanish. But the point, the sting, of the insult may come not from the belief that women are inherently cowardly but that men who behave as cowards are unmanly. Such thinking remains alive and well today. In Kevin Powers's 2012 novel *The Yellow Birds*, an soldier who went to combat in the recent American engagement in Iraq (in which Powers himself served) tells himself that "cowardice got you into this mess because you wanted to be a man and people made fun of you and pushed you around in the cafeteria and hallways in high school because you liked to read books and poems sometimes and they called you fag and really deep down you know you went because you wanted to be a man." Allowing oneself to be bullied, being thought queer or intellectual: such apparent unmanliness could be overcome by joining the military.[53]

Cowardice is not nearly as much of a problem for women. One seldom hears them labeled cowards, and when one does, it sounds strange, begging for qualification.[54] A character in Emma Dunham Kelly-Hawkins's 1898 novel *Four Girls at Cottage City* observes that "you will very often find the spirit of a mouse concealed in the frame of a large woman, while your little, slender, wiry one is as courageous as a lion...." Women *can* be cowardly, in this character's opinion, but they cannot be as cowardly as men: "And the rule holds good with the other sex, only timidity in a man is a hundred times more contemptible than in a big woman. The woman's sex excuses her to a certain extent, but what is more despicable than a cowardly man—especially if he is a big one?"[55] Body size, Kelly-Hawkins implies, influences the attribution of cowardice. The bigger the body, the less excusable the cowardice.

Partly this must have to do with simple physics. Even babies as young as ten months old, a recent study found, will predict that the bigger cartoon character will defeat the smaller one, so if the bigger one loses or flees, some explanation is required.[56] The theory of natural selection also helps explain the connections among body size, gender, and the attribution of cowardice. Some primate group behavior is organized by dominance hierarchies that are themselves shaped by the fact that in some species (including our own) male primates are on average larger than females. The size difference suggests to one scientist that "the male on average should be better than the female at displaying dominant behaviour and worse at displaying subordinate behaviour, i.e. the male should be more aggressive and less fearful than the female."[57] If this hypothesis is true, then biology underlies the human cultural norm that stigmatizes the display of fear in men but tolerates it in women.[58]

Consider attitudes toward men crying. Edward B. Hughes, a private in the Union Army, was found guilty of desertion in the face of the enemy and cowardice at Chickamauga in 1863 because he "did skulk behind a tree, and when ordered to come into ranks by his Captain, say in words to this effect 'I can see as well here' and while there in the rear of his company did bemoan himself in a cowardly manner by crying and other manifestations of cowardice." The trial returned to the matter of his crying several times.

> Q: Was the accused crying when you saw him behind the tree?
> A: I believe he was, I saw tears or water coursing from his eyes.[59]

There may have been a certain kindness behind the witness's clinical precision, his reluctance to use the word *crying*, a behavior often thought unmanly for reasons that appear to be both natural and cultural. Current research indicates that girls and boys cry with the same frequency until puberty, when both sexes begin to cry less, but the decline in male crying is much sharper than the decline among females. This gap may reflect a physiological cause, or it may be that cultural expectations of manhood assert themselves powerfully at adolescence.[60] Or perhaps nature and culture converge to powerful effect. Men may be naturally less inclined to admit and less able to display fear than women are, and society reinforces, to a lesser or greater extent, this natural tendency. Whatever the case, and despite increasing acceptance of soldier's tears in recent years, the idea that real men don't cry is stubbornly persistent.[61] Private Hughes was found guilty and sentenced to be shot, a sentence commuted to prison and hard labor for the duration of the war.

Cowardice may indeed be the crucial link in the chain binding courage and gender. William Ian Miller notes that "we will know that women are accepted as official players at aggressive combative courage" not when they receive medals for bravery, for such accolades are often politicized, but "when it is fully believed that [women] can be subject to court-martial for cowardly conduct."[62] As Miller has it, the price of the privilege of courage is the risk of being deemed, and punished as, a coward; eligibility for cowardice is fundamental to eligibility for courage. Yet the maleness of the courage/cowardice club may reflect not the special importance of males but their dispensability. It has been speculated that a prime survival strategy for early humans was to employ adult males as sentinels. Because they are bigger they can see farther and fight more effectively—and because they are males they are, reproductively speaking (eggs being rarer than sperm), more expendable.[63]

Eligibility for cowardice and the consequent fear of it can also complicate access to certain kinds of courage. "Many a man has not the moral courage to plead for peace," wrote Hannah J. Bailey of the Woman's Christian Temperance Union, a critic of the Spanish-American War, "for fear he shall be accused of effeminacy or cowardice." Not having such fear makes women more natural and effective peace advocates.[64]

Sex—or the withholding of it—can be a powerful weapon in such advocacy. Aristophanes's *Lysistrata* tells the tale of women who refuse to have sex with men who go to war. Their tactic of making themselves as alluring as possible for their husbands only to deny them the pleasures of the bedroom was revisited in the United States during the Vietnam era in a famous poster depict-

Division of Political History, National Museum of American History,
Smithsonian Institution

ing the Baez sisters—Joan Baez, Pauline Baez Marden, and Mimi Fariña—sitting bare- but cross-legged under the words, "GIRLS SAY YES to boys who say NO."[65]

When "girls" say yes to war by becoming soldiers themselves, they find it a challenge to remain women and soldier on. In her 2005 memoir *Love My Rifle More Than You: Young and Female in the U.S. Army*, Kayla Williams notes that military training taught her "how not to be like a woman, how not to be weak, how not to cry, how not to have PMS or even periods, as if to be female meant to put forth a constant effusion of unpleasant secretions, as if to be a man was to withhold."[66] Gender here brings us to the association of cowardice with a bodily function as vital as reproduction—excretion.

The origin of the American usage of "yellow" as a synonym for cowardly is obscure, but that the term endures may owe something to its connection to involuntary urination, or enuresis. An American World War II veteran remembered worrying that his "bladder would surely empty itself and reveal [him] to be the coward that [he] was."[67] The 1954 film *The Caine Mutiny* (based on the 1951 novel by Herman Wouk) evokes this phenomenon on a grand scale when, on orders from the panicky Captain Queeg, the minesweeper USS *Caine* drops yellow dye overboard to signal to the boats it's leading that they should proceed with caution. The *Caine* then speeds to safety, leaving behind it a huge expanse of yellow-colored ocean, treacherous waters that the other boats have to navigate without the minesweeper's help. This act of cowardice inspires Queeg's men to call him "Old Yellowstain" and to sing a song in his dishonor:

I've got those Yellowstain blues
those silly Yellowstain blues.
When someone fires a shot
it's always there I am not . . .

Encopresis, involuntary defecation, is the stuff of crude current slang and age-old cliché too.[68] Aristophanes's *Peace* has great fun with a strutting commander who flees battle and turns his scarlet cloak a darker color.[69] One Union colonel accusing another of cowardice said, "Ye have more shit in your breeches than you do in your guts."[70] As World War II memoirist John Ellis notes, "stereotypes of 'manliness' and 'guts' can readily accommodate the fact that a man's stomach or heart might betray his nervousness, but they make less allowance for his shitting his pants or wetting himself."[71]

The habits and beliefs connected with our early toilet training lead us to (so to speak) keep our shit together—or to try to—even in the face of mortal danger. James Jones reported that during combat in Guadalcanal he stood up to urinate as his company was being barraged. "Even with death staring me in the face," he remembered, "I had to go through the whole customary procedure of urinating to keep from getting it on me. So strong was the early training of my childhood. At any moment I might be dead, but I could not just piss in my pants (which were already wet) or not even just lay down on my side to piss."[72] An important stage in each person's development is becoming continent and learning to disapprove of those who do not.

Sigmund Freud might say that our contemptuous feelings about cowardice are the result of a "reaction formation" that occurs quite early on in life. We envy the coward because, deep down, we want to indulge incontinence of every kind and be cowardly ourselves. Deep down we *are* cowardly, and so we build a wall of disgusted contempt to protect ourselves from such revelations. It's part of growing up.

We do not like to contemplate the other end of life either, growing old or debilitated: the loss of bowel and bladder control, of the cough reflex, of hair; tear ducts overflow, our very cells break down.

The coward does not manifest all these symptoms, but he does present some of them, and in so doing he brings us an unwelcome preview of our own imminent loss of bodily integrity, what Philip Larkin called the "whole hideous inverted childhood" of aging.[73] Displays of cowardice offer us a disturbing reminder of human frailty and boundedness, the "abject finitude" of our existence.[74]

The connection between incontinence and cowardice is still in a way surprising. The fearful tendency to empty bowels and bladder has adaptive value. It relieves the fearful creature of excess weight so that it then has less to carry as it flees or fights.[75] Of the 2,095 men in one American division in the South Pacific during World War II, over two hundred reported having urinated in fear; over four hundred admitted to having lost control of their bowels.[76] The phenomenon is accepted in some circumstances. After a shelling in Erich Maria Remarque's *All Quiet on the Western Front*, a soldier reveals that he has soiled himself. "That's no disgrace," says another soldier. "Many's the man before you has had his pants full after the first bombardment."[77]

Incontinence can even be worn as a strange badge of courage. "Only the laundry knew how scared I was," reported U.S. Army Air Force lieutenant Louis Zamperini about his incontinence during a plane crash—but such a confession emphasizes the strength of will behind the acts performed in spite of fear's power over the body, further evidence of the fact that Zamperini was, as the title of Laura Hillenbrand's best-selling book put it, "unbroken."[78]

The best way to avoid the charge of cowardice is to wound the enemy, or to be wounded by him. A soldier who upon his return from battle wears the enemy's blood will generally not be suspected of cowardice; his own blood will protect him from this suspicion as well. One might think in the first case of Hector in the *Iliad* praying that his son may someday return from a battle with the bloody armor of some vanquished foe, and in the second of the Hollywood hero's bloodied face—usually a flesh wound that accentuates the cheekbones.[79] The American poet and World War II veteran Louis Simpson writes of

> war-heroes, of wounded war-heroes
> With just enough of their charms shot away
> To make them more handsome. The women moved nearer
> To touch their brave wounds and their hair streaked with gray.[80]

Wounds provide inoculation against the charge of cowardice and can even serve as the aphrodisiac that cowardice decidedly does not.[81]

It is possible to game this system, of course. In a comical portrait, Theophrastus (a disciple of Aristotle) depicts the coward as someone who will do anything to avoid battle. He will forget his sword, then hide it, then make a long show of looking for it, then care oversolicitously for a injured comrade. Then, when the battle is over, "covered with blood from the other's wound, he will meet those returning from the fight, and announce to them, 'I have run some risk to save one of our fellows.'"

A more extreme ploy is depicted in an 1862 popular print of the unsubtly named "Adam Cowherd" having his finger cut off so he can get a medical exemption certificate like the one in the left hand of the other man in the picture. This other man's right hand shows that he has already had this procedure performed: he's a damn coward too.[82] As in other wars, self-injury was a significant problem during the Civil War, with numerous court-martial cases for

CANDIDATES FOR THE EXEMPT BRIGADE.—

Library of Congress

cowardice made against soldiers who shot their fingers, thumbs, hands, or feet to escape duty. Their files often include testimony from doctors noting the damning gunpowder in their wounds.[83]

Legitimate wounds are themselves not all equal. How and where one is injured matters. Instead of proving one's courage, being wounded in the back can suggest cowardice. In Morford's *The Coward*, Carlton Brand is finally redeemed when he leads a charge at the Battle of Culpeper and is struck by a bullet that "passed from breast to back,—thank God not from back to breast!"[84] (The novel ends with him being lovingly nursed by his former fiancée and presumably future wife, Margaret Hayley.) Not everyone in the Civil War era believed that being wounded in the back suggested cowardly flight. One Union officer called the idea "humbug. A mounted officer is as likely to be hit in the back, and more likely to be hit in the side than in the front"; condemning him for such an injury would be unjust. But *The Coward* was not alone in promulgating this humbug.[85] One Confederate soldier remembered, "Oh, how I ran! I was afraid of being struck in the back, and I frequently turned half around so as to avoid if possible so disgraceful a wound." His captain ran backward with him.[86]

Curiously, though, turning tail can actually increase the likelihood of getting killed. The Greek poet Tyrtaeus pointed out that "once a man reverses and runs in the terror of battle, / he offers his back, a tempting mark to spear from behind. . . ."[87] The back may tempt the spear because, as lieutenant colonel Dave Grossman speculates in *On Killing*, a book sometimes used for combat training, soldiers find it easier to overcome their reluctance to kill when they can't see the face of their victim; turning one's back can also excite potential attackers' "chase instinct."[88] A target with his back turned is, furthermore, no threat to the targeter. All this only adds to the stigma of the wound in the back: "it is a shameful sight when a dead man lies in the dust there," Tyrtaeus notes, "driven through from behind by the stroke of an enemy spear."[89]

As its title suggests, Crane's *The Red Badge of Courage* takes on the idea of the redemptive wound directly. Crane wrote that he intended the book to present "a psychological portrayal of fear," a project that necessarily put into question the moral judgment of fear implied by the idea of cowardice and the idea that a wound could be a sign of courage.[90] Young Henry Fleming envies the injured: "He conceived persons with torn bodies to be peculiarly happy. He wished that he, too, had a wound, a red badge of courage."[91] Henry gets his wound, to be sure, but not in the course of a heroic leap beyond duty into the glorious fray of battle, not in the course of duty at all, and not from an enemy weapon. Rather, he is hurt by the butt of the rifle of a fellow soldier in the course of a massive and frantic retreat as he makes his halfhearted return from desertion. Crane presents Henry's wound not as a badge of courage but of, at best, the arbitrary violence of war.

James Jones had read *The Red Badge*—he wrote a paper on it for a class while he was a soldier[92]—

University of Virginia Library

but *The Thin Red Line* is even more skeptical about what in World War II came to be called a million-dollar wound. Corporal Fife—like Henry Fleming, half-obsessed with cowardice—thinks through the optimal ways to be injured: a major wound that almost kills you so you can get out of the war but not be crippled for life, or a "minor wound which would incapacitate or cripple you slightly without crippling fully. Fife could not decide which he would prefer. He didn't really prefer any, that was the truth."[93] Jones's goal in this novel was, as he said while he was writing it, to liberate the men who grew up after World War II from "from the horseshit which has been engrained in them by my generation," which had served in it.[94]

"Cowardice" and "courage" were essential to the horseshit. In a harrowing scene based on his own experience, Jones sought to show that they were not "terms of human reference any more" by associating some of the archetypal features of cowardice with an act that seems to be the very epitome of courage: victory in hand-

Harry Ransom Center, University of Texas

to-hand, one-on-one combat.[95] A Japanese soldier attacks young Private Bead while he is squatting to defecate in the woods. When the emaciated Japanese soldier comes after the indisposed Bead with a bayonet, Bead tackles him and finds him easy to overpower but hard to finish off. "My god," Bead wonders, "how much killing did the damned fool require?" All the while sobbing and trying to keep his unfastened pants from falling, Bead beat the Japanese soldier, "kicked him, choked him, clawed him, bayoneted him, shot him." Finally, "[s]tanding above him spraddlelegged to keep his pants up," Bead finishes the job. The other man dead at last, he falls to the ground and vomits.

A more inglorious battle to the death is difficult to imagine. Bead is spattered with blood—the mark of the triumphant warrior—but he is "terrified someone might think he had crapped his pants from fear." "Ashamed and embarrassed by the whole thing," he resolves not to tell anyone about it.[96] In associating paradigmatically courageous behavior with a reviled symptom of cowardice, Jones deflates, even denatures, these moral categories.

But Jones knew that they were not to be gotten rid of. "One day one of their number would write a book about all this," reads the last sentence of *The Thin Red Line*, "but none of them would believe it, because none of them would remember it that way."[97] War stories would continue to glorify conventional courage and, drawing on all the archetypal associations of manliness and shame, they would continue to condemn cowardice. And wars would continue.

Perhaps he should not have been quite so despairing. A number of recent books have argued that war is becoming less common. Proportionally speaking, death in combat has declined precipitously since World War II; the trend can be traced back before that, for centuries even, and violence outside of war has also decreased. Thanks to our instinctual altruism, and to a variety of civilizing factors such as urbanization, education, commerce, and organized systems of justice, human beings have expanded the range of people they feel sympathy for, far beyond kin or tribe. According to this line of thinking, we have become more likely to listen to "the better angels of our nature"—to borrow the title of Steven Pinker's 2012 book—and to abhor violence.[98]

Henry Fleming seems to anticipate the trend (or be aware that it's already happening) when he laments that he wouldn't get to see "a Greek-like struggle." Such "would be no more," he thinks. "Men were better, or more timid. Secular and religious education had effaced the throat-grappling instinct, or else firm finance held in check the passions." Henry would get to see combat, but the struggle he has isn't exactly Greek-like, and the whole of his story hints at the arc of progress spelled out by Pinker and others. Henry engages in an "eternal debate" through much of *The Red Badge*: will he give in to fear and run or "discover that he had been a fool in his doubts, and was, in truth, a man of traditional courage"? What he ultimately discovers is that the debate itself is foolish, ill-premised. When he thinks that having made his "mistakes in the dark" meant that he was still a man, the implication is that any sin so thoroughly a matter of social perception is no sin at all. At the end of the novel, Henry "felt a quiet manhood," Crane writes, "nonassertive but of sturdy and strong blood. . . . He had been to touch the great death, and found that, after all, it was but the great death. He was a man."[99] This newfound sturdiness comes from reckoning not only with his fear of death but also with his fear of being thought a coward.

Decades later, when we reencounter him in "The Veteran" (a short story published a year after *The Red Badge of Courage*), Henry jokes about cowardice. Accompanied by his grandson at the grocery store, he is asked, "Mr. Fleming, you never was frightened much in them battles, was you?" Henry's answer, "You bet I was scared," provokes laughter. "Yes sir," he goes on, "I thought every man in the other army was aiming at me in particular, and only me. . . . So I run!" At this, Crane tells us that "wrinkles appeared at the corners of his eyes. Evidently he appreciated some comedy in this recital."

The Red Badge of Courage makes the traditional ideas of courage and cowardice seem adolescent, and Henry, in "The Veteran," has grown up. It's a nice story—a wise old man sees the folly of his earlier vainglory and of his shame at cowardice—and it ends with

Henry's heroic death in the course of saving animals from a burning barn. "When the roof fell in," Crane writes,

> a great funnel of smoke swarmed toward the sky, as if the old man's mighty spirit, released from its body—a little bottle—had swelled like the genie of fable. The smoke was tinted rose-hue from the flames, and perhaps the unutterable midnights of the universe will have no power to daunt the color of this soul.

But though Henry Fleming's spirit seems triumphant, the story is haunted by an earlier moment. When Henry made light of his cowardice in the grocery, his grandson "was visibly horror-stricken. His hands were clasped nervously, and his eyes were wide with astonishment at this terrible scandal, his magnificent grandfather telling such a thing. . . . His stout boyish idealism was injured."[100] This stout boyish idealism, and the scandal of cowardice that forms the dark backing of that idealism, seems to be reborn with every generation. If we take the story to be set in the year it was published, 1896, Henry's grandson might a few years later have joined Theodore Roosevelt on San Juan Hill, or he might have waited to test his idealism in the Great War.

Chapter 3

THE WAYS OF EXCESSIVE FEAR

Before the Civil War, lieutenant Moses Powell of the First Regiment Michigan Sharpshooters had been known for his bravery as a deputy sheriff in his small hometown, and he looked every bit the stalwart leader of men—tall and with "a large, handsome head, graced with a long, beautiful beard, and altogether a very prepossessing looking person," as one of his fellow soldiers put it.[1] Powell proved the opposite of prepossessing when battle came, however. "[W]hen we went into position" for combat, according to a witness at Powell's court-martial for cowardice, "he was very seldom with the Company." One of the doctors who examined him said he regarded his case as "peculiar" since Powell's "mental excitement had as much to do with his disordered state as physical reasons." The court preferred simpler terms.

Q BY COURT: What did this mental excitement arise from?
A: I interpreted it to arise from the action in front [.]
Q BY COURT: Was not this excitement what is commonly known as fear?[2]

The damning implication of the question—that fear made Lieutenant Powell morally suspect—reflected a venerable idea that endured during the Civil War,[3] when, as Gerald Linderman contends, soldiers generally equated fear with cowardice.[4]

It is a strange equation. Fear is a natural adaptive response to danger. It increases the heart rate and secretion of adrenaline, and concentrates blood in large muscles and the brain rather than the intestines and skin (thus

Collection of John Buckbee

does the face go "pale with fear"). Arms and legs are energized for fighting or fleeing. Profuse sweating helps cool the body in case it needs to undertake arduous action.[5] These phenomena typically occur when one simply *feels* fear; *expressing* fear also has adaptive benefits. Fearful eyes widen and pupils dilate to take in as much visual information as possible.[6] The speed of eye movements also increases, which enhances "target localization." The fearful face typically enlarges the nasal cavity, augmenting what neuroscientists call "one of the most basic and primitive forms of sensory intake, nasal inspiratory capacity."[7] In these and other physiological manifestations, fear can enhance both our awareness and our ability to act.

Sometimes military authorities have recognized the inevitability and utility of fear. A booklet issued to U.S. Army soldiers during World War II showed that American military authorities thought it best to accept and acknowledge fear, and to deny explicitly the equation of fear and cowardice. **"YOU'LL BE SCARED,"** it read in bold caps. "Sure you'll be scared. Before you go into battle, you'll be frightened at the uncertainty, at the thought of being killed. Will it hurt? Will you know what to do? If you say you're not scared, you'll be a cocky fool. Don't let anyone tell you you're a coward if you admit being scared."[8] It was army policy during World War II to cultivate tolerance about fear among the troops.[9] And this included fear and anxiety about being cowardly: "Have you been hiding some very dark thoughts about yourself?" the pamphlet asked. "Have you called yourself a coward?"[10]

Permissiveness about fear arose at least in part from a sense that war had become more fearsome. War has always been hell, and Martin van Creveld, for one, doubts that "modern war is harder to bear than its predecessors."[11] But the scale of war, in time and space and might, has increased significantly, and this can make it harder to bear—or at least make it seem so. Well into the nineteenth century, battles were measured in hours or days. By 1916 they often stretched for months. As World War I "dragged on," Captain Charles Wilson of the Royal Army Medical Corps observed, "fear was no longer an occasional and exotic visitor but a settler in our midst."[12] Its cumulative effect led Wilson (later Lord Moran) to think that a man's ability to hold up against it—his courage—was not an absolute quality of his character but something he had a certain amount of, like money in a bank account, and which could be depleted slowly or suddenly by the hardships and horrors of war.

The proliferation of ever more destructive and far-ranging weapons and ever more efficient and devious means of deploying them also enlarged the zone of danger and saturated it with hazards as never before.[13] Death could come from the sky, from over the horizon, from under the water; in the form of poison gas, it could come from the very air. Twentieth-century combatants experienced and witnessed the appalling damage done to human beings by weapons designed to demolish the ever larger and more heavily armored machinery of twentieth-century war.[14] According to John Keegan, weapons were also increasingly designed with cruel intentions in mind: "Weapons have never been kind to human flesh, but the directing principle behind their design has usually not been that of maximizing the pain and damage they can cause.... It is now a desired effect of many man-killing weapons that they inflict wounds as terrible and terrifying as possible." Keegan cites as an example napalm, the 1942 American invention engineered to cling more closely to human skin as it burns.[15] In 1946 the word *overkill* came into the English language, an American coinage first used (as a verb) in the military context.[16]

The fearsomeness of war did not change everyone's views toward what constituted excessive fear. At the same time American authorities were cultivating tolerance toward fear, the Japanese Imperial Army, reviving and reshaping the Bushido ethic to compel its soldiers during World War II, "simply rejected" fear[17]—an attitude that helps explain Japanese soldiers' banzai charges and kamikaze attacks and their contempt for surrender. Better to die by your own hand, plunging your sword into your bowels, or even by your own foot, pulling the rifle's trigger with your toe, than to allow yourself to be taken alive. Japanese authorities did not provide troops guidance about white flags or the other conventions of surrender, for surrender was held to be almost unthinkably cowardly. This attitude helps explain a startling disparity: at Saipan and Iwo Jima, one Allied soldier was taken captive for every three who were killed; the ratio among the Japanese was 1 in 120.[18] The war itself did not end with surrender, in the prevailing Japanese view;

rather, the emperor merely decided to "terminate" hostilities. It took a decade before the Japanese state would acknowledge the actual conditions of its defeat.[19]

Soldiers' circumstances and experience can also soften or harden what they deem to be excessive fear. Prolonged exposure to the hardships of combat in the Civil War led to a "readiness to narrow the definition of cowardice," according to Linderman. By the end of the war, he argues, soldiers did not equate fear with cowardice nearly as much as they had at its beginning.[20] In World War II, it seemed to work the opposite way. When actual battle came, American soldiers became less tolerant of displays of fear in their fellows.[21] Perhaps combat corrects to the mean: the Civil War soldiers found themselves too ready to judge others as cowardly, the World War II soldiers not sufficiently so.

Yet beneath the contingent and changing nature of our judgment about fear and fearful behavior, it is possible to discern a principle that generally prevails: fear in the context of battle is generally viewed as excessive when a soldier reveals it in a way that threatens to spread it.[22] At Shiloh, a Union colonel reported, "We formed again on the Purdy road, but the fleeing mass from the left broke through our lines, and many of our men caught the infection and fled with the crowd."[23] The metaphor is apt, though as the young field of social neuroscience is beginning to explore, fear infects more quickly than any virus, thanks to operations both in and *between* brains. Discoveries about so-called mirror neurons may have been overhyped, but they have shown our nervous systems to be less self-contained, more permeable than previously believed.[24]

A practical understanding of the social psychology of fear long predates such neuroscientific thinking, of course. The book of

Deuteronomy shows an awareness of the infectiousness of fear in its advice that "officers . . . shall say, What man is there that is fearful and faint-hearted? Let him go and return unto his house lest his brethren's heart faint as well as his heart" (20:8). A lieutenant in the Indiana Cavalry said in an 1864 court-martial case, "If anyone ever finds me showing the white feather I hope he will shoot me before my example creates a panic."[25]

Perhaps the most obvious way to show the white feather and so create panic is by running.[26] Stephen Crane's *The Red Badge of Courage* shows how quickly and automatically this happens. While he was in camp, Henry Fleming had "tried to mathematically prove to himself that he would not run from a battle," but when battle comes and a soldier near him flees, he takes no time to do any calculating. Fleming

> turned his head, shaken from his trance by this movement as if the regiment was leaving him behind. He saw the few fleeting forms.
>
> He yelled then with fright and swung about. For a moment, in the great clamour, he was like a proverbial chicken. . . .
>
> Directly he began to speed toward the rear in great leaps. His rifle and cap were gone. His unbuttoned coat bulged in the wind. The flap of his cartridge box bobbed wildly, and his canteen, by its slender cord, swung out behind. On his face was all the horror of those things which he imagined.

There's a self-infecting process happening here too. The more Henry runs, the more he fears, and so the more he runs: "Since he had turned his back upon the fight his fears had been wondrously magnified."[27] Crane's psychology of fear accords with a theory that William James and Carl Lange were both promulgating at around the same time as Crane wrote—one that has recently seen renewed interest in neuroscience.[28] These men held that emotion followed physiological arousal, rather than the other way around. Generations of Psych 101 students have been given this shorthand for this theory of emotion: "I run, therefore I fear." It's hard for them to wrap their heads around this theory, because it runs counter to "common sense" and what feels like personal experience. After one beholds a frightening object, one's body responds with an elevated heartbeat or by automatically performing some action; this bodily response is then interpreted by the mind as fear. Ambrose Bierce defined a coward as "one who, in a time of perilous emergency, thinks with his legs."[29]

Henry's cowardice seems to be made all the worse by the fact that, as he flees, he lightens his load by dropping his rifle. In throwing away arms the soldier was "both disarming himself and arming the enemy," as Roman law had it.[30] It must make causing panic in others more likely, too. Yet despite all the damning details that show Henry to be "like a proverbial chicken" (not to mention the explicit damnation itself), Crane complicates the judgment of Fleming's flight as cowardice. Recalling this episode, Henry actually thinks he acquitted himself quite admirably. He remembers "how some of the men had run from the battle. As he recalled their terror-stricken faces he felt a scorn for them. They had surely been more fleet and more wild than was absolutely necessary." Their style showed the excessiveness of their fear. His fellow fleeing soldiers "were weak mortals," Henry thinks. "As for himself, he had fled with discretion and dignity."[31]

Fleeing—or at least retreating—with discretion and dignity is not impossible. Socrates famously did so at the Battle at Delium, "quietly on the lookout for friends and foes, [making] it plain to everyone even at a great distance that if one touches this real man, he will defend himself vigorously."[32] For ably leading the retreat of British troops routed in battle against the French and Indians in 1755, George Washington was known as the "hero of the Monongahela."[33] But Henry's view of his own flight is distinctly generous to himself. He's no Socrates or Washington.

Henry's vanity and grandiosity provoke our laughter and make us question not just his judgment of his fearful conduct, but the very categories—courage and cowardice—that he brings to that judgment. Compare the description of the proverbial chicken Henry, "speed[ing] toward the rear in great leaps.... The flap of his cartridge box bob[bing] wildly," with one of Henry taking part in an attack, in which we read that "he ran desperately, as if pursued for a murder. His face was drawn hard and tight with the stress of his endeavor. His eyes were fixed in a lurid glare. And with his soiled and disordered dress, his red and inflamed features surmounted by the dingy rag with its spot of blood, his wildly swinging rifle and banging accouterments, he looked to be an insane soldier."[34] Both scenes depict Fleming in a desperate run, the difference in the second instance being that he keeps his gun and participates not in a frenzied flight but a frenzied assault. Cowardice and courage become merely arbitrary names we give to physiological reactions to environmental conditions. One recent sociological study of violence has even gone so far as to call group aggression a "forward panic" in which the physiological symptoms are the same as for panicked flight.[35] Louis-Ferdinand Céline, in *Journey to the End of the Night* (1932), writes of the "flight *into* collective murder" of World War I, and the narrator of this (semiautobiographical) work wasn't having any of it: "I wasn't very bright myself, but at least I had sense enough to opt for cowardice once and for all."[36]

The GI's that James Jones depicted in *The Thin Red Line* had apparently not read their Céline or their Crane. A conventional idea of cowardice figures as powerfully in the thoughts of this group of American soldiers serving on Guadalcanal in World War II as it did for Henry Fleming, but Jones is even more explicit than Crane in showing how prevalent the preoccupation with cowardice was—and how quickly it could disappear in the heat of combat. "[S]omewhere in the back of each [soldier's] mind," Jones writes, "like a fingernail picking uncontrollably at a scabby sore, was the small voice saying: but is it worth it? Is it really worth it to die, to be dead, just to prove to everybody that you're not a coward?"[37] That quick riff on death inflects the question of cowardice with a wicked poignancy. "To die" is a dramatic and finite act, perhaps worth doing to avoid the shame of cowardice; "being dead," on the other hand, is a duller matter, a permanent condition, and so not as acceptable an exchange for one's reputation.

When it comes to actual combat, Jones's novel makes it explicitly clear that soldiers do "not worry about being brave or being cowardly." Such notions do not guide or explain their behavior; biology does: "Their systems pumped full of adrenaline to constrict the peripheral blood vessels, elevate the blood pressure, make the heart beat more rapidly, and aid coagulation, they were about as near to automatons without courage or cowardice as flesh and blood can get."[38] This is literary naturalism with a vengeance—what one scholar aptly calls "medical realism."[39] In Jones's vision, the physiology of fear supersedes any thoughts about cowardice or courage. "Numbly, they did the necessary."[40] This numbness is today understood as a stress-induced elevation of hormones and neurotransmitters that impairs functioning of the prefrontal cortex, a part of the brain important in reasoning, reflection, and other high-level mental and emotional processing—functions that enable moral judgment.[41] What Crane and Jones and current neuroscience tell us about fear is that although soldiers may think about cowardice before combat, it's far from their minds when they reach the heat of battle.

Cowardice has also become less of a concern in modern warfare because some archetypically cowardly actions, particularly running, are no longer effective ways of escaping danger. Consoled by the sound of the footsteps of others behind him who are also fleeing, Henry Fleming "felt vaguely that death must make a first choice of the men who were nearest; the initial morsels for the dragons would be then those who were following him. So he displayed the zeal of an insane sprinter in his purpose to keep them in the rear. There was a race."[42] Whether this race is winnable or not is another question, and the answer seems increasingly to be no. Despite the warnings of old about the cowardly back tempting the spear, if one is fleet enough or gets a good enough head start, one *can* get out of range of a spear or arrow. Modern weaponry makes getting out of the way much more difficult. The Civil War saw the first widespread use of the rifled musket and also improvements in bullet shape that made kills possible from more than half a mile away. Artillery shelling could launch shots over the horizon. The twentieth century saw dramatic improvements in the range and power of such weapons.[43] Rocket missiles deliver themselves faster than sound.[44] A soldier, indeed an entire platoon, could now be wiped out before danger was even suspected.

There is no longer any race. One does not even have the chance to run, and the mobility of one's own machines can be deceptive, and, indeed, ultimately immobilizing. One can literally fly in an airplane, of course, or go inhumanly fast and far on land or water in some motorized vehicle, but within that vehicle one is stuck. Nor does range or speed help when, as James Jones wrote of World War II, "there was nowhere to run. Just about every nation was involved, one way or another. The whole world was caught up. Had some sanctuary existed, transportation to it would have been impossible under the government control being exercised."[45]

The futility of running narrows the possibilities for cowardice. We might recall here Samuel Johnson's explanation for why, compared to recklessness, cowardice was "always considered as a topic of unlimited and licentious censure": because cowardice, unlike recklessness, is not easily checked. When there are fewer places to run, when running can be easily checked, we need no longer waste "unlimited and licentious censure" on those who would flee.

Hiding and its close associate cowering (not etymologically related to cowardice, but often linked with it) constitute another archetypal cowardly behavior that has been largely destigmatized in the context of modern war. The American rebels' habit of fighting guerrilla style—hiding in the forest, raiding, and then scurrying off—against a red-coated foe arrayed in the open has often been cited as a crucial reason the colonists won the Revolutionary War.[46] In James Fenimore Cooper's novel of the Revolutionary War, *The Spy* (1821), the hero Harvey Birch reports that in one battle the British "Rig'lars were all cut to pieces, for the [American] militia were fixed snugly in a log barn." The loyalist to whom Birch speaks has doubts that the British lost this or any other battle, but she does not "doubt the rebels got behind the logs."[47] She speaks with contempt. The rebel practice of taking cover and firing from behind trees and buildings and rocks was, in the British view, cowardly.[48] Birch responds "coolly" to the loyalist's implicit accusation:

"I think . . . it's quite ingenious to get a log between one and a gun, instead of getting between a gun and a log."[49] Birch's wit, coupled with the changing conditions of war, wins the point.

Although *The Spy* was the first novel written by an American to become a best seller in the United States, the fact that Birch was a spy who hid and frequently disguised himself made it difficult for early nineteenth-century readers to think him heroic.[50] At Waterloo in 1815, it was only when one was ordered to lie down that lying down was acceptable; otherwise, it was deemed cowardice.[51] During the Civil War, as one historian notes, men's tendency to take cover was "widely recognized by both officers and privates, and no one was prepared to criticize the men for this natural act,"[52] but taking cover was still sometimes condemned.

Union Army colonel David H. Williams's habit of hiding behind trees led his own men to taunt him: "Come out from behind that tree, Stumpy Williams, you coward, you are not competent to command."[53] He was found innocent in his court-martial, unlike private Edward B. Hughes, who while crying (as noted in chapter 2) "did allegedly . . . skulk behind a tree, and when ordered to come into ranks by his Captain, say in words to this effect 'I can see as well here.'" Hughes defended his actions as prudent. "As regards taking shelter behind a tree," he said in his closing statement, "when nothing but straggling shots were coming over, I do not believe [it] was even censurable, and I assert that I did it with my captain's consent." But as we have seen he was found guilty and sentenced to be shot, a sentence commuted to imprisonment and hard labor during the war.[54] First lieutenant Ferdinand Ornesi was supposed to lead his men into battle, but when enemy fire came near, he hid himself "in the house like a man afraid of bullets." Found guilty of cowardice before the enemy and conduct unbecoming an officer, Ornesi was sentenced to lose his "rank and honors" and be shot, though the death penalty was remitted.[55]

Such cases show that, even in the face of the terrible and growing power of modern war—why shouldn't a man be afraid of bullets?—there remained something in men that resisted the obvious utility of concealing oneself. Trenches were sometimes tactically necessary during the Civil War, and shovels were necessary to dig trenches—and yet shovels came to be symbols of cowardice.[56] Crane picks up on the resistance to hiding in *The Red Badge* in an episode when

> many men in the regiment began erecting tiny hills in front of them. They used stones, sticks, earth, and anything they thought might turn a bullet. . . .
>
> This procedure caused a discussion among the men. Some wished to fight like duelists, believing it to be correct to stand erect and be, from their feet to their foreheads, a mark. They said they scorned the devices of the cautious. But the others scoffed in reply, and pointed to the veterans on the flanks who were digging at the ground like terriers. In a short time there was quite a barricade along the regimental fronts.

The next time this matter comes up, Crane does not note any debate at all: "The men curled into depressions and fitted themselves snugly behind whatever would frustrate a bullet."[57] Experience taught them that modern weaponry makes using the "devices of the cautious" a kind of prudence untainted by cowardice.

The rapid increase in weapons' range and power over the nineteenth century pushed armies to shed their brightly colored uniforms and eschew close formations on open ground,[58] and the value of concealing and sheltering oneself would seem to have been irrevocably confirmed by World War I and its thousands of miles of trenches. It was this war that gave the English language, in 1917, a word that endorsed strategic concealment: "camouflage."[59] But still the stigma against hiding survived. One of Joseph Stalin's henchmen forbade Red Army troops from digging trenches in the Crimea during World War II; it was a "defeatist" tactic.[60] General George S. Patton was known for riding around combat zones in an open command car, and for standing out in the open in his eye-catching uniform while shells fell nearby.[61] In *The Thin Red Line*, Corporal Fife makes what he thinks of as a "heroic decision" to stand up and risk being shot rather than risk being thought a coward. He is not alone in worrying that to hide might be cowardly. Under attack from warplanes, a captain "did not know whether as an officer and commander he should stay up in the open or get down in his hole like everybody else. It was a constant battle every night, and every raid."[62] The captain always winds up in his hole, but his nightly battle with himself reflects the surprisingly persistent connection of crouching or hiding with cowardice.

Our developmental and evolutionary history may help to explain this persistence. In crouching to the ground, the coward undoes our progress from the helpless immobility of the newborn, to the crawling of the infant, to the upright posture of an adult, standing tall. In evolutionary terms, the stigma attached to crouching or taking cover may draw some of its power from the way it reverses the eons it took for our ancestors to become bipedal. An officer at Waterloo captured the equation of cowering and flight with evolutionary backsliding when he expressed contempt for a military doctor who "dropped on his hands and knees" when he was frightened by a passing shot, and, to the delighted derision of all, "away he scrambled like a great baboon."[63]

The cowering soldier also violates what Van Creveld calls an "age-old military tendency toward magnificence," a tendency he notes may parallel what zoologists call the handicap theory—in which, for example, the male peacock flourishes his tail even though doing so may attract a predator because it may also scare off a rival and attract a mate. The erect epauletted soldier in his plumed helmet presents a tall, wide target—but his ostentation impresses his enemy and his fellows, and maybe their sisters too, thereby increasing, at least hypothetically, his chances of reproducing.[64] He who cowers misses this opportunity. Perhaps what makes a lowered posture in war seem cowardly is that the cringing soldier has not actually been defeated, but his action constitutes a kind of premature surrender.

The instinct to hide—or run, for that matter—becomes obsolete in the event of nuclear war. When it comes to courage, one's bank account, to use and perhaps abuse Lord Moran's metaphor, does not just get emptied out; the bank itself is demolished. When it comes to cowardice, the terrible prospect of nuclear annihilation flips the conventional view on its head. During the Cuban missile crisis, after advising president John F. Kennedy to offer to remove America's nuclear weapons from Italy and Turkey if the Russians would pull theirs out of Cuba, U.S. ambassador to the United Nations Adlai Stevenson observed that most of the men in the room when he gave that advice "will probably consider me a coward for the rest of my life for what I said today, but perhaps we need a coward in the room when we are talking about nuclear war."[65]

Yet if no fear can be excessive when it comes to nuclear war, conventional warfare has perhaps become—or may become in the future—a less fearful enterprise. Military training has become more sophisticated about managing fear; "battle inoculation" involves habituating soldiers to danger by, for example, using live ammunition. Such training emphasizes competence and professionalism rather than the shame of cowardice.[66] Scientific advances promise to produce fear-suppressing drugs.[67] More and more soldiers perform their duty by facing computer screens rather than enemy guns.[68] Robots are becoming more able to perform combat functions once left to human soldiers.[69] War itself is becoming "unmanned."[70] Specialists who operate drones sit thousands of miles away from their target, far from the danger that for millennia came to anyone who dared to attack enemy warriors. Fear doesn't seem to enter the picture.[71]

More generally, beyond the military context, there is also reason to think that the quantum of fear in the world, or at least in many parts of the developed world, has diminished. Between 1850 and 2008, life expectancy at birth for American males doubled, from 37.2 years to 75.5 years.[72] Among the effects of such an increase is to make the greatest fear, that of death, seem distant and vague. The "decrease in frequency of proper occasions of fear" that William James said characterized civilized life has continued apace since he made the observation in 1884.[73]

Yet a diminution of fear is not an absolute good. Though our working definition of cowardice requires excessive fear, a seeming *deficit* of fear can also be seen as cowardly. Consider the case of Moses Powell's fellow lieutenant in the First Regiment Michigan Sharpshooters. In May 1864, Hooker DeLand refused to fight, telling a fellow officer that he would not go into battle because "he thought it was too warm for him, that he did not want to get killed just then." A few days later he told this same officer "that he did not calculate to go into any fight, that he had earned his commission by serving as a private and that he had something else to live for, that he had a mother and sister to support and that he was not going to be killed in this war, that he would resign if permitted, that sooner than go into a fight he would be dishonorably dismissed, or words to that effect." DeLand's audacious declaration on the battlefield that he did not want to die "just then" suggested a defiance that persisted through his

Collection of John Buckbee

drumming out, when one witness reported that he "seemed to brazen it out with a foolhardy manner."[74] Resolution is an oddly discordant quality in a supposed coward, sometimes comically so, but there it was in Lieutenant DeLand.

DeLand seems to fit William Ian Miller's description of a "fearless coward"—someone who has the courage to buck the pressure to conform, or who lacks shame. "[S]uch a person," Miller writes, "does not run away. The image is wrong; even the notion of fleeing misrepresents the insolence, even the fearlessness, with which he walks, sullenly saunters, but manifestly does not run away, while muttering, 'fuck this.'" DeLand also fits Miller's argument that for the fearless coward the originating excessive fear becomes "only a fillip, a hypothesis, that set in motion his fearless determination to avoid combat by any means necessary."[75] Yet Miller's formulation does not remove fear from the idea of cowardice. Outside observers' attribution of inner states such as fear is always hypothetical, and "initial fear" is, however submerged, still fear. In DeLand's case his fear of war had hardened into tenacity, and it did not help him in his encounter with the military justice system.

Corbis Images

The case of Eddie Slovik, whom Miller cites as a fearless coward, also shows how initial, excessive fear can change into something else. When he turned himself in after deserting, Slovik scrawled a candid confession that captured the originating fear (the "scared nerves and trembling" that practically paralyzed him when under shell fire) and, in its final words ("AND ILL RUN AWAY AGAIN IF I HAVE TO GO OUT THIER"), the transformation of that fear into a kind of defiance.[76] The day he submitted the confession an officer recommended he retract it, but Slovik refused. At his court-martial, the document was admitted as evidence without objection from the defense, and Slovik did not say anything to explain or qualify it; in fact he did not say anything at all. Slovik was, his widow said, "the unluckiest poor kid who ever lived." But his defiance helps explain how he became the only American soldier since the Civil War to be executed for desertion—the only one of the 40,000 American soldiers who deserted during World War II, the only one of the few thousand who were court-martialed for deserting, the only one of the forty-nine whose death sentences for deserting were approved.[77]

Another version of seemingly fearless cowardice was posited by the Reverend Samuel Davies, and the word he associates with it rings strangely to twenty-first-century ears: "security." Davies's main

I Pvt Eddie D. Slovik #36896415
Confess to the Desertion of The
United States Army. At The Time
of my Desertion We Were in
Albuff in France. I come to
Albuff as a Replacement. They
Were Shilling The Town and we
Were Told To dig in For The Night
The Flowing Morning They were
Shilling us again. I was so
Scared Nerves and Trembling
That at The Time The other
Replacements Moved out I
Couldnt move. I Stayed They
in my Fox hole Till it was quite
and I was able To move. I Then
Walked in Town. Not seeing any of
our Troops So I Stayed over night at
a French hospital. The next Morning I
Turned myself over to The Canadian
Provost Corp. After being with Them six
Weeks I was Turned over To American
M.P. They Turned me Lose. I Told my
Commanding my Story. I said that if
I had To go out Their again I'd
Run away. He said Their was nothing he
Could do For me so I Ran away again
AND I'll RUN AWAY AGAIN IF I
HAVE To go OUT Their   5555
Signed Pvt Eddie D. Slovik
A.S.N 36896415

- 1 -

worry about fear in May 1758 was not its excess but its lamentable absence among his "countrymen."

To judge by the text of Davies's sermon *The Curse of Cowardice* and the difficult time British authorities were having in recruiting Virginia colonists to battle the French and their Indian allies, many Virginians did not think they had anything to fear. Davies insisted otherwise. In his summary of the "present Circumstances of our Country," he described the horrors of the frontier, where many British colonists "lie dead, mangled with savage Wounds. Others have been dragged away Captives, and made Slaves of imperious and cruel Savages." In Hanover County and points east, danger may have seemed to be far away, said Davies, but it would come, and it would expose the folly of not having been properly fearful: "Some cry, 'Let the Enemy come down to us, and then we will fight them.' But this is the trifling excuse of Cowardice or Security...."[78]

Security and cowardice have not always seemed such an odd pair. The word *security* comes from the Latin *se cura*, "without care." After the familiar primary definition, "The condition of being protected from or not exposed to danger; safety," the *Oxford English Dictionary* gives for *security* a third definition: "culpable absence of anxiety, carelessness."[79] For Davies, being secure meant refusing to feel fear for fear of the responsibility such a feeling would entail. He was not alone in his usage or his worry. Those concerned with protecting their well-being and interests in Revolutionary era America tended to form so-called Committees of Safety, and security and safety were held to be at odds. As Benjamin Franklin wrote in the 1757 edition of *Poor Richard's Almanack*, "The way to be safe, is never to be secure."[80]

Good fortune seems to exacerbate cowardly security. Colonial Virginians, Davies noted, "rest in the quiet unmolested Possession of their Liberty and Property, without anyone daring to disturb them, and without their doing any Thing for their own Defence: or as if neither God nor Man could strip them of their Enjoyments." Davies had to admit that Virginians had good reason to think this way. Thanks to God, they live in "a Land of Liberty and Plenty; a Land, until lately, unalarmed with the Terrors of War, and unstained with human Blood: Indeed, all Things considered, there are but few such Happy Spots upon our Globe."[81] Life in North America for British colonials was indeed good, relatively speaking, especially in Virginia, the richest British colony in mainland America, and one that had seen very little of war for decades.[82]

But the good life can make one soft, as Davies was not the first or last to observe. William Shakespeare wrote that "Plenty and Peace breed cowards."[83] The most famous American critic of this phenomenon was Theodore Roosevelt, who at the turn of the twentieth century railed against "ignoble ease" and "timid peace"— dangers that followed from not leading a "strenuous life."[84] Plenty and peace create a kind of obliviousness that may be abetted, in the American case, by geographical isolation. In making a case for invading Iraq after 9/11, president George W. Bush took up this theme: the idea that "prior to September the 11th, we were confident that two oceans could protect us from harm" became a kind of mantra for the White House.[85] The lesson of 9/11, Bush said, was that "[t]he dangers of our time must be confronted actively and forcefully, before we see them again in our skies and in our cities.... The danger posed by Saddam Hussein and his weapons cannot be ignored or wished away."[86] Bush's case for confronting actively and forcefully—by invading Iraq—echoed Davies's case against those who refused to go fight out on the frontier. Such people, Davies noted, like to say, "Let the enemy come down to us, and then we will fight them," but if the enemy did come, they "would be as forward in Flight, as they are now backward to take up Arms."[87]

Bush and Davies both issued urgent calls to arms against an enemy that seemed far away, but there is one glaring difference in their rhetoric. Davies was speaking out *against* security in a sense that has entirely disappeared from American discourse, whereas Bush spoke to champion security in a sense that sometimes seems to dominate American discourse, to the dismay of some. Andrew Bacevich notes that the current "cult of national security" exaggerates the threats against the United States in order to justify extreme measures to eliminate those threats. The cult simultaneously exploits fears and promises to free us from them.[88] Davies's sermon against security reminds us that freedom from fear has its costs: we might become too secure, in the old sense of culpably lacking fear, about security.

Fear is, of course, far from gone, and it will never disappear; death will never seem *that* distant or vague. Thousands of American soldiers have experienced fear (and injury or death) in Iraq and Afghanistan, and millions in those and other countries live in fear as a result of war. As a deadly drone or a kitchen-made bomb reminds us, humanity's destructive ingenuity remains fearsome, and there will always be crime, disease, and natural and man-made disasters. "Most fearsome is the ubiquity of fears," the sociologist Zygmunt Baumant writes; "they may leak out of any nook or cranny of our homes and our planet. From dark streets and from brightly lit television screens. From our bedrooms and our kitchens. From our workplaces and from the underground train we take to get there or back. From people we meet and people whom we failed to notice. From something we ingested and something with which our bodies came in touch."[89] Bauman's account of what he calls the "liquid fear" of our time goes on to the point that, without wishing to discount it, one cannot help but start to feel the extreme opposite of security, paranoia. While Davies's secure coward denies fear, a paranoid obsesses over it. Conspiracy theory can help the paranoid manage this great burden by focusing his efforts against one evil force: communism, Islamo-fascism, the United Nations. Even when others refuse to acknowledge the enemy's existence, he emphasizes its vastness and terror.[90] No one can accuse *him* of cowardly security.

But then, if the paranoid decides to act, it may be because he feels compelled by a fear that not to act would be cowardly. Driven by excessive fear, he may behave recklessly, as Aristotle warned that cowards sometimes could. Thinking more carefully about coward-ice can help us think more critically, more realistically, about fear and how society should respond to it. Doing so might help us avoid the dangerous complacency of the overly secure, and the dangerous vigilantism of the paranoid.

Chapter 4

DUTY-BOUND

Against the force of fear, the idea of cowardice sets the call of duty. For each mention of fear in Samuel Davies's *The Curse of Cowardice*, for example, duty comes up three times—as when Davies calls the men to "our duty in the sight of God" and "the dreadful, but important Duty of shedding human Blood."[1] Davies uses the term *duty* in a sense common then and today, fairly expressed in the 1911 *Encyclopedia Britannica*: "a term loosely applied to any action or course of action which is regarded as morally incumbent, apart from personal likes and dislikes or any external compulsion."[2] Yet external compulsion is not foreign to an idea of duty. Nowhere is duty more important than in the military context, and nowhere is the element of coercion stronger; nowhere is one more "duty-bound."

Cowardice exposes what might be called the paradox of duty: duty is compulsory, but it is also expected to be performed voluntarily. On one hand, the rules against cowardice and the ways it is prevented or punished smack of strong external compulsion. On the other hand, the accusation of cowardice and the contempt behind it assume individual autonomy: the accused could have done otherwise and chose not to. Military law codifies the importance of volition in its consideration of misbehavior before the enemy: "The act or acts, in the doing, not doing, or allowing of which consists the offence, must be conscious and voluntary on the part of the offender."[3] Strong external compulsion can strengthen the sense of duty and cowardice, but it can also vitiate this sense by suppressing the play of free will, an essential component of moral responsibility. A man should be courageous because being so is noble, not because he is acting under compulsion, Aristotle said.[4] One ought not to be cowardly under compulsion, runs the corollary, but because cowardice is ignoble.

Weak external compulsion and correspondingly strong respect for free will also have a mixed effect. They can heighten what might be called the personal power of cowardice and duty but also undermine the clear definition of these concepts and the rigorous enforcement of them. When men raised in a democratic individualistic culture are faced with the great external—and in many cases internalized—compulsions of modern total war, the importance of duty seems to diminish or come into question. Examining specific mentions of "duty" in relation to cowardice suggests an increasingly common understanding that duty is trivial, absurd, or downright pernicious.

Compulsion's ability both to make duty and cowardice significant and to render them moot is far from an exclusively modern phenomenon. The ancient phalanx shows how compulsion can both weaken and strengthen the ideas of duty and cowardice. In the classic image of the phalanx, men are closely ranked in row upon row, forming a mobile armored wall.[5] Deployed in broad daylight across from a similarly arrayed force on a field selected by mutual agreement to give no cover to either side, men in phalanx warfare always had a clear and unambiguous duty: to charge the other

Canfield Design

side or to defend against a charge. It was the ultimate battle of will; failure in this endeavor on the part of an individual soldier would be immediately evident to his fellows—up to eight of whom he might be physically touching, with many more very close by.[6] Because all those nearby were vulnerable to the contagion of fear that the cowardly man introduced, cowardice in the phalanx had great potential to do harm. If one man flees, the Greek poet Tyrtaeus said, "the spirit of the whole army falls apart."[7]

But the phalanx that gave duty and cowardice such significance could also squeeze away that significance. Among the Greeks and Romans it was common practice to do what Homer depicts Nestor doing in the *Iliad*: placing brave men on the outsides of the phalanx and putting the cowardly in the middle, "so that willing or not they would be forced to fight."[8] The absence of agency deprives such men's actions of their moral content. In its comprehensive external compulsion, the phalanx solves the problem of cowardice by overriding individual human will.

One need not be in an actual phalanx to feel so constrained. Stephen Crane's *The Red Badge of Courage* shows how a kind of mental phalanx can work. Henry Fleming feels that his regiment "enclosed him. And there were iron laws of tradition and law on four sides. He was in a moving box." The awkward repetition of "law" suggests the way history, society, and authority can reinforce each other and bind the individual. Henry had not been conscripted but somehow he thinks that he "had not enlisted of his free will. He had been dragged by the merciless government. And now they were taking him out to be slaughtered."[9] The moving box makes him feel as if he has no control over his conduct, and, accordingly, that terms such as *cowardice* are not applicable to him. The meaning of *courage* collapses under such pressure too. In *The Thin Red Line,* Corporal Fife dreams that he gets bombed to death: "they had trapped him into bravery and killed him."[10] The timid man stuck in the middle of an advancing phalanx might well feel something similar.

Prohibitions against cowardice represent what must be the most important and dramatic side of the box—the back side, as it were, pushing the soldier forward so he doesn't wind up like the Pennsylvania private who "had shown the white feather." His wrists were tied tightly then looped over his knees, a stick or musket slid over his arms and under his knees, a piece of wood or a bayonet placed in his mouth and held tight there by a lanyard. This "bucking and gagging" was just the beginning of his punishment. "In this position," we read, "he is at the mercy of any one desiring to have fun at his expense. The colonel now summoned the captain of the company and commanded everyone to file by and spit in the man's face. Some of the comrades gave him the full benefit of all that tobacco chewing could bring forth, others scarcely reached his face with any spittle, but the colonel stood by, and as the men filed past ordered them to spit lively." The author of this account presents it as evidence of "the inventive genius of some of the regimental commanders."[11] Such humiliating punishments used shame to strengthen the sense of duty. Any soldier who had to line up and spit lively on his comrade-in-arms would want to avoid being on the receiving end of such punishment, and presumably the spat-upon soldier would not want to repeat the experience.

Part of the power of shaming punishments came from the irony that the convicted coward was allowed, indeed condemned, as Plato noted, to the "pitiful clinging to life" that had gotten him accused of cowardice in the first place.[12] A slight twist of such reasoning has been used to justify a very different punishment. A 1942 German article noted that the best "cure for cowardice" was to deprive the convicted coward of "the very thing man is trying to retain, namely, his life."[13] When a *group* of men is deemed guilty of cowardice, the death penalty for all is often simply impracticable. Killing too many of your own soldiers can, of course, seriously weaken your side. In such cases, the Greek historian Polybius described what struck him in the second century BCE as a novel response, one that enforced discipline through calculated terror: decimation. Most of those who were deemed cowardly would be rebuked and put on barley rations and made to dwell out the camp's walls. A tenth of them would be selected to be punished "with the fustuarium without mercy." This involved the leader taking a cudgel and just touching the condemned coward, writes Polybius, "whereupon all the soldiers fall upon him with cudgels and stones. Generally speaking men thus punished are killed on the spot...."[14] Decimation was practiced as late as 1942, in Stalingrad, when some Russian soldiers were fleeing the front until their divisional commander stopped them and scolded them for their cowardice. Then, as he walked in front of the men, he counted out loud until he reached the tenth, whom he shot point-blank in the face. He continued until his gun was empty of bullets.[15]

Capital punishment for failure of duty both invests duty with supreme importance and makes a mockery of the idea that duty should be performed "apart...from any external compulsion." The story of admiral John Byng showed this dramatically. Byng had served in the Royal Navy for over thirty years when what became known as the Seven Years' War was declared in 1755. In 1756, Byng led an expedition to protect the British fort at Minorca, which was under threat from the French by both land and sea. Ordered to use "all possible means in his power" to save the fort, Byng retreated as soon as he saw French ships. A fellow admiral led an attack against these ships, but Byng failed to provide support and, deciding that Minorca was lost, sailed for Gibraltar. The fort surrendered shortly thereafter. Upon his return to England, Byng was indicted under Article 12 of the Naval Code: "Every person in the fleet, who through Cowardice, Negligence or Disaffection shall in time of Action withdraw or keep back, or not come into the Fight or Engagement; or shall not do his utmost to take or destroy every Ship which it shall be his Duty to engage...every such person so offending, and being convicted thereof by the Sentence of a Court Martial, shall suffer Death."[16] For six months after the indictment, the question of Byng's cowardice was the subject of pamphlets, sensationalist journalism, riots, and political posturing. A sign on one of the Byng figures read, "Acts of Cowardice in those who are esteemed their country's defenders should always be treated in this manner."[17] He was burned in effigy all over England. "Let B——g securely bear his fleet away," wrote one of Byng's critics, sarcastically evoking security in the same negative sense that Samuel Davies would a year later, "And keep his ships to fight another day."[18]

Duty for those who are especially esteemed as a country's defenders—namely, military officers such as Byng—is often more complicated than their underlings' duty. On one hand, they are expected to show great zeal in combat, risking their lives so that their men do the same. On the other hand, because their lives are strategically more valuable than their men's, duty sometimes requires them to refrain from risking themselves and to risk, even deliberately to sacrifice, their men. Byng was criticized for not doing so. One balladeer referred sarcastically to *great Rear-Admiral Byng* who "would not risk a man," but "[k]ept cautiously snug in the rear." [19] Not risking a man suggests excessive fear for not so much his own life as his men's, but the two were conflated by many of Byng's accusers.

Byng deeply resented the accusation of cowardice: "No Symptom of Cowardice, that odious and capital Part of my Charge," as he put it during his trial, "has hitherto appeared to the Court."[20] But the belief that he was cowardly seems to have doomed him. Toward the end of his shortened life, more and more of his countrymen came to sympathize with Byng, but by then only King George could grant him clemency, and he chose not to—because he thought Byng a coward. He was not found guilty of cowardice but of failing to do "his utmost to take or destroy every Ship which it shall be his Duty to engage," a distinction largely overlooked at the time and ever since.[21] Byng was shot to death at noon on March 14, 1757. He did not want to wear a blindfold ("No; it is my

Royal Greenwich Maritime Museum

fate; I must look at it and receive it"), but out of consideration for his executioners he put one on, and signaled his readiness for the end by dropping a handkerchief.[22]

Byng's timing was awful. The law requiring execution for any violation of Article 12 had been in place only since 1749. The language making the death penalty optional ("or such other punishment as the nature and degree of the offense shall be found to deserve") was restored in 1779.[23] British military discipline was famously harsh, especially during the Seven Years' War. One study notes that the rate of pardons dropped after 1754, while the rate of corporal punishment increased.[24] Another study estimates that the average British Army soldier sentenced to be flogged in 1758 received 720 lashes; more than a third of such men received more than a thousand lashes.[25] This practice gave the term *redcoat* a terrible connotation. Byng's execution showed that naval officers would be held to the same severe standards as men in the ranks, and that doing one's duty to the utmost was imperative. It has been argued that after the execution of Byng, British admirals became more aggressive in their tactics, turning the war around for the British and leading to a series of great victories, even into the nineteenth century.[26] The most famous victory for the British Navy and along with it its most famous exaltations of duty came in 1805. As admiral Horatio Nelson led the navy against the French at Trafalgar, the last signal he raised up to his fleet took the form of a phrase that, as his biographer Robert Southey put it, "will be remembered as long as the language, or even the memory, of England shall endure ... :—'England expects every man to do his duty!'" A shot from a French ship fatally wounded Nelson, and among his last words were, "Thank God, I have done my duty."[27]

But if the execution of Byng enforced an ideal of duty, it could also be seen as making a mockery of this ideal. It was Byng's case that inspired Voltaire's famous line in *Candide* that "in this country they think it's good to kill an Admiral from time to time, to encourage the others."[28] "Encourage" here emphasizes the irony that severe punishments meted out for failure of duty offer a choice—doing or dying—that is really not a choice. The admirals are not being encouraged to fight; they are being forced to. The same could be said of their underlings, those eighteenth-century British sailors and soldiers (those "lobsters" and "bloody backs," as they were sometimes called[29]) who, as one historian puts it, were "brutally trained and flogged into a sense of duty."[30]

A year after Byng's execution, Samuel Davies in his 1758 recruiting sermon went to great lengths to present ideas of duty and cowardice largely free of external compulsion. He did ask, if the men failed to answer his call, "what remains but that you must be *forced* to it by Authority?"[31] Such a threat may have carried some weight. There had been conscriptions in Britain in 1756 and 1757,[32] and

Davies's audience would probably have known about Byng's execution, and they would have encountered redcoats in Virginia. But the men and Davies would also have known that British or colonial authorities would have a very difficult time forcing them into military service: first, because the sprawling backwoods offered ample refuge for evaders; second, because most men owned guns, which, as James Titus puts it, "vastly complicated the task of compelling them to do anything."[33] Antirecruitment riots in Virginia in late 1755 came as a surprise to royal governor Robert Dinwiddie, an "old school imperialist," in the words of one biographer, who "had assumed that the riffraff would meekly do their 'duty'; that is, they would do whatever their 'betters' told them to do."[34] Instead the riffraff were known to beat recruiting officers.[35]

Duty, perhaps especially that of a soldier, is not a single discrete obligation, which being met can be so disposed of,[36] but as members of a militia, a force always intended to be ad hoc, Davies's audience was not known for its discipline or steadfastness.[37] When they did serve, the British forces—and their officers especially—often found them insubordinate if not outright cowardly, and sometimes cowardly precisely because they were insubordinate. As brigadier general James Wolfe, a leader of British forces fighting the French in Canada, wrote in 1758, "The Americans are in general the dirtiest most contemptible cowardly dogs that you can conceive. There is no depending on them in action. They fall down dead in their own dirt [probably meaning "excrement"] and desert by battalions, officers and all."[38] Just a week before Davies delivered *The Curse*, brigadier general John Forbes, the man who would lead the expedition for which Davies was recruiting, expressed doubt that Virginia would fill its rolls; he also predicted that even if the colony "shou'd draft their Militia to compleat the two thousand

Men . . . these Men will not stay eight days with us."[39] Malingering was common, and desertion was rampant.

Given the circumstances, Davies hoped to elicit more than the passive and temporary acquiescence that an appeal to political or spiritual authority would bring.[40] His strategy was to take a two-pronged approach to defining duty and showing how the neglect of it could be cowardly. To establish the men's duty to join the company, Davies refers to the second half of his sermon's biblical text, "*Cursed be he that keepeth back his Sword from Blood*" (Jeremiah 48:10), claiming that it's intended for the "Coward, who, when God, in the course of his Providence, calls him to Arms, refuses to obey, and consults his own Ease and Safety, more than his Duty to God and his Country."[41] Thus does Davies dispense with the obvious coward, who would avoid military service altogether; such an artless dodger might not be easy to catch, but he's easy to identify since his failure of duty is blatant.

To account for the more subtle cowardice of those who would join but not do their utmost, Davies then quotes the other half of the Jeremiah verse: "*Cursed be he that doth the Work of the Lord deceitfully*." This statement, he notes, addresses "another Species of Cowards; sly, hypocritical Cowards. . . . They commence Soldiers, not that they may serve their Country, and do their Duty to God, but that they may live in Ease, Idleness and Pleasure, and enrich themselves at the public Expence." Davies wanted men not merely to join but "according to our respective Characters, to carry on with Vigour," and this sly sort of cowardice undermined such vigor.[42] It could not be quashed by force or discouraged with an appeal to authority; it might, though, be less common among soldiers who freely chose their duty.

Wanting the men to join "as *Volunteers*" (his emphasis), Davies proposed soldiering as a contractual matter, as an agreement involving mutual obligations and specific expectations for a prescribed duration.[43] Colonists wanted to know under whom they would serve, on what mission, for how long, and for how much pay. Davies covered all the elements. Officers would be men "from among yourselves, from whom you may expect good Usage." This meant that the recruits would not be under the immediate authority of cruel and disdainful army regulars. They would serve fairly briefly, too, for less than six months.[44] The men would help make up a force that would march under Forbes on Fort Duquesne. And, as Davies noted, "Ye that would catch at Money, here is a proper bait for you; ten Pounds for a few Months Service, besides the usual Pay of Soldiers."

To clinch his argument, Davies conceded that Great Britain was "interested in our Protection; but can she be as interested as ourselves?"[45] He was not afraid to ask and answer an age-old but perhaps especially American question: What's in it for me? In trying to balance the greater interest with self-interest, in arguing that the men before him should fight not only to help the crown and their distant fellow subjects, but also to save their liberty, their "Plenty" and "Property," and their own skins, Davies fit Alexis de Tocqueville's description of "American moralists." They "do not claim that one must sacrifice oneself ... because it is great to do it; but they say boldly that such sacrifices are as necessary to the one who imposes them upon himself as to the one who profits from them." Tocqueville reasoned that since the typical American was driven to self-concern "by an irresistible force," leaders could hope only to direct this self-concern, not stop it.[46]

A prototypical American moralist, Davies presents prototypically American versions of duty and cowardice. In aiming to get the men to decide *for* themselves, in both senses of the phrase, he infuses duty and "the curse of cowardice" with a sense of personal power. Men who volunteered would own their duty more fully, and more fully condemn cowardly dereliction of that duty. But a rich mixture of freedom and self-interest can also undermine the power of duty and cowardice. Vital questions remain: What, exactly, is the duty? How should the duty be performed? The word *duty* shares a root with *due*: it is what is owed. But what does one person in this New World owe to country and king? And who decides?[47] Duty to oneself can coincide with one's larger duty, as Davies argues, but there can come a time when these duties diverge. A man who joins an army believing it will benefit him personally may have his belief sorely tested when mortal danger presents itself: How can *dying* be in his self-interest?

The tension between self-interest and the common interest, between doing what you want and obeying authority, characterized the sense of duty in the Revolutionary era, too. For all his talk of liberty, Davies in 1758 also addressed his audience as "subject of the best of kings."[48] By 1776, such an attitude would, among the independence-minded, be equated with rank cowardice.[49] Tom Paine wrote, "Every tory is a coward, for a servile, slavish, self-interested fear is the foundation of toryism...."[50] But linking obedience with cowardice posed a problem for American military leaders, for to win the war they needed soldiers to follow orders. Baron Von Steuben, engaged to revamp the training of undisciplined American troops during the Revolutionary War, observed that in the Old World one could say to a soldier, "'Do this,' and he doeth it, but [to the American soldiers] I am obliged to say, 'This is the reason why you ought to do that,' and then he does it."[51] One senses a mixture of admiration and exasperation in this statement. The informed and willing obedience of citizen-soldiers may be superior to uninformed and unwilling obedience; they may fulfill their duty more fully. Such is Davies's hope. Yet reasoning with one's men rather than simply ordering them can make doing battle more difficult than it already is.

The conflict between respect for autonomy and the need for obedience is evident in Continental Army disciplinary practices. The Continental Congress adopted its Articles of War from the British articles almost wholesale on June 30, 1775, with one significant change intended to distinguish the Continental Army from the cruel and tyrannical British force. Punishments in the Continental Army were much more lenient, reducing the number of crimes punishable by death and the maximum number of lashes from one thousand to thirty-nine.[52]

This limit did not last long. Military leaders attributed defeats to lax discipline. After George Washington and others complained that the thirty-nine-lash limit was too low, it was raised to one hundred when Congress passed new Articles of War on September 20, 1776.[53] On that same day, as he was trying to rally troops for a (doomed) defense of Manhattan, Washington issued a statement from Harlem Heights saying of each soldier that "the Grounds he now possesses are to be defended at all events; Any Officer, or Soldier, therefore, who (upon the Approach, or Attack of the Enemy's Forces, by land or water) presumes to turn his back and flee, shall be instantly Shot down, and all good officers are hereby authorized and required to see this done, that the brave and gallant part of the Army may not fall a sacrifice to the base and cowardly part, or share their disgrace in a cowardly and unmanly Retreat."[54] The exigencies of war trumped the ideology of the republic. Independence would require fierce external compulsion. A year later, Washington would reffirm the principle when he ordered that if a soldier "turns his back upon the enemy, and attempts to run away, or to retreat before orders are given for it, . . . officers are instantly to put him to death.[55] Yet I know of no cases of cowards being shot down on the field in the Revolutionary War, and none of the American Revolutionary court-martial cases for cowardice ended with the execution of the accused.[56]

American authorities preferred to foster what Davies had tried to foster, and what Edmund Burke, in arguing for "conciliation" with Great Britain's restive colonies in North America in 1775, called "liberal obedience," founded not on fear of authority or on desire for profit but on "kindred blood," cultural and social ties, and a common love of freedom. Such an obedience would be characterized by a more profound "bravery and discipline" than fear of authority or coercion could ever inspire.[57] Correspondingly, it also inspires a more profound contempt for cowardice. American citizens in arms would do their duty out of idealism and patriotism, not fear of punishment. To the same degree that the conduct of "free Citizens in arms" should be superior, as Washington put it in 1778, their failures of duty, their "effeminate shrinking," their cowardice, should be condemned.[58]

The tension between autonomy and obedience was perhaps even more pronounced during the Civil War, when millions of men who had no experience of military service joined the armed services.[59] Whether they enlisted voluntarily or were conscripted,

Union and Confederate soldiers felt their loss of freedom keenly, but they also thought it was their duty to serve.[60] Perhaps the most famous volunteer was Robert E. Lee, alleged to have written to his son that "duty" is "the sublimest word in our language. Do your duty in all things. . . . You cannot do more, you should never wish to do less." (The so-called "Duty Letter" turned out to be a forgery, but while it may not have achieved quite the fame that Lord Nelson's proclamations on duty did, as a prominent piece of American scripture it was compared to Abraham Lincoln's Gettysburg Address.[61])

There is some disagreement among historians about how the sense of duty weathered the Civil War. Gerald Linderman argues that the extended horrors of the war exhausted soldiers not only physically and mentally but morally too. By 1864 soldiers were less idealistic about their cause, their country, and their duty. James M. McPherson acknowledges the growing rates of desertion and the jaded attitudes of some soldiers, but he also notes an enduring respect for duty. He quotes one veteran from Maine who explained re-upping for another three years by writing, "*Do your duty is my motto* even though it may clash with my own personal life." An Illinois soldier wrote, "Because I have done my Duty for the last 23 months, that is no reason why I should not return to the regiment and do my Duty again."[62] To the contrary: having done one's duty was reason to keep doing it.

This virtuous circle was broken in cases of cowardice, as Hooker DeLand's story shows. DeLand, that soldier who in 1863 refused to fight, telling a fellow officer that he would not go into battle because "he thought it was too warm for him, that he did not want to get killed just then," had volunteered for the Union Army as a private in 1861, became a sergeant in 1862, then a second lieutenant, and then a captain—all this before turning twenty-one. He had fought well, and by 1863 he felt he had *done* his duty. This was not for him to decide, however. Reviewing DeLand's case, judge advocate general Joseph Holt allowed that fear could overwhelm "men who are disposed to do their duty." The problem with De-Land was that he "appears to have acted deliberately" when he left his command. As we have already seen, Holt had solid grounds for this observation. DeLand had allegedly told a fellow officer that he would rather be dishonorably discharged than go back into combat. Noting that Deland "absented himself from his command," Holt concluded, "It is not to be wondered at, that a Court composed of soldiers who have done their duty should impose a severe punishment for such offences." [63]

Prior good service could help mitigate punishment for a military crime such as cowardice—but if anything it hurt DeLand. DeLand had shown he *could* fight, but now he was refusing to do so. He was rejecting duty, and for this he was not only dishonorably discharged but also sent to prison for the duration of the war.

The nature of the moving box changed in the twentieth century, when advances in military technology and consequent adaptations in tactics led students of war to speak of the "empty" or "naked" battlefield, where dispersed soldiers felt not only fear but isolation as well. As Dwight D. Eisenhower observed, "Except for unusual concentration of tactical activity, such as at a river crossing or an amphibious assault, the feeling that pervades the forward areas is loneliness. There is little to be seen; friend and foe, as well as the engines of war, seem to disappear from sight when troops are deployed for a fight. Loss of control and cohesion are easy, because each man feels himself so much alone, and each is prey to the human fear and terror that to move or show himself may result in instant death."[64] This phenomenon has contradictory effects on the question of cowardice. Isolation deprives soldiers of the visible support of their comrades, support that can help keep them from being cowardly. But a soldier's cowardice was also less likely to be witnessed by others, and less likely to do widespread damage by causing a panic.[65]

Other twentieth-century developments, however, tended to fortify the moving box and limit the operation of free will. We have seen that the British government in 1758 could not easily force a Virginian to do anything; there was a vast wilderness to escape to, and the comparatively primitive military technology of the eighteenth century meant that he possessed or had access to most of the same weapons the British government had.[66] In the twentieth century, getting hold of or operating a tank or plane or one of the other more complex, expensive, and powerful weapons of industrialized war was an altogether more challenging proposition. The twentieth-century state could also control the means of transportation that brought soldiers so far away from their homeland. "It is a function of the impersonality of modern war," John Keegan writes, "that the soldier is coerced more continuously and more harshly by vast, unlocalized forces against which he may rail, but at which he cannot strike back and to which he must ultimately submit: the fire which nails him to the ground or drives him beneath it, the great distance which yawns between him and safety, the onward progression of a vehicular advance or a retreat which carries him with it willy-nilly. The dynamic of modern battle impels more effectively than any system of discipline which Frederick the Great could have dreamt."[67]

The feeling of being impelled was increased by psychological and social forces put into play by propaganda and indoctrination, which sought to make external compulsion internal. The twentieth century's world wars gave rise to what one historian has called "the axial age of propaganda." In an age of industrial, total war, nations needed to convince masses of people to join the war effort, and new methods of communication—radio, film, television—helped make this possible.[68] Like propaganda, indoctrination, which aims to inculcate soldiers with particular military and political values, must also be as old as war itself. But systematic indoctrination is a relatively new phenomenon, first instituted by American authorities in 1941. The Cold War saw a proliferation of propaganda and indoctrination efforts.[69]

James Jones's *The Thin Red Line* depicts contempt for cowardice as essential to indoctrination's success. Corporal Fife is "as bound and tied by his own mental processes and social indoctrination as if they were ropes, simply because while he could admit to himself privately that he was a coward, he did not have the guts to admit it publicly." Jones captures the way the physical and mental forces of modern war controlled individuals without them even knowing it. After taking a hill at the cost of several of his men's lives, and more of the Japanese's, a captain in *The Thin Red Line* has a "horrifying vision" of "all the soldiers doing the same identical thing, all of them powerless to stop it, all of them devoutly and proudly believing themselves to be free individuals. It expanded to include the scores of nations, the millions of men, doing the same on thousands of hilltops across the world. And it didn't stop there. It went on. It was the concept—concept? the fact; the reality—of the modern State in action." Believing themselves to be free makes the coercion harder to see and, when seen, all the harder to take, and it makes a mockery of duty. "But what the hell?" thinks one soldier. "If a man's government told him he had to go and fight a war, he had to go, that was all. The government was bigger than him and it could make him. It wasn't even a matter of duty; he *had* to go."[70] For Jones, the overwhelming power of war and the modern state, yoked to capitalist interests, bureaucratization, indoctrination, and media saturation make "duty" nonsensical.

Joseph Heller's *Catch-22* captures the nonsense in all its absurdity in the case of a soldier who repeatedly goes AWOL and is repeatedly caught and sentenced to "dig and fill up holes six feet deep, wide and long." In indiscriminately equating his ditch-digging to the travails of a front-line soldier, flattens the significance of duty into nothing. Digging ditches is "a matter of duty," he says, "and we each have our own to perform. My duty is to keep digging these holes. . . . Your duty is to screw around in cadet school and hope the war ends before you get out. The duty of the men in combat is to win the war, and I just wish they were doing their duty as well as I've been doing mine. It wouldn't be fair if I had to go overseas and do their job too, would it?"[71] For Heller, duty was dilemma. You had to be certifiably crazy to get relieved, but "[a]nyone who wants to get out of combat duty isn't really crazy." That's the catch-22.

Perhaps the worst duty was to have to execute one of your comrades who had not done his. It was a common practice among some countries in World War II. More than fifteen thousand German soldiers were shot for dereliction of duty. In the last days of the war, even German civilians were subject to execution for cowardly conduct—such as surrendering to Allied troops.[72] Joseph

Stalin followed Adolf Hitler's example in forming "penal companies from soldiers who were guilty of breaches of discipline because of cowardice or bewilderment," as he put it in the infamous
"Not one step back!" proclamation (Order No. 227). These penal
companies were often sent on dangerous, even suicidal missions,
such as trampling minefields. Order No. 227's rule that "panic-
mongers and cowards should be exterminated in place" was followed.[73] Soviet executions for cowardice and desertion number
in the hundreds of thousands.[74] Such fierce and inescapable compulsion could turn the idea of cowardice on its head. "In the Red
Army," as the Russian marshal Georgi Zhukov put it, "It takes a
very brave man to be a coward."[75]

The contrast on the American side, where Eddie Slovik was
the lone soldier shot for desertion, is striking. Yet between 1957
and 1974, three American directors made graphic films about this
power of the modern state to coerce in the most terrible way—to
execute its own soldiers, and to make its own soldiers do the most
terrible duty of executing. The most well-known of these is Stanley
Kubrick's *Paths of Glory* (1957). After a regiment falters while making a suicidal charge in World War I, the ambitious general who
ordered the attack is outraged and wants to execute one hundred
men from the regiment. Ultimately the decision is made to execute
three soldiers as examples. One of the soldiers is chosen because he
knows too much about his superior's misconduct on a previous
mission, another because he is a "social undesirable," and the third
is chosen by lot, even though he had received citations for bravery
in previous battles. Kirk Douglas plays Colonel Dax, the officer who
was put in the impossible position of leading the attack, and then
of defending the three men in a farcical court-martial. The last of
the three soldiers fractures his skull in a fight the night before the

United Artists

execution, and is rendered unconscious. He is brought out for the execution strapped to a stretcher, and a pinch to his cheek rouses him only momentarily before all three of the men are shot to death.

The 1964 British film *King and Country*, directed by the American Joseph Losey, may be even more harrowing. It tells the story of Arthur Hamp, a deeply pitiable private in World War I, a cuckolded cobbler who went off to war because his wife and mother-in-law dared him to. He's the only surviving member of his company when he decides to "go for a walk" and desert the western front. The movie depicts the rainy, corpse- and rat-filled trenches where Hamp is imprisoned and where his court-martial takes place. Despite the best efforts of Captain Hargreaves to defend him, Hamp is found guilty. Mercy is recommended, but then word from headquarters comes that the company is moving into line and that, in order to "maintain morale," the prisoner should be shot early the next morning. Hamp's fellows get him and themselves drunk that night, and the company medic injects him with something. When they bring him out the next morning, he is unconscious, tied to a chair. The men who shoot at Hamp don't do their job well. Instead of killing him, the bullets knock him down and wake him up. Hargreaves walks over to where Hamp lies in a puddle. He pulls up the blindfold and cradles Hamp's head. "Isn't it finished yet?" the officer asks Hamp. To which Hamp replies, "No sir, I'm sorry." Hargreaves, the man who had defended him, at first reluctantly and cynically, but finally sympathetically and earnestly, puts a pistol in Hamp's mouth and shoots. Hargreaves is played by Dirk Bogarde, but an advertisement for the movie removed him from the scene—the better to put the viewer in his place. There's just the hand with the gun in Hamp's mouth and a statement: "Go ahead . . . kill him—you're the only friend he has!"

British Home Entertainment

The 1974 television movie *The Execution of Private Slovik*, directed by Lamont Johnson, is even more overt than these other two films in conveying how execution victimizes not just the condemned man but also those whose duty it is to kill him. The title of the film is apt: we see poignant scenes of Slovik before he became a soldier, but the movies dwells at great length on his execution and the preparations for it. Because American authorities were worried, as William Bradford Huie put it, "about whether in 1945 American youths ... could ... be trusted to shoot the heart out of a fellow,"[76] they took numerous measures to ensure that the execution proceeded flawlessly: the selection of dependable "combative" marksmen, a practice session, and pep talks of a kind to the marksmen. "Nobody is asking you to like it," the chaplain tells them, "but you're going to do as you're told. . . . None of us made this decision, but we're the men who are ordered to carry it out because a higher authority has accepted the moral responsibility." The attending medical officer taps on the chest of a man chosen because he is Slovik's size. "It might help if you think of the heart as a circle," he tells the marksmen; "it's a semiround organ and it's found in the area of the lower third of the breast bone. In other words, here—not up here, as some people think—but here. Right here." At the execution site, an odd-looking piece of equipment, a sort of cross-shaped stretcher, provokes a question from the chaplain. It's a "collapse board," he is told. "The man is a condemned coward, father. He may not be able to walk out here under his own steam." Slovik does go out under his own steam. The film suggests that it was Slovik's executioners who might have needed the collapse board by depicting it being carried out and set cross-like behind the officer in charge who reads the order to kill him.

Despite all their preparations, the twelve marksmen do not do their job well. None hit Slovik's heart. For a few excruciating minutes, as the film depicts, he lives on: he gasps, his head bobs. The doctor attends him with his stethoscope and the soldiers are ordered to reload, at which the chaplain shouts, "Sure, do it again, if you like it so much!"[77] Slovik dies as they are reloading, a moment captured in the film by the rosary slipping from his bound hands and falling into the snow.

Universal Studios Licensing LLC

The film was heavily promoted, with full-page newspaper advertisements that showed Slovik, played by Martin Sheen, being readied for execution, and when it was aired it became, according to some sources, the most-watched made-for-television movie in American history.[78] The audience got bigger as the movie progressed, with numbers peaking in the final excruciating execution scene.[79] This grim film met a deep need in a country that felt conflicted about military duty and what to do with those who evaded it—a category that included not only those young men who had deserted or who had evaded service altogether, but perhaps the nation as a whole, too, as it left behind its allies in South Vietnam. Peace with honor seemed impossible. And if the nation was withdrawing from Vietnam, what could it do with all those young men who had had the good sense to withdraw earlier, or never go? The movie dramatized how trapped Americans felt by conventional notions of military cowardice and showed the terrible price that making an example of a man exacts, and not just from the man. All this in the name of duty?

Appeals to conventional duty suffered from their association with the proverbial "just following orders" defense of many an accused war criminal, from the Nuremberg Trials to the My Lai Massacre and beyond. The forces of mental and physical compulsion that could bolster the sense of duty also seemed less effective. Young men subject to a draft could not escape to the Virginia wilderness, but it wasn't a case of there being "nowhere to run," as James Jones had said of World War II. There were Canada and Mexico, and other ways to defer and evade. Americans, soldiers and civilians alike, increasingly came to believe that the war in Vietnam was neither just nor in their nation's best interest.

Some who did become soldiers found ways to do their duty with less than the "vigour" that Samuel Davies called for; they turned "search and destroy" missions into "search and avoid" ones. Sometimes soldiers went beyond negligence to overt resistance. "We don't have too many cases of battle fatigue," wrote one army captain in 1966, "but we do have a goodly number of people who after a certain point just refuse to go out anymore. . . . And to tell the truth it's hard to blame them." There were also instances of "combat refusal" by entire companies. Mutinies rose markedly beginning in 1968.[80]

The most dramatic cases of resistance to authority came when soldiers "fragged" their officers. These assassinations were attempted for a variety of reasons, but the most common was targeting gung-ho officers. The mere threat of such assassinations could make officers think twice about being too zealous.[81] The contrast with the case of Admiral Byng is striking. In 1757, high authorities in the British government had an admiral shot to encourage other admirals to do their duty to the utmost; in Vietnam in the 1960s and '70s, soldiers in the ranks murdered their superiors to encourage them to do the bare minimum.[82]

Conventional ideas of duty remained, of course, but at some point "dutiful" became used most often in a pejorative sense to describe something done well, or well enough, but for the wrong reasons. Duty was also sometimes subject to radical revision, and the sense of cowardice along with it. Tim O'Brien gave the reformulation its most memorable expression in his 1988 fictionalized memoir *The Things They Carried*, when the narrator decides not to flee the Vietnam draft by going to Canada. "I was a coward," he writes, ending one story with a statement that turned the call to duty on its head: "I went to the war."[83]

Indeed, cowardice in much twentieth-century literature of war figures does not figure as a fearful evasion of one's duty to authority or even one's brothers-in-arms. For John Andrews in John Dos Passos's 1923 novel *Three Soldiers*, the coward is one who fails in the duty to be himself: "What right had a man to exist who was too cowardly to stand up for what he thought and felt, for his whole makeup, for everything that made him an individual apart from his fellows, and not a slave to stand cap in hand waiting for someone of stronger will to tell him when to act."[84] In *The Thin Red Line*, the radical cynic Welsh articulates a similar notion. "Fife," Welsh thinks with characteristically obscene bitterness,

> while also being a punk kid and an ass, was a coward. Welsh did not mean coward in the sense that he would shit his pants and run away. Fife wouldn't do that; he would stay. . . . When he said coward, what he meant was that Fife had not yet learned—if he ever would—that his life, and himself, his He, didn't mean a goddamned thing to the world in general, and never would. . . . Fife was smart enough to know it, or at least learn it, but he wouldn't let himself admit it. And in Welsh's dictionary, that was the worst kind of coward there was.[85]

This version of cowardice recognizes and even concedes the enforced passivity of the individual. Stuck in a moving box one cannot do anything, so the duty one owes is interior, a clarity and honesty in how one sees the world and one's trivial and helpless place in it. Welsh's idea of cowardice directs contempt toward those who refuse to see reality clearly—that is, as Welsh sees it. Dos Passos, Jones, and O'Brien all redefine cowardice as a failure of a different kind of duty—a duty to oneself, or to truth, or to the truth about oneself.

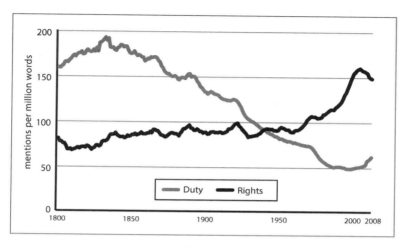

Canfield Design

Such redefinition of duty is part of a larger political and cultural shift from a duty-based republicanism to a liberalism that emphasized rights. Patton in 1940 worried about America's ability to fight a war because, he said, "We've pampered and confused our youth. We've talked too much about rights and not enough about duties."[86] And this was before the rise of rights movements for African Americans, women, gay men and lesbians, and other minorities in the second half of the twentieth century. The Google Ngram graph for *rights* runs in the opposite direction for that of *duty*, which is strikingly similar to that of *cowardice*. From its peak in the early 1800s, the term *duty*'s prominence decreased by a factor of five by 2000.

Like *cowardice*, *duty* shows an uptick in usage over the past decade or so. Some of this recent increase must be a result of the invocation to duty after 9/11. Exaltations of duty like Lord Nelson's or Robert E. Lee's can sound archaic or grandiose, but they have not disappeared. For the sake of duty, men and women still devote and sometimes sacrifice their lives, joining the military or engaging in other forms of public service. *Call of Duty* is also the name of a popular video game in which players take on missions as infantry-men during World War II. It first hit the market in 2003. In 2011, a new version of the game was launched with a multimillion-dollar ad campaign and a compelling catchphrase: "There's a soldier in each of us."

Chapter 5

THE RISE OF THE THERAPEUTIC

Having focused on the force of fear and the call of duty, we now turn our attention to what is caught between them—namely, he who acts or fails to act, and how that person and his conduct are judged or not judged. Is there a soldier in each of us? Perhaps, but it has long been recognized that when fear conflicts with the call of duty, each soldier's ability to answer the call varies. In the *Iliad*, Hector observes, "No one ever said men are equal in war."[1] Aristotle noted that some people are by nature more timid than others.[2] The same recognition informed the practices of putting the timid soldier in the middle of the phalanx (chapter 4) and the book of Deuteronomy's recommendation that "fearful and fainthearted" men be kept away from battle (chapter 3). It has also always been recognized that, no matter the man, some fears are simply too much to overcome. Aristotle noted that we should forgive those who perform a "wrong action because of conditions of a sort that overstrain human nature, and that no one would endure."[3]

Such awareness has always informed thoughtful assessment of alleged cowardice. But there is a difference between our own era and that long stretch from ancient times to the nineteenth century: an institutionally sanctioned medical vocabulary now gives greater force and definition to alternate ways of explaining "improper" fearful conduct. Coupled with and to an extent caused by developments already discussed (including the perceived increase in the terrors of modern war), this medical vocabulary, and the diagnostic, therapeutic trend of which it is part, has in the past century helped diminish the scope and force of the idea of cowardice in the context of war. Cowardice seems less relevant to battle than it used to be, and less a cause for shame. In American history, the first glimmers of an official diagnostic vocabulary appear during the Civil War. These beginnings were very fitful, and before turning to them we need to acknowledge the often fierce resistance to any mitigation of cowardice at that time.

Perhaps the fiercest and most highly placed resister on the Union side was Joseph Holt, judge advocate general of the United

Library of Congress

States from 1861 to 1864. A Kentuckian and arch-Unionist who helped keep Kentucky away from the Confederacy or neutrality, Holt put the preservation of the Union and the judicious enforcement of its laws above all other considerations.[4] He had broken with his family over the question of secession, and there was in his devotion to the Union cause, notes one biographer, "something of the fury of the scorned added to the zeal of the convert."[5] Accusations of cowardice tended to provoke Holt's fury and zeal both. When a Union captain shot dead another officer who had derided him as "a coward and a slacker," Holt restored the captain to duty on the grounds that an honorable man should not have to abide such attacks on his character.[6] When a charge of cowardice was leveled responsibly and the accused was found guilty, Holt never favored mercy.

Hooker DeLand offers a case in point. After he was found guilty of cowardice and sentenced to hard labor, many sought to have his sentence reduced. A petition from his company, signed by many officers and enlisted men, noted that he was just twenty-one and "that he has a sister an orphan like himself, who is and has been to a certain extent dependent upon his exertion for a livelihood." In a last appeal for clemency, a congressman (DeLand was "very respectably connected") noted in a letter to president Abraham Lincoln that DeLand "says that his crime was not from choise but from a *constitutional* weakness" (emphasis in the original). Holt had had enough. "This case," he wrote, "has received three careful examinations by this bureau + in each it was found that the sentence was justly merited. If any mitigation is granted, it must be as an act of pure grace." As was noted in chapter 4, pure grace was not forthcoming for DeLand.[7]

Holt also resisted mitigation in the case of lieutenant Henry Barker of Pennsylvania, who was charged with cowardice for his conduct at Chancellorsville in 1863. Despite his contention that he was sick and had "marched under difficulties ... my feet were sore and I gave out," Barker was found guilty and sentenced to be shot to death. Brigadier general John C. Robinson approved the verdict and the sentence, but since Barker's regiment had been "mustered out of service + his execution as an example rendered unnecessary," Robinson recommended that Barker be merely dismissed from the army and that details of his case be published in his home state of Pennsylvania. Holt was outraged. The lieutenant's "reason for leaving his company," he wrote in a letter to President Lincoln, "was that his *feet were sore*. This may have been the case but they were not too sore to run to the rear, it appears. A more humiliating confession or admission could hardly be spread upon the record of a Court Martial."

A letter from a family friend testified to Barker's kindness and noted that he was "the youngest of three brothers and the [sole] support of a widowed mother. . . . " But Holt was not moved by this appeal, or by the idea that the mustering out of Barker's regiment rendered his punishment "unnecessary." Patriotism in Holt's view dictated steadfastness, and he thought that letting Barker off easy would undermine discipline throughout the army. "The frequent exhibition of such cowardice weakness or infirmity," he wrote, "whichever it may be termed, demands that officers shall find no escape from the obligations which their position fidelity and highest duty bind upon them." For Holt, the distinctions among cowardice, weakness, or infirmity were too fine to bother with when, as he wrote, "the highest interests of the government, the endurance, nay the safety of the Republic" were hanging in the balance.[8] Mitigation was a luxury the Union couldn't afford.

The most poignant Civil War case of unmitigated punishment for cowardice must be that of private Samuel Clements. When he enlisted in February of 1864, Clements claimed to be forty-four years and nine months old—an age perhaps too conveniently close to the maximum age for enlisting, which was forty-five, but lying about one's age was not uncommon among men who were either too young or too old to serve. He was married, five feet five inches tall, a rope maker with a light complexion, gray eyes, and light hair.[9] Clements was mustered into the Thirty-Second Regiment of Maine Volunteers of the Union Army in April 1864 but had "been left sick" in Maine. He did not join the rest of his regiment in Virginia until June 14. Two days later he was in the ranks but complaining, according to a fellow private, "that his foot or leg pained him Severely." The enemy was a mile away, within cannon range, and musket fire could be heard. An hour before the regiment went into action, Clements disappeared. For more than six months he hid with a few others in a swamp a couple of miles behind the battle lines. On January 2nd, 1865, Clements was arrested and charged with desertion and cowardice. A few weeks later, at the end of his trial, he gave a statement in his defense.

It is worth quoting at length.

National Archives

Jan. 20th 1865

May it please the Honor of the court to hear a short statement of facts from Samuel Clements the Prisoner.

In the first place I aver, that, I am, at times, both mentally and physically unable to perform the duties of a soldier

> 1st by reason of my age being 53 years ~~of age~~ old; and further debilitated by a severe cut recieved in the foot, some years ago.
> 2ndly In addition to never possessing by nature, a strong intellect, I labor under a mental infirmity caused by a serious fracture of the skull bone recieved from the machinery of a rope factory in Mass., which at times seriously impairs the vigor and clearness of my mental understanding

Further, being at times addicted to intemperance, I, was (at an evil hour) while under the influence of excessive drinking, decoyed into the service by speculators, contrary to my intentions and to the prejudice of the public service; but after being brought to realize my situation, as an enlisted man, I, after consoling myself as well as circumstances would admit, resolved to do the duties required of me as well as my abilities would allow.

After some months service, my debilities began to work heavily upon me, and not having much acquaintance with the proper course to be pursued, I listened to the advise of bad, or ignorant men— perhaps both; ... which I have long since (to my sorrow) found to be ill advised, and more stupidly followed.

When once back in the rear, I chose to remain til well rested; and then report back to my command: as my officers were aware of my lameness, I thought it would be all right,

If the court please to consider these facts; and desire fuller explanatory information I will [be] happy to appear, and give minuter details: and for further satisfaction, undergo a surgical examination.

In view of this statement of facts I trust it may be the good pleasure of the honorable Court, to exercise clemency towards me, beautifully illustrating the Golden rule of our Savior.

National Archives

The eloquent if slightly legalistic and florid prose, written in a fine hand, makes the reader wonder: How can a self-professed mental deficient have produced such a document? This mystery is poignantly resolved at the end of the letter. Far to the left side of the page appear the letters "Sa." Someone looking over Clements's shoulder—perhaps the same man who had written the letter for him—must have interrupted him and told him to sign directly under the valediction. There in a shaky and untutored hand Clements wrote his full name.

The letter did no good, apparently. Clements was found guilty of desertion and cowardice and sentenced "to be shot to death with musketry at such time and place as the Commanding General may direct."[10] This sentence was carried out on February 10, 1865.[11] There may have been "aggravating circumstances" in Clements's case. A note on his file claims that he and the others hiding with him had "lived by begging, or marauding," and commanding general George Meade approved the execution in the hope that it would be "sufficient warning to all stragglers and hangers-on about the lines of this army." But the trial transcript itself makes no mention of any marauding, and he was found guilty only of cowardice and desertion.[12] Clements's claim that he had been tricked into joining the military, his professed mental deficiency and alcoholism, advanced age, injuries to head and foot, his contrition and appeal for Christian mercy: none of these did anything to soften the judgment of the court-martial or of those who reviewed its verdict and sentence.

Cases like DeLand's, Barker's, and Clements's show how cowardice resisted mitigation, how, when the safety of the republic or of a company of soldiers was at risk, infirmity or weakness might not excuse cowardice; they *were* cowardice. Cowardice, furthermore, defined the man. Gerald Linderman has argued that Civil War soldiers believed that battle was "a litmus test revealing their single essence, either courage or cowardice."[13] In the court-martial case of private Simon Snyder of the Sixth New Jersey Volunteers, one witness was asked about Snyder's "character for bravery." He replied, "It seems to be the idea in the company that he is a coward." One could not be tried for *being* a coward, though; one had to do something cowardly. In Snyder's case it was falling out to get water just as his company came under fire that confirmed the prejudgment.

> Q: Did he desert you in the most cowardly manner in this instance?
>
> A: I think he did sir.

Snyder was sentenced to death, a sentence that was commuted with the end of the war.[14]

The most dramatic illustration of the belief that cowardice was a single, defining essence was the practice of branding, which could make one cowardly act mark a man for the rest of his life. Branding assured the congruity of conduct and character, inner vice with outer appearance. The Romans tattooed deserters with the letter "D." The British codified the same practice before the end of the seventeenth century. During the Revolutionary War, the Continental Army does not seem to have branded soldiers, but military law historian William Winthrop noted that the practice of branding or otherwise marking became quite extensive in the American military, with soldiers marked or branded with D for deserter or drunk, "H D for habitual drunkard, M for mutineer, W for worthlessness, C for Cowardice," and so on.

Many Civil War soldiers were sentenced to be branded for desertion and cowardice. It is less clear how often the sentences were carried out.[15] Daniel J. Webber of the First Battalion of the Eleventh Regiment of the U.S. Infantry was sentenced to have his head shaved, to carry a placard reading "Coward," and to have a

C branded on his hip. Privates Joseph C. Waldron and Andrew Whack of the Fortieth New York Volunteers disregarded their superior officer's orders to advance at North Anna in June 1864. The officer had even gone so far as to strike one of them on the shoulder with his sword to push him into the fray. Both were found guilty of cowardice and sentenced "to be branded with the letter C ¾ of an inch in length on [their] forehead[s]."[16]

It is hard to tell if the sentence was carried out, though. Most instances of branding occurred in the first year or so of the war, and it seems to have been generally considered extreme and unmilitary.[17] Brands on the face were subject to special scrutiny. Found guilty of cowardice and desertion at Fredericksburg in 1862, private Andrew Cronan of the New York Fortieth was sentenced to (among other things) have a letter D branded onto his right cheek. "The court" explained that it deviated from

> the usual practice of branding culprits on the hip and decided . . . that the brand in this instance be made on the cheek for the reason that sentences of the former character have been already executed in this Division and do not appear to have had that salutary effect which the severity of the sentence would promise; numbers of enlisted men have been heard to declare that they would gladly undergo such a degradation, could they thereby escape from the service[.] The Court changes the brand from the hip to the cheek in the hope that the perpetual publicity of the disgrace the prisoner has suffered may restrain others from the commission of the same offence and thereby prevent the necessity of a resort to the last method of punishment contemplated in the articles of war.

But this decision was overturned by division headquarters.[18] Holt himself thought branding "was against public policy" and "not conducive to the best interests of the service."[19] It was officially prohibited in the American military as of 1872. (Britain prohibited it in 1871.)

Even when the safety of the republic was in danger, rigidly punitive views about cowardice did not always prevail in the Civil War. When Holt voiced his intent to deal harshly with deserters, Abraham Lincoln is said to have replied, "Deal gently with these leg cases, Judge, for no doubt many a pair of cowardly legs has run away with a valiant heart."[20] Linderman argues, "By 1864 the new tolerance for men whose behavior would earlier have brought condemnation had achieved informal incorporation in the military justice system."[21] Words like *disheartened, nervous, played out, used up, melancholy,* and *badly blown* gave soldiers nonjudgmental terms for behaviors that otherwise might have been judged cowardly.[22] The "constitutional" problem DeLand spoke of also sought to deflect moral judgment. There was a difference between cowardice and infirmity, and justice demanded distinguishing the two.[23]

DeLand's comrade-in-arms lieutenant Moses Powell had tried the same "constitutional" defense DeLand did. A witness reported his saying, "relative to his being in the rear so much, that it was a constitutional thing with him and he couldn't help it. That when the shot and shell came around he could not stand it."[24] Powell made a habit of consulting regimental surgeons; he even seems to have done a bit of what might nowadays be called "doctor shopping." What was he hoping to find? The most well-recognized terms that could be used when dismissing or excusing men from military service were *insanity, nostalgia, irritable heart,* or *sunstroke.* The distinctions among these diagnoses are blurry. Eric T. Dean sees in *sunstroke* a predecessor to *combat fatigue.*[25] *Nostalgia* has been described as predecessor to posttraumatic stress disorder and as the first official alternative to cowardice.[26] Union medical authorities used the term to explain a pathological longing for home, which sometimes drove soldiers to desertion or other behaviors or emotional states that might otherwise be explained by cowardice. Among them were hypochondriasis, "a succession of morbid feelings which appeared to simulate the greater part of disease; panics; exaggerated uneasiness of various kinds" as well as "disordered digestion" and being "serious, sad, timid, apprehending on the slightest grounds the most serious results."[27]

There were many reasons for the "new tolerance" suggested by such nonmoralistic explanations for unsoldierly conduct. Recognition of the terrors of modern war and of the increasing power and range of weapons and length of battles was coupled with recognition of the challenge that the shift from civilian to military life presented to millions. This awareness was accompanied by a reluctance to punish citizen-soldiers too severely, a reluctance that was both a matter of liberal democratic principle and practical political thinking. During the Revolutionary War, this reluctance manifested itself in the Continental Army's relatively lenient punishments. In the Civil War, cowardice was a common charge and desertion still more so, but death sentences for these offenses remained rare, and actual executions rarer still. As Lincoln said, "You can't order men shot by the dozens or twenties. People won't stand it, and they ought not to stand it."[28]

The new tolerance was also part of a larger historical shift, one not confined to the United States or the Civil War era. From the mid-eighteenth century, Western societies had been moving away from corporal punishment, torture, branding, and spectacular public executions and toward more seemingly mild treatment of criminals and other outcasts. They increasingly sought to understand transgression as a consequence of human error or sickness rather than of curse or sin, and moved away from a retributive toward a rehabilitative sense of justice, a growing willingness to treat human behavior medically rather than judge it morally.

This shift was characterized by a diagnostic spirit, as reflected in terms like *nostalgia*, which sought (at least in theory) not to condemn misbehavior but to explain its underlying cause. *Diagnosis* (from the Greek *dia* meaning "through, thoroughly, asunder," and *gnosis*, "to learn to know, perceive") implicitly questions the idea that a man is a "single essence," and the honor-shame culture's assumption that external appearance reveals inner character. One's character was not branded, metaphorically or literally, on one's face. *The Oxford English Dictionary* notes the first appearance of the verb *diagnose* in 1861. Before that, one had to "make a diagnosis."

Still, though the creation of a verb to cover the job reflects the rise of the idea, the date of its coinage also suggests that it named something new, something rare and fragile. The appeal to the constitutional obviously did nothing for Powell or DeLand, and there is no record of a Union soldier who actually tried to use *nostalgia* as a defense against an official charge of cowardice.[29] Clements's apparent disabilities did nothing to help him either. Indeed, rather than diagnostic thinking invariably leading toward more lenient punishment and rehabilitation, it could cloak a deeply moralistic, shame-based, retributive approach. The medical patina of the word *nostalgia*, for example, proved to be just that—a patina, beneath which sometimes lurked the full force of moral judgment. One Union Army surgeon suggested that soldiers presenting the symptoms of nostalgia should engage in vigorous exercise, and that they be convinced "that their disease is a moral turpitude; that soldiers of courage, patriotism and sense should be superior to the influences that brought about their condition . . . that their disease was looked upon with contempt—that gonorrhea and syphilis were not more detestable." Such treatment, according to the surgeon, "excited resentment, . . . and the patients rapidly recovered. Within two years not a single case of nostalgia has occurred, which may be attributed to the fact that idleness is unknown in the regiment, while the odium attached to the disease has played a part in causing the men to overcome the influences which tend to its production."[30]

What seems at first to be a medical explanation for acts that would otherwise be deemed and punished as cowardly becomes a judgment of cowardice by another name. This link between the moral and the medical was hardly new. At least since Plato connected good health to good character, human beings have mixed therapeutic and moral judgments.[31] But what the surgeon does here goes beyond mixing; in equating disease with turpitude, the therapeutic serves the punitive. Nostalgia neatly follows the pattern in which "scientific discourse," as Michel Foucault put it, "becomes entangled with the practice of the power to punish."[32]

Neither *nostalgia* nor any other nineteenth-century medical term gained significant currency as an alternative explanation for cowardice. That would wait for World War I. By the twentieth century, having become better able to heal the human body, medical science increasingly laid claim to the assessment and treatment of human conduct and character (which it knew as "psychology"). This development, when combined with advances in weapons technology that made the modern battlefield seem different from anything that had come before, laid the groundwork for a deeper reassessment of supposedly cowardly behavior. "The present war is the first in which the functional nervous disorder ('shell-shock') have constituted a major medico-military problem," wrote Thomas W. Salmon, the chief consultant in psychiatry for American forces in Europe, in 1917. "As every nation and race is suffering from the symptoms, it is apparent that the new conditions of war are chiefly responsible for their prevalence."[33]

As its name suggests, shell shock was thought to be caused by artillery shells, which had become much more powerful, accurate, and far-reaching since the Civil War.[34] In 1915, doctors pointed to explosives to explain soldiers' paralysis, flight, or uncontrollable weeping. As the seminal article on the topic put it, "It would be contradictory to expect the human organism to be unaffected by violent explosions which produce such an effect on surrounding objects, animate and inanimate."[35] The apparent physiological basis of shell shock helped give it credibility in the minds of soldiers and civilians alike. Doubt about its etiology arose soon after, when doctors observed that soldiers who had clearly suffered physical wounds did not show symptoms of shell shock and were in fact generally quite cheerful, while apparently shell-shocked soldiers did not seem to have been physically concussed, with many of them never having even been near a shell explosion. But by the time medical authorities concluded (perhaps mistakenly, as we shall see) that shell shock was a purely psychological disorder, the concept had achieved a general currency.[36] The United States came late to the Great War, but Americans readily adopted the term.[37]

Once again, though, in a pattern similar to that with nostalgia being deemed a "moral turpitude," the medical approach did not always preclude moralistic judgment and treatment. One American doctor advised that "any appearance of such symptoms as tremors, paralysis, etc.," in those thought to be suffering from neurosis "should be rigidly discouraged." Measures such as curtailing leaves, putting soldiers in isolation, and administering electric shocks should be undertaken to "suppress the self-indulgence which is so often" the cause of the soldiers' condition. They should be urged to "give up their symptoms." He wrote, in short, that the idea was to "[c]heck the development of neurosis by denying its existence from the start."[38]

Still, by attributing conduct that might otherwise have been considered cowardly or crazy (paralysis, uncontrollable weeping) to medical phenomena such as shell shock or war neurosis, doctors "for the first time recognized a grey area" between the two, as Ben Shephard puts it.[39] Many people showed genuine sympathy for the men who suffered from shell shock, and the term stuck, giving substance to an alternative way of thinking in which judgment of soldiers' conduct was not reflexively moralistic.[40] In both its official promulgation, which was rather brief, and in its establishment as a phrase universally recognized in the English language, shell shock reflected a new appreciation for the horrors of war and for the limits of human endurance in the face of those horrors, and a corresponding reluctance to judge too harshly those who faltered in battle.[41] Acceptance of *shell shock* and, after it, terms such as *battle fatigue* and *war neurosis* meant that the label *cowardly* was not applied as widely as it might have been, nor perhaps with the same certainty or ethical weight. Samuel Stouffer found that roughly three quarters of American enlisted men and officers surveyed during World War II agreed that (as the survey put it) "men who crack up in action . . . get shell-shocked, blow their tops, go haywire . . . should be treated as sick men." Fewer than 10 percent said such men "should be treated as cowards and punished."[42] Medical assessment of what might otherwise have been a moral matter (a question of cowardice) had gained widespread acceptance.

The acceptance was not total. Upon reading James Jones's account of his war-induced psychoneurosis, Ernest Hemingway referred to him as "a psycho and not a real soldier." He wrote to Charles Scribner, who published both Hemingway and Jones, "All I hope is that you can make all the money in the world out of him before he takes that over-dose of sleeping pills or whatever other exit he elects or is forced into."[43] This was in 1951, after Jones had become famous for his phenomenally successful debut novel, *From Here to Eternity*, and Hemingway may have been jealous. But he was also showing an enduring suspicion of mental illness and resistance to the therapeutic that is never hard to find.

The most famous backlash had come in 1943 when general George S. Patton encountered private Charles H. Kuhl, a soldier who professed to be a psychiatric casualty. Patton slapped Kuhl's face with his glove and literally kicked him out of the hospital tent. A week later, Patton met private Paul G. Bennett, in hospital because of his "nerves." "Your nerves, Hell, you're just a goddamned coward," Patton told him, "you yellow son of a bitch. Shut up the goddamned crying.... You are a disgrace to the Army and you are going back to the front to fight, although that's too good for you. You ought to be lined up against a wall and be shot." Pulling out a pistol, Patton added, "In fact, I ought to shoot you myself right now, goddamn you." Patton then twice slapped Bennett across the face.[44]

Patton had his reasons—personal, practical, and ideological. In 1918, he had been *decorated* for his part in an action in which he threatened to shoot men who hesitated to advance.[45] Also, in the moments before each of the slapping incidents, Patton had been visiting with soldiers who were badly—physically—wounded, and he was dealing with grave manpower shortages. Patton also disliked

Library of Congress

the risk-averse strategy of the American military and what he thought this strategy and the claims of psychiatric injury reflected: a larger dilution of the warrior spirit. At president Dwight D. Eisenhower's insistence, Patton apologized to both of the soldiers he had slapped, and also made a series of apologetic-sounding speeches to his troops.[46]

In a letter to his wife, however, Patton was not contrite about what he called "the incident." Looking at the original letter on file at the Library of Congress is revealing. The editor of *The Patton*

Kay says that you are all shrunk up (not her words but the
idea) over the incidentI Am sorry it hurt you but personally I know Damned
well I did my duty and if more people did it the same way we would win
a war instead of just fight one. My little dictionary has not got
Sycotpast in it but every division now has.The war weariness will be
fierce,more deadly than the huns.

Love,

Library of Congress

Papers deciphers that strange word in the second-to-last sentence as "sycophant"—mistakenly, in my view.[47] "Psychiatrist," a biographer's guess, strikes me as closer to the mark.[48] But I think "sucotrast" is exactly what Patton meant to type; the handwritten corrections seem intentionally haphazard too, so as to dramatize that "psychiatrist" was so *not* in his dictionary that he could not and would not spell it correctly. Patton, after all, thought that "a large proportion of men allegedly suffering from battle fatigue are really using an easy way out. . . . Any man who says he has battle fatigue is avoiding danger and forcing those who have more hardihood than himself the obligation of meeting it." Judge advocate general Joseph Holt would certainly have agreed. "If soldiers would make fun of those who begin to show battle fatigue," Patton went on, "they would prevent its spread, and also save the man who allows himself to malinger by this means from an after life [*sic*] of humiliation and regret."[49]

Patton's last words in the letter do reflect his worry about the mental cost of prolonged exposure to combat: "The war weariness will be fierce," he wrote, "more deadly than the huns." But it is not clear if he means soldiers' weariness, his own, or both. In any case, with "weariness" he eschews the medical term a "sucotrast" would have offered.

Patton died in 1945. Had he lived, he would not have been pleased by the continuing ascendance of the therapeutic "easy way out." When the feature film *Patton* opened in theaters, the slapping incident was back in the news. It was 1970, and the United States was involved in the deeply unpopular war in Vietnam. On Memorial Day weekend of that year, the *Richmond News Leader* ran a brief editorial about Kuhl, now fifty-four. Looking back, Kuhl said of Patton, "I think he was suffering from a little battle fatigue himself." The editorial asserted, "Unquestionably, Kuhl is correct in his assumption. Patton always drove himself as hard as he drove his men—to the outer limits of human endurance. Patton's difficulty was that he refused to acknowledge in himself the battle fatigue he deplored in his men. And so when the exhausted general met the exhausted private, the difference between the *slapper* and the *slappee* was only a matter of rank."[50] One can easily guess what Patton would have thought of this.[51] The *Richmond News Leader* was not a liberal paper: on the same page as the comment on Patton and Kuhl there appeared a list of American prisoners of war being held in North Vietnam. "Wouldn't it be reassuring if, just today, those who scream their denunciation of the Vietnam War would say a few words in denunciation of Communist treatment of American prisoners? But they won't. . . . "[52] That even such an editorial board would presume to diagnose Patton suggests how pervasive the diagnostic ethos had become.

Patton would not be sanguine about the warrior spirit since Vietnam. Actual psychiatric casualties among American soldiers in Vietnam were quite low—an estimated 12 per 1,000 compared to as many as 101 per 1,000 in World War II[53]—but in the aftermath of the Vietnam War, the creation of a new diagnostic category would continue the medicalization of battle experience and apply it even to those who had never seen battle. Posttraumatic stress disorder (PTSD) became an official diagnosis in the American Psychological Association's third *Diagnostic and Statistical Manual* (*DSM-III*) in 1980. The proliferation of what two English psychiatrists call "medically unexplained" war syndromes such as Gulf War syndrome and Bosnia War syndrome might have led Patton to lament that each war seems to have its own eponymous psychological affliction.[54]

One could try to reassure him by saying that the diagnostic can actually *serve* the warrior spirit in a couple ways—first by cloaking moral judgment in medical language, as we have already seen in attitudes toward nostalgia or shell shock, when diagnosis becomes a vehicle that might delay but ultimately delivers moral condemnation. Even today, whether congenital or caused by war trauma, mental illness can carry a terrible stigma. A recent study of PTSD among Iraq War veterans needed 440 volunteers; researchers could find only twenty, and attributed the shortfall to "stiff resistance in the ranks to acknowledging mental wounds in combat soldiers."[55] Brain injury helped cause depression and PTSD in one army sergeant, but he observed that amputees received most of the attention at Walter Reed Army Medical Center.[56] Physical injury is still a red badge of courage; psychological injury remains something else. A marine veteran testified before Congress in 2009 about "the personal attacks veterans, including myself and many others, had to encounter once we were willing to be treated for PTSD within our unit. The idea of being a real Marine that does not complain when coming back home and who sucks it up and just does the job that we were tasked to do, this mentality resulted in many of the marines I served with, including myself, turning to drugs and alcohol. . . ." At that same hearing, another Marine observed, "When we all come back from Iraq and we seek help from our command, they call us 'weak' and 'cowards.'"[57]

The second way that diagnosis can serve the warrior spirit is by confirming the suspicion of cowardice by ruling out medical explanations. Marine lance corporal Thomas H. King appealed on medical grounds his 2004 court-martial conviction for cowardice and other charges. When his unit was about to go into "an area teeming with Iraqi insurgents," King refused orders to accept bullets for his rifle, refused to carry a loaded weapon, and refused the option of driving unarmed—all, it was alleged, because he was afraid of dying. He originally pled guilty to the charges against him, but he contended in his appeal that when he had misbehaved and when he pled guilty he was having psychological problems, specifically PTSD and bipolar disorder. The members of the appeals court considered the possibility that these problems should excuse the soldier's misconduct and render his plea "improvident," but they found no evidence of PTSD in the record and noted that the diagnosis of bipolar disorder came after the soldier's misconduct; there was no evidence that he had the disorder during his service. Their due consideration of these medical explanations did not dilute their belief that the accused was cowardly; if anything, it fortified it.[58]

Cases like King's show how considering and rejecting medical explanations can contribute a sense of openness and fairness in trial and thereby make moral judgment stronger and more certain. Saying that in some instances cowardice no longer applies implies that in other instances it still does. And there can be a more general effect: rather than merely reducing the scope of cowardice, PTSD and similar diagnoses can serve at times, in an ever-changing combat environment and in light of new insights about human psychiatry, to adapt and so save the concept of cowardice.

Patton would probably not buy such reasoning. He would agree with the British field marshal who wondered in the early 1990s if "so-called Gulf War Syndrome [was] a genuine medical condition, a psychological delusion or a ramp to extract money from the Ministry of Defence," and who worried that "the insidious influence of today's compensation and counseling culture," "the idea that the answer to stress is professional counseling," diminished soldiers' ability to overcome their fears and do their duty.[59] Imagine Patton's outrage at the National Vietnam Veterans Readjustment Study, which reported in 1988 that close to one million American soldiers who had served in Vietnam had suffered from "full blown" posttraumatic stress disorder—a number more than three times that of the soldiers who had been in combat units. Subsequent studies estimated that three out of every four Vietnam "veterans" being compensated for PTSD were "pretenders"; some had never been to Vietnam; some had never even been in the military.[60]

The *DSM-IV* (1994) advised doctors to beware of "malingering" in possible PTSD cases, but it has become clear that this is easier advised than accomplished. It is also clear that doctors and other diagnosticians, the government, and indeed society as a whole would rather not worry too much about it. Although psychologists have warned that self-reporting is not a reliable way to assess trauma or traumatic disorder and that independent evidence of a "stressor" is needed, self-reporting is typically the primary source of data for diagnosis. A 2010 change to Veterans Affairs policy asserted that as long as soldiers' testimony about trauma sounded plausibly related to their military service, the PTSD diagnosis should stand.[61] When there is "any reasonable doubt" about the veracity of a soldier's claim of PTSD, Veterans Affairs authorities are now "legally bound to resolve [it] in the veteran's favor."[62]

Even more galling to Patton would be the practice of applying current diagnostic ideas to soldiers in previous wars. The most famous recent instance of this involved the 306 soldiers executed by the British for desertion, cowardice, and other military crimes in World War I. One was private Harry Farr, who had been hospitalized three times for shell shock and who, as one advocate stated in 2006, "was very obviously suffering from a condition we now would have no problem in diagnosing as post traumatic stress disorder."[63] After he refused to participate in an attack on German lines in 1916, Farr was found guilty of cowardice and executed. He and the other 305 soldiers were pardoned in 2006 after fierce debate that did not end with the official parliamentary pardon. George Haig, grandson of field marshal Douglas Haig, who had confirmed Farr's sentence, was outraged by the decision. He allowed that "some of these soldiers were genuinely shell-shocked. But many were rogues, persistent deserters and criminals, or they were guilty of cowardice. They had to be made an example of."[64] He and others also protested the unfairness of judging those such as his grandfather, who had had to make difficult wartime decisions.

Still, the pardons were granted, and the proponents of such retroactive diagnosis can point to new research that conflicts with the idea that shell shock had no physiological basis. When World War I soldiers behaved strangely after being near an exploding shell, and doctors could not detect evidence of physical injury, they ascribed their problems to psychological trauma or distress. But recent advances in neurology have helped researchers see physical evidence of traumatic brain injury that would have gone undetected even ten years ago. As a 2006 report in the *Journal of the Royal Society of Medicine* put it, "the recent experience of blast injuries in Iraq and Afghanistan makes it clear, in retrospect, that many of these [World War I] soldiers did indeed experience actual brain injuries." Had doctors in 1916 had the benefit of such advances, they might have concluded that shell shock was indeed a physiological consequence of an exploding shell, that Harry Farr was indeed physically injured.[65]

Leon Hawley

Farr and the other 305 soldiers who were pardoned are commemorated by the Shot at Dawn Memorial, erected in 2001 at the National Memorial Arboretum in Alrewas, England.[66] At the center of the memorial is a sculpture based on the likeness of private Herbert Burden, who had joined the military in 1914 at the age of sixteen, having lied about his age. In 1915, he left his regiment to console a friend in another regiment whose brother had reportedly been killed.[67] He was found guilty of desertion and executed in July 1915 at the age of seventeen, still not legally old enough to serve in his regiment.[68] The white concrete sculpture depicts him blindfolded, hands tied behind his back, a target on his chest—not a coward but a victim, a boy done in by insidious, powerful forces that duped him into war and then punished him for being human. Behind him are wooden stakes, each bearing the name, rank, regiment, age, and date of death of the other executed soldiers.

Eberhard Hauff

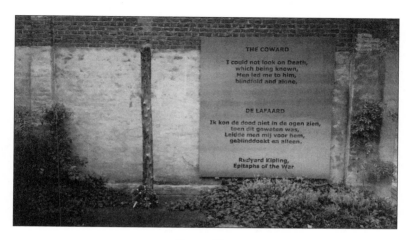

Norman Date

There are similar monuments elsewhere in Europe.[69] Numerous memorials in Germany honor deserters of the Wehrmacht, who were "rehabilitated" by the German parliament in 1997.[70] The memorial in Stuttgart depicts the thick, flat figure of a soldier and, behind him, the hole his absence has created in a block of granite. This vivid depiction of someone who has escaped what Stephen Crane called the moving box, but not without cost to his person, is "dedicated to deserters of all wars."[71]

In Belgium, in Flanders Fields, the centerpiece of a monument to executed soldiers is a lone pole and a plaque on which appears in English and in Flemish translation one of Rudyard Kipling's epitaphs for the war, "The Coward": "I could not look on Death, which, being known, / Men led me to him, blindfold and alone."[72] The quietly turned couplet as Kipling wrote it simply bears witness; it does not seem to judge one way or another. Set in the monument, however, it seems to seek not only sympathy but exculpation.

These monuments and the increasing tolerance or even celebration of deserters may reflect the hypothetical global shift, explored in chapter 2, away from violence and toward increasing empathy and peacefulness. The trend away from violence seems most evident in Europe, which has seen a dramatic transformation into what has been called a "nonwar community." As James Sheehan puts it in *Where Have All the Soldiers Gone?*, "The blend of commitment and coercion that once motivated [Europeans] to fight and die for their nations is gone forever."[73] Given the bloody history of Europe in the twentieth century, this is understandable. Why shouldn't the memory of those soldiers who deserted the Wehrmacht be honored? Why did it take the German parliament so long to reverse its convictions?

But the practice of memorializing and pardoning, sometimes even celebrating soldiers who avoided combat has provoked some alarm. Michael B. Oren asserts that in Europe a just sympathy for deserters from unjust wars has turned into "an admiration for desertion as a general practice." And he wonders "whether Europe's eagerness to immortalize deserters will reverberate elsewhere. It sounds far-fetched," he adds, "but it is impossible not to wonder: Will visitors to Valley Forge someday see a single pole" such as the one commemorating "The Coward" in Belgium?[74]

My guess is that there will not be such a monument at Valley Forge or anywhere else in the United States. By and large, and for sometimes contradictory reasons, Americans have generally not gone in for celebrating desertion. On one hand, Americans have not been too harsh, generally speaking, in the treatment of cowardly or cowardly seeming soldiers in the past. Having no 306 executions, no thousands shot on the front, Americans have less to feel guilty about and compensate for, less to reassess. On the other hand, the United States has not become a nonwar community in the way Europe has; it has by far the largest military in the world, and it can even be said that America has sponsored the European move away from war by remaining a "war community" itself. As president Barack Obama put it rather pointedly in his 2009 Nobel Peace Prize acceptance speech before a European audience, the United States has "helped underwrite global security for more than six decades with the blood of our citizens and the strength of our arms."[75]

Yet what Sheehan writes of Europeans—that in the twenty-first century they have come to think of national defense not as the duty of all, or even of every male citizen, but of the citizens who choose that duty and are trained and paid to perform—sounds true of Americans as well. There was never a golden age when the burden of war was evenly distributed among the entire population, but compared to the Civil War or the period of the two world wars and Vietnam, the American military today draws on a far smaller proportion of the population, and a more narrow stratum of it. During the run-up to the invasion of Iraq, just one out of the 635 men and women in Congress had a child who might have seen combat; the proportions are similar for the privileged families of business, media, and academia.[76]

Neither the elite nor indeed the majority of the population has shouldered or even felt the cost of war in other senses either. "War taxes are the only ones men never hesitate to pay, as the budgets of all nations show," William James said.[77] But as has often been noted, the latest wars in American history have been waged without asking civilian America to pay anything like an extra "war tax." President George W. Bush never actually called on Americans to beat the terrorists by going shopping, but many observers thought that his administration emphasized commerce rather than sacrifice. There were no recruiting posters asking, as they had in World War I, "On Which Side of the Window Are You?" Being inside the shop was fine, an act of citizenship—though a white-board in a U.S. Marine post in Ramadi, Iraq, showed soldiers' resentment of such a notion. "America is not at war," read the sign. "The Marine Corps is at war; America is at the mall." A photograph of it became common on military blogs.[78]

John Moore/Getty Images

This disconnection between the general population and the all-volunteer military helps explain American enthusiasm for seeking military solutions. We are militarily active because most of us don't have to pay the price for our military activity. This disconnection also helps explain why cowardice in the military is a topic too obscure and tender to ponder for nonmilitary Americans. We are willing to have other people and other people's children put themselves in harm's way, but we feel both ignorant and guilty about it, and that is enough to keep us from presuming to judge soldiers for failures in the heat of combat, even really to think about such failures. (It is hard to imagine a film like *The Execution of Private Slovik* being made today, much less setting any ratings records; the film has not been reissued on DVD in the United States.) The members of the volunteer military force earn our indiscriminate and unthinking gratitude. To cover for our unwillingness to sacrifice ourselves, we call all the soldiers heroes and leave it at that.[79] Pondering the cowardice of a soldier might also lead all too readily to the question of why we ourselves have not answered or even heard the call to duty and joined the fight, or actively supported those who do. Or, if we think that "cowardice" should not be punished, that not fighting is morally correct, then the question becomes why we aren't campaigning against the war.

A case that briefly became national news in 2003 revealed the enduring stigma of cowardice; it also revealed a man spurred on by that stigma to fight for more enlightened views about the effects of trauma on soldiers. Georg-Andreas Pogany enlisted in the U.S. Army in 1996 and in 2003, in the early days of the invasion of Iraq, he volunteered to serve as an interrogator for a team of Green Berets. Around midnight on September 29, on his second night in Iraq, Pogany saw a group of American soldiers dragging an Iraqi man's corpse. "From his waistline to his head, everything was missing," he said. "It was incomprehensible. I couldn't believe that had once been a person." Some of the soldiers were laughing, but not Pogany.[80] He became nauseous and panicky, vomited and got the shakes, hallucinated. "I couldn't function," he said. "I had this overwhelming sense of my own mortality. I kept looking at this body thinking that could be me two seconds from now." A psychologist diagnosed him with "normal combat stress reaction" and prescribed rest and a return to duty, a program Pogany wanted to follow.

But his superior officer "went Patton on him," as Pogany said later.[81] He called him a "shitbag" and a "coward"—"a fucking coward, I'm going to make sure everyone in the rear knows you're a fucking coward."[82] And so on, for roughly an hour. Pogany was sent back to the States; his gun was confiscated and he was put to work sweeping parking lots and cleaning bathrooms at Fort Carson in Colorado. He also consulted with a lawyer.

Steve Peterson/*New York Times*/Redux (2003)

On November 6, 2003, Pogany's image appeared at the beginning of a CNN newscast, paired with that of Jessica Lynch, an American soldier who had been held prisoner in Iraq and whose rescue was being celebrated. "Heroes and Cowards in War" was the title of the "In Focus" segment.[83] But the day this story aired, the charges against Pogany were reduced to dereliction of duty. The next year they were dropped altogether. The year after that Pogany was honorably discharged, and subsequent evidence has come to light that he (and other soldiers) had experienced an adverse reaction to malaria medication.

Michael Ciaglo/*Colorado Springs Gazette*, 2013

Since leaving the military, Pogany has made it his life's work to advocate for soldiers suffering from PTSD and other "invisible wounds" such as traumatic brain injury. When such soldiers are ill-treated he puts his military training into action. He "assesses the enemy situation" and strategizes how to "outmaneuver" the military bureaucracy that behaved unjustly toward him and toward other returning soldiers who were denied the care and benefits they deserved. Pogany has learned the intricacies of the military's medical retirement process and studied the *DSM*, which "still sits within arm's reach of his desk at home."[84] As of this writing, he is director of military outreach and education for Give an Hour, which recruits volunteers to counsel soldiers coming back from war.

Pogany has been described as an angry man. "They frigging labeled me a coward in front of the entire goddamned country," he said in 2004.[85] But now he is "even somewhat thankful because the branding made him who he is today"[86]—a man driven to get his fellow veterans the compensation, treatment, and respect they deserve, and to fight the stubbornly lingering notion that asking for help is a sign of weakness. He insists that his work since leaving the military "has never been about payback . . . but rather the very thing the military preaches: Duty." He speaks of feeling "an obligation to help those who came home and struggle. We must help them, because if we don't . . . not only are we breaking a sacred promise we've made to them, we're also dishonoring the memory of those who have not come home."[87] It is not enough to put a yellow ribbon up for the troops, he told one radio reporter. "The soldier's creed says 'I will never leave a fallen comrade.' At the end of the day, when I put my head on my pillow, I can say that the yellow ribbon is not just a magnet that I put on my car." The story ended with a pointed question from Pogany. "I actually put my yellow ribbon into action," he said. "What have you done to support troops?"[88]

Chapter 6

SO LONG A FILE

Cowardice Away from War

The cases of Georg-Andreas Pogany (chapter 5) and John Callendar (chapter 1) invite comparison. Like Callender, that soldier court-martialed for his cowardly conduct at Bunker Hill who later fought so bravely for the Continental Army that George Washington erased the court-martial from his record and restored him to his officership, Pogany was motivated by the shame of cowardice to act courageously. There are, of course, significant differences between the two cases. Callender was actually found guilty of cowardice, and apparently with some reason. Pogany was never officially charged with it, and even the suspicion of cowardice proved unfounded. While Callender fought war in its conventional form, Pogany today fights what William James called the "moral equivalent of war." James felt that "martial virtues" such as "intrepidity, contempt of softness, surrender of private interest, obedience to command" were essential to keeping society together, but that it would be a better world if we exploited these virtues to fight not each other but more worthy enemies such as disease, poverty, and injustice.[1] Where Callender erased the stain of cowardice on the battlefield, Pogany chases the shadow of cowardice from the homes and hospital rooms of veterans.

Both men, though, were soldiers. Before joining the army, in fact, Pogany had served for four years in the marines and had been in the navy reserve. (He had also worked as a volunteer fireman.) He was the man, to paraphrase Walt Whitman; he suffered, he was there, and he had learned the hard way that the therapeutic or diagnostic approach is often exactly the proper response to someone who has been traumatized. That some soldiers who were not traumatized pretend to be, as discussed in chapter 5, seems an inevitable hazard of an otherwise worthwhile enterprise. But there is also considerable concern among some that the therapeutic approach applied properly in the military setting has been improperly, even promiscuously applied outside of it. While concepts such as shell shock and battle fatigue stipulate combat experience explicitly in their very names, *posttraumatic stress disorder* (PTSD) and related terms do not. British commentator Ben Shephard notes that PTSD created a "bridge ... between 'war neurosis' and the victims of civilian trauma that had never really existed before."[2] Trauma has proven vulnerable to "conceptual bracket creep." In PTSD's first articulation in the American Psychological Association's third *Diagnostic and Statistical Manual* (*DSM-III*, 1980) qualifying "traumatic stressors" included experience "outside the range of usual human experience": living in a war zone or experiencing a natural catastrophe, say, or being raped or beaten or witnessing violence firsthand. In 1994, the *DSM-IV* broadened the criteria so that being frightened by "learning about the misfortunes of others, including strangers" can be said to constitute trauma.[3] Elaborations on the PTSD guidelines in the 2013 *DSM-5* have been criticized by some (and praised by others) for making the PTSD criteria still easier to meet.[4]

Beyond noting an alarming proliferation of the trauma diagnosis, some commentators also lament how the "traumatized" are treated and taught to think of themselves—as victims. In *One Nation under Therapy*, Christina Hoff Sommers and Sally Satel deliver a polemic against what they call "therapism" that "valorizes openness, emotional self-absorption and the sharing of feelings" and embraces the idea that "vulnerability, rather than strength, characterizes the American psyche."[5] The "culture of trauma," Shephard writes, "undermines the general capacity to resist trauma," and he thinks it is "too late" to fight against this culture. "Trauma has been vectored into the wider society by the law and the media; armies of half-trained counselors now live off it." Thus does the therapeutic triumph, and thus does the "culture of trauma" reign supreme.[6] By depriving us of a main defense against cowardice—the fear of being cowardly—the culture of trauma threatens to make cowards of us all.

At this point in American and indeed modern Western moral history, cowardice seems to be severely attenuated in its archetypal setting, war. Without this model as a ready reference—a setting where duty is defined so clearly, fear felt with such force, and the cost of cowardice felt so keenly—can cowardice figure with any clarity and power in everyday moral discourse? Some commentators believe that if the idea subsists at all it must be in profoundly distorted and diluted form. James Bowman wrote in 2006 that "what passes for mortal insult—at least in its capacity to generate genuine-looking emotion—lives on not in the charge of cowardice itself but in the charge that you have charged someone else with cowardice and so, presumably, damaged his self-esteem."[7]

This would give new meaning to an eighteenth-century aphorism that warned of the danger of the insult of cowardice: "As cowardly as a coward is, it is not safe to call a coward a coward."[8] Back then the insult might lead to a duel; today it might get you called before a sensitivity committee. Other observers feel the term has vanished altogether; the word *cowardice*, Jeffrey Snyder observed in 2001, has "largely disappeared from public discourse."[9]

Yet Snyder's observation appears in an article he titled "A Nation of Cowards." He knew (or hoped, anyway) that the term retained power—power made very evident in the labeling of the 9/11 attackers and the Boston Marathon bombers as cowards. A foggy sense of cowardice also seems to inform the common understanding of crime. Criminals are often called cowards in the same loose way the 9/11 terrorists were. Recently in Boston an elderly woman was mugged and thrown to the ground. "It's despicable," said the district attorney. "Only a coward would attack a 73-year-old woman from behind."[10] The murderer or rapist or pickpocket, though he failed no duty out of fear, and indeed may have endangered himself to commit his crime, is often called a coward. The term is also used on occasion to describe white-collar criminals. I think we call criminals "cowards" for the same reason we use the term for terrorists and bullies. If the criminal or bully really acts out of fear, then perhaps we have power over him. This comfort is largely illusory. It may well be that the thug is in some way insecure, afraid of revealing a hidden vulnerability. But he's not physically vulnerable to the person he assaults. Most often the bully hurts you not because he is afraid but because he can. He wants *you* to be afraid.[11]

Cowardice is not just a label for some criminal behavior after the fact; the fear or shame of cowardice can cause crime as well.

A fifteen-year-old boy breaks into a house to vandalize it, thinking there's no one home. When he hears a sound, he runs away into the woods until he can run no more. "But here's a strange thing now," he says later,

> Why does a natural coward suddenly change and decide he wants to be brave, can you tell me that? You know what I was when I was puffing and blowing and trying to catch my breath back sitting on the tree? I was ashamed of myself, that's what. Ashamed that the moment I heard a noise somewhere in the rest of the house I turned like a chicken and ran. I didn't have the dignity to walk at a rapid pace or anything. . . . That was a downright disgraceful thing for me to face: I'd been a coward, least that's what I looked like to myself. So I had to disprove it right there and then, I had to go back and find me another house and trash that one straight away. Nothing else would do, the coward had to prove himself to be brave.

In the next house he breaks into, the boy winds up murdering an old woman.[12]

A similar feeling leads Raskolnikov to kill the pawnbroker in Fyodor Dostoevsky's *Crime and Punishment*. The theme is announced on the opening page of the novel, when Raskolnikov fears even to meet his landlady, to whom he owes back rent: "I want to attempt such a thing, and at the same time I'm afraid of such trifles," he thinks, "Hm . . . yes . . . man has it all in his hands, and it all slips through his fingers from sheer cowardice."[13] The idea of murder had occurred to him when he overheard a conversation between a military officer and a student friend of his. The student says the pawnbroker should be killed and her money used to help needy people. "You're talking and making speeches now, but tell me: would you *yourself* kill the woman or not?" "Of course not," says the student, to which the officer replies, "Well, in my opinion, if you yourself don't dare, then there's no justice in it at all!" And they go back to playing billiards.[14] But the conversation stays with Raskolnikov, who agrees that the pawnbroker's death would make the world a better place. He also believes himself a superior being with certain severe but exalted duties, and that he should control his own fate and that the pawnbroker prevents him from doing so. To believe all this and *not* dare to kill her: that would be cowardly.

Coward and similar terms are the most "violence-provoking" insults among criminals, according to the psychiatrist James Gilligan.[15] Sometimes the insult need not be spoken but simply "in the air." In *In Cold Blood*, Truman Capote recounts the true story of two men who, independent of each other, might not have been capable of murder, but who together kill four innocent people. One of the men, Perry Smith, wants the other, the blustery Dick Hickok, to argue him out of killing and thereby show that he, Hickok, "was a phony and a coward." "See," said Smith, "it was something between me and Dick."[16] That something at the bottom of this slaughter was not a desire to kill but a game of chicken revolving around cowardice, the belief that, in the circumstances, not being violent would be cowardly.

One way to break the cycle of violence is to forfeit in such a game, to embrace or to surrender to appearing cowardly. The 1938 film *Angels with Dirty Faces* offers a dramatic illustration. Rocky Sullivan (played by James Cagney), is a toughened criminal who is friends with Jerry Connolly (Pat O'Brien), a priest. Much to Father Jerry's dismay, the neighborhood boys he is trying to steer away from a life of crime look up to Rocky, even after he's convicted of murder and sentenced to death. The prospect of death by electrocution does not faze Rocky. "It'll be like sittin' down in a barber's chair," he says. Father Jerry pleads with Rocky to go to "the chair yellow" so the neighborhood boys, and thousands like them across the country, will no longer think of him as a "glorified hero": "They've gotta despise your memory. They've gotta be ashamed of you." Rocky vehemently declines his friend's request, but as he is brought to the electric chair he screams and begs just as Jerry had asked, a moment the film depicts in silhouette.

Whether Rocky faked his fear or not remains unclear, but the film does make clear that, at least for the short term, his seeming cowardice had the desired effect on the boys who had admired him. When Jerry confirms the newspaper reports ("ROCKY DIES YELLOW; KILLER COWARD AT END!"), the boys are shocked and dismayed. The film ends with celestial music playing as Father Jerry leads the boys out of their basement hideout, up toward the light of day.

Such an approach to juvenile rehabilitation contrasts starkly with the approach popularly known as "scared straight," in which veteran jailed convicts try to terrify young delinquents in an attempt to push them away from a life of crime. But being "scared straight" in this way has been shown not to work very well, and in fact it may actually lead to increased criminality.[17] Perhaps it would work better to introduce "at-risk" youth to convicts who behave abjectly, sniveling and begging and weeping and moaning like Rocky Sullivan. Maybe that would scare them straight. To my knowledge, this tactic has not been attempted.

Compared to some other countries, there seems to be more room in the United States for the cowardice-violence dynamic to operate among the law-abiding. In requiring one to flee a threatening person in most circumstances, the English common-law tradition of the duty to retreat makes doing violence against someone who is or may do violence to you illegal in most cases. This tradition has been overturned in the United States, where the right to kill in self-defense was legally justified by authorities who thought the duty to retreat reflected and fostered cowardice. The duty to retreat was Old World doctrine that ill-became brave citizens of a frontier nation.[18] Many states have laws that allow individuals who think they are in danger to "respond with deadly force." A recent incident in Florida, in which "neighborhood watch captain" George Zimmerman shot and killed an unarmed teenager, Trayvon Martin, brought no-duty-to-retreat laws into the news. Opponents of the statute in Florida call it the "shoot first" law, emphasizing its potential to justify reckless violence; proponents refer to it as "stand your ground," emphasizing its defensive and courageous nature.[19]

The absence of a duty to retreat in the American context puts cowardice into play in interesting and complicated ways. In a 1934 case when the self-defense defense seemed especially thin, a Georgia jury was advised, "To justify a homicide the fears of the slayer must be those of a reasonable man ... and not those of a coward."[20] But conversely, the absence of a duty to retreat leaves room for one to wonder if one is actually obliged *not* to retreat, to defend oneself, or even to attack. One should act out of regard for one's assailant's potential future victims, for example, or for reasons of self-respect, to avoid being cowardly.

Such thinking infuses the myth of the Old West as well as *Dirty Harry* and other vigilante-justice movies. It also informs the argument against gun control that Snyder advances in "A Nation of Cowards." In his defense of the right to bear and use arms, Snyder laments how eagerly we accept the advice that "when confronted with lethal violence, we should not resist, but simply give the attacker what he wants." How, he asks, can we "address the problem of rampant crime without talking about the moral responsibility of the intended victim"? Must we farm out what might be our most fundamental impulse and right, to defend ourselves, to specialists? The doctrine of no-duty-to-retreat may stand legally, but to Snyder, the cultural tradition behind it has faded, indeed reversed, become a duty not just to retreat but to surrender. Thus it is he notes that we have become "a nation of cowards and shirkers," all of us victims waiting to happen.[21]

One time-honored response to such a charge is a kind of hearty acceptance, an inversion of cowardice such as is expressed in the 1964 film *The Americanization of Emily* (based on a 1959 novel of the same name by William Bradford Huie). Lieutenant commander Charlie Madison is a wised-up World War II naval officer who says that when he was in combat at Guadalcanal, "I discovered I was a coward. That's my new religion. I'm a big believer in it. Cowardice will save the world. You see, cowards don't fight wars. They run like rabbits at the first shot. If everybody obeyed their natural impulse and ran like rabbits at the first shot, I don't see how we could possibly get to the second shot.... So, I preach cowardice. Through cowardice, we shall all be saved."[22] Two centuries before that, Samuel Johnson had observed that "mutual cowardice keeps us in peace. Were one-half of mankind brave, and one-half cowards, the brave would be always beating the cowards. Were all brave, they would lead a very uneasy life; all would be continually fighting: but being all cowards, we go on very well."[23] The individual, private vice makes a social and public virtue.

Yet there is a kind of cowardice whose commonness does not redeem it. In a 1901 polemic against lynching, Mark Twain wrote of "man's commonest weakness, his aversion to being unpleasantly conspicuous, pointed at, shunned, as being on the unpopular side. Its other name is Moral Cowardice, and is the supreme feature of the make-up of 9,999 men in the 10,000."[24] The notion of moral cowardice has remained mostly implicit in this book, where physical cowardice has been in the foreground, if also in retreat. The moral versus physical distinction is a fraught one. Moral *courage* is typically understood to involve social rather than physical risk.[25] But someone acting out of moral courage (denouncing her corrupt boss even when she'll get fired for it; defending a view so unpopular that his reputation and material fortunes may suffer) may well experience emotional and even bodily symptoms like those a soldier in mortal danger experiences. And a soldier doing something that everyone would call physically courageous may feel no such physiological consequences. As British lawyer and judge James Fitzjames Stephen has noted, "The distinction between moral and physical courage is, in fact, a distinction without a difference."[26]

But there may be a significant distinction between these kinds of courage, and it may well lie in cowardice—the weak link that proves to be the crucial one. William Ian Miller speculates that in some cases you don't have to be physically courageous to be morally courageous, but you can't be too much of a physical coward either. Standing your ground, even metaphorically, requires not caving in to fears that one experiences bodily.[27] One wants to stick up for some cause, but gives in to his fear of public speaking or of ridicule. Worry about making fools of ourselves leads us to fail our friends, family, faith, or selves in countless ways. In such cases prudence or tact or politeness or decorum or discretion is the better part of valor, we may tell ourselves, corrupting a proverb as Falstaff did after playing dead in battle.[28] But such rationalization doesn't necessarily stop us from feeling cowardly. After writing that moral cowardice governs 9,999 men out of 10,000, Twain added, "I am not offering this as a discovery; privately the dullest of us knows it to be true."[29]

The worst moral cowardice may not be failing out of fear but instead not attempting anything at all. Even doing evil is better than that, as Dante implies in making the *Inferno*'s neutrals envy the fate of everyone else, even those across the river in the circles of hell. T. S. Eliot was more explicit about the superiority of choosing iniquity to not choosing at all when he praised Charles Baudelaire as a poet who was man "enough for damnation." "[I]t is better, in a paradoxical way, to do evil than to do nothing," wrote Eliot; "at least, we exist."[30] The souls in hell's anteroom never really did exist.

When Virgil tells Dante not to speak of them, just to look and pass on, he does as he is told. He passes on, remains silent—but he does look. What he sees is a banner racing through the air, and behind it innumerable sorry souls running. Wasps and horseflies sting these wretches. Blood and tears streak down their faces, down their naked bodies, to their feet, where the vile mixture feeds worms. There is a terrible aptness to the punishment. Not having acted or chosen, these souls neither truly live nor die, so they have no names and no hope. How fitting it is that, despised by both God and his enemies, these nobodies cannot check in or out of hell. They who were too afraid to march behind a banner now race after a banner that says nothing. Or is it that those who abjectly followed the majority in life follow it now for eternity?[31] They are condemned in death to flail forever—at that banner, at those wasps and flies—because they never extended themselves in life.[32]

The decidedly undramatic ways the cowardice of these souls manifested itself in their lives does not make them less cowardly;

Marco Beck Peccoz; Collezione Perizzi, Parma, Italy

it may in fact make them more so. The trimmers never ran away, never dropped their swords or shields, never shit their pants—but only because they never came close to the fray. To desert you first need to join up, to choose one side or the other; at least Falstaff was on the battlefield. Instead of hiding behind a tree trunk like Army colonel David "Stumpy" Williams (chapter 3), Dante's cowards hid behind convention, behind whatever passed for common sense and normalcy. The cowardly neutrals whose tears trickle down to the worms may never have cried in life, for tears signal a committed feeling that they lacked. On earth perhaps they smiled. Primates show their teeth not as a gesture of menace but of deference. Jane Goodall compares the chimpanzee's "full closed grin," in which the jaws are closed and the lips retracted, to the "human nervous or social smile."[33] The zoologist-artist who sketched it for her, David

Bygott, wonders how this "classic 'fear face' across many primates . . . has become recognized as a 'happiness face' in our culture."[34]

David Bygott

Those "sorry souls" who make such a terrible noise in Dante's ears did not make a peep in life. The unavoidable example of the cowardice of silence is the Holocaust. By the definition used in this book, cowardice does not apply to those in Nazi Germany who believed it their duty to perpetrate genocide. But the label has been applied convincingly to those who knew or should have known that their duty lay in doing something to stop the mass murder, and yet did nothing. As Primo Levi put it,

No one will ever be able to establish with precision how many, in the Nazi apparatus, could *not not know* about the frightful atrocities being committed, how many knew something but were in a position to pretend they did not know, and, further, how many had the possibility of knowing everything but chose the more prudent path of keeping their eyes and ears (and above all their mouths) well shut. Whatever the case, since one cannot suppose that the majority of Germans lightheartedly accepted the slaughter, it is certain that the failure to divulge the truth about the Lagers represents one of the major collective crimes of the German people and the most obvious demonstration of the cowardice to which the Hitlerian terror had reduced them: a cowardice which became an integral part of mores and so profound as to prevent husbands from telling their wives, parents their children. Without this cowardice the greatest excesses would not have been carried out, and Europe and the world would be different today.[35]

Rather than being (in Daniel Goldhagen's phrase) Adolf Hitler's *willing* executioners, the perpetrators of this "major collective crime" failed by *not* asserting their will.[36] Without such cowardly abdication, the "banality of evil" would be impossible. "[T]he greatest evil perpetrated is the evil committed by nobodies," Hannah Arendt wrote, "that is, by human beings who refuse to be persons."[37]

Martin Luther King made similar arguments about those who failed to fight injustice in the United States. He did not spare his fellow African Americans from the charge of cowardice, saying at a memorial service for a slain civil rights worker, "Yes, he was murdered even by the cowardice of every Negro who tacitly accepts the evil of segregation."[38] In lamenting Americans' apathy about U.S. involvement in the Vietnam War, King said he "agreed with Dante that the hottest place in hell is reserved for those who in a period of moral crisis maintain their neutrality. There comes a time when silence becomes betrayal."[39] Dante actually makes no mention of the temperature of this particular spot in the *Inferno*, nor, as we have seen, are the neutrals actually *in* hell. But King's point is clear.

As King shows, the shame associated with cowardice can be stoked and used even by those who are skeptical about cowardice conventionally defined. Mark Twain showed his skepticism when he told the tale of his own abortive attempt to join the Confederate side in the war in "The Private History of a Campaign That Failed," a tale of would-be soldiers who do little but raise false alarms and constantly retreat. When faced finally with real danger, Twain writes, "Our boys went apart and consulted; then we went back and told the other companies present that the war was a disappointment to us and we were going to disband." They then disbanded.[40] "The human race is a race of cowards," Twain wrote elsewhere, adding with characteristic wryness, "and I am not only marching in that procession but carrying a banner."[41]

Yet Twain does not laugh cowardice off altogether. His indictment of 9,999 out of 10,000 as moral cowards was in earnest. Even if he held out little hope that talking about moral cowardice would help reduce it, he used the term as if it had viable ethical value. His assertion in a notebook that "[y]ou are a coward when you even *seem* to have backed down from a thing you openly set out to do" may give more practical guidance;[42] "even *seem*" (the italics are his) and "openly" acknowledge the importance of social context and of witness in enforcing a contempt for cowardice, moral or physical.[43] But if one wants to use contempt for cowardice to motivate oneself or others, social perception is a helpful reinforcement. If you pick it well, the crowd can be your friend. The moving box can sometimes get you where you want—or *should* want—to go.

This is not to say that the crowd, however well chosen, need have the final word in defining cowardice and enforcing that definition. When Twain defines the coward as one who shrinks from something he himself "set out to do," he allows for, perhaps even obliges, the autonomous self to choose. We saw how Samuel Davies emphasized respect for autonomy and how that respect gave a special charge to his version of cowardice. It may be that with the rise of individualism (with attendant shifts in cultural emphasis from, depending on which historian or sociologist you read, shame to guilt, sincerity to authenticity, honor to dignity, respect to self-respect) we have come to worry more and more about this individual sort of cowardice. The advancing Spartan army considered cowardly anyone who did not stay in rhythm to the pipes;[44] Henry David Thoreau observed that someone who does not seem to stay in rhythm may be marching to a different drummer. Cowardice remained relevant, though. A different drummer can still take the measure of a man, or a woman.[45] "Whatever your sex or position," Thoreau wrote, "life is a battle in which you are to show your pluck, and woe be to the coward."[46] Speaking of the often arduous project of self-realization, William Ian Miller is no doubt right to say that it "need hardly involve courage; more likely it is a less glorious matter of plain hard work."[47] But even if courage does not figure, cowardice can, if the project is understood as a duty, and the plain hard work is avoided out of fear (of difficulties, say, or of plain hard work). Being courageous may not be necessary to realize yourself, but not being cowardly is.

Worry about an individual sort of moral cowardice may be characteristically American, but it is not uniquely so. Samuel Johnson lamented the "mean and cowardly dereliction of ourselves," our tendency to convince ourselves that some worthy venture is impossible, when really we're just afraid to try. Do not bother, this sort of cowardice says; this endeavor will be frustrating or futile; there will be insuperable hurdles. You can't see them from here, but they're just around the first bend, and every single bend after that. We typically despise and condemn those who, out of fear, flee in battle or otherwise fail in their duty to the group, reserving for them "all the virulence of reproach"; but we seem to tolerate this individual sort of cowardice quite readily. What Johnson calls a "cold despondency," a pusillanimity in which excessive fear leads to an evasion of duty to the self, does not pose a limitless danger to the group. It may in fact make us feel better about our own similar evasions. But just because such dereliction "flatters us by that appearance of softness and imbecility which is commonly necessary to conciliate compassion" does not mean it is noble.[48] It does mean that those who would indict it have to work harder.

Certainly Dante indicts it. Before he contemplates those suffering in hell's anteroom, he contemplates the cowardice of his own would-be pilgrim self. He begins his journey having lost his way in middle age. He was "full of sleep," and now he finds himself in a dark dense forest, beset by beasts. There he encounters the shade of his hero Virgil, who promises to guide him. Despite this guarantee, though, despite being promised the protection of three blessed women, and despite being convinced that his journey is the only way to salvation, Dante is daunted by the prospect of going through hell. Before entering the gate, he protests to Virgil that he is not worthy. "For I am not Aeneas, am not Paul," he says. "Nor I nor others think myself so worthy." Here humility serves or masks what Johnson might call a mean and cowardly dereliction.[49] Such small-spiritedness can manifest itself in the equivocations of those who would let planning and pondering replace actual doing. Dante wants to turn back, "for thinking ate away the enterprise / so prompt in the beginning to set forth."[50]

This is the cowardice that Hamlet says conscience makes.[51] Overthinking leads to indecision, which leads to procrastination, which leads to more overthinking and indecision. Søren Kierkegaard anatomized the cycle compellingly: "What cowardice fears most of all is the making of a resolution, for a resolution instantly dissipates the mist. The power cowardice prefers to conspire with is time; for neither time nor cowardice finds any reason for haste." Such cowardice can disguise itself with many names to justify forestalling or forgoing.[52] Cautiousness is an obvious one. Humility is another, so readily evident in Dante's I-am-not-worthy protestations. A kind of humble cowardice can worm its way into the self-deprecation required of those who do not want to seem pretentious or hubristic. But self-effacement when taken too far can actually efface the self.

A still more insidious species of moral cowardice takes the form of a high-mindedness that evades dealing with the quotidian details of life. Kierkegaard pairs such an attitude with a seemingly very different vice, pride: "How proud to be able to stare constantly into the clouds without ever needing the head to look at the feet!"[53] A version of this strangely elevated sort of cowardice was memorably dramatized by Henry James in "The Beast in the Jungle," a story that depicts John Marcher, a man who refrains from living his own life as he awaits some big thing he is convinced will happen to him. The only person Marcher tells about this belief is a woman named May Bartram. The beast in the jungle is Marcher's "sense," as she puts it to him, "of being kept for something rare and strange, possibly prodigious and terrible, that was sooner or later to happen to you." His preoccupation with the beast keeps him from doing much of anything with his privileged life, and what he does do he does with a detachment that characterizes even, or rather especially, his relationship to May. It is as if they sit side by side, fellow spectators, waiting for the beast to leap. John never quite fully looks at her, and when she becomes seriously ill, he thinks foremost that she will be deprived not of her life, but of the privilege of witnessing his: "What if she should have to die before knowing, before seeing—?"[54]

May dies. And gradually—excruciatingly gradually—John Marcher meets the beast. "It wouldn't have been failure to be bankrupt, dishonoured, pilloried, hanged," he thinks; "it was failure not to be anything. . . . No passion had ever touched him, for this was what passion meant; he had survived and maundered and pined, but where had been *his* deep ravage?" His deep ravage comes when he finally understands, a couple of years after May's death,

"*She* was what he had missed." Looking at her grave he sees "the sounded void of his own life."[55]

Marcher makes a fine candidate to join Dante's neutrals. The fitting "consummation of infinite waiting" that James describes as his lot after May Bartram's death aptly describes the anteroom of hell, for what are anterooms for but to wait in?[56] Yet no James scholars have compared Marcher's conduct and fate to that of the cowards in the *Inferno*.[57] No one has observed that John Marcher and May Bartram's story might have had a happier ending if someone had given Marcher a good slap and told him not to be such a coward. Marcher is an extreme character, a very Jamesian one, but his sense of being a spectator of his own life is not so extraordinary; it makes him a figure of the modern, hyper-self-conscious individual, estranged within, forcing the ape smile, the closed grin, without: "What it had come to was that he wore a mask painted with a social simper," James writes, "out of the eyeholes of which there looked eyes of an expression not in the least matching the other features."[58]

Marcher also reminds us how rife with opportunities for cowardice—as rife, perhaps, as war, to which it is so often compared—is love. The first comes when the would-be lover lets the fear of rejection or of looking like a fool overcome the duty to heed the heart's desire. The coward slinks away, maybe writes the valentine, but definitely doesn't send it. Next, sometimes, comes the refusal or failure to—as contemporary parlance has it—commit. This sort of cowardice is typically, but not exclusively, male. At the end of Junot Diaz's book of linked stories, *This Is How You Lose Her* (2012), the philandering macho narrator ponders why he failed to be faithful to the woman he really loved: "You are surprised at what a chickenshit coward you are. It kills you to admit it but it's true."[59] The love villains of romantic novels and soap operas are often portrayed as cowardly in this way.

It isn't just the failure to forgo other lovers to commit to one that can make one a coward. In one of his "lines" (he didn't like to call them "poems"), Stephen Crane explored how worldly concerns could compromise devotion:

And you love me
I love you.
You are, then, cold coward.
Aye; but, beloved,
When I strive to come to you,
Man's opinions, a thousand thickets,
My interwoven existence,
My life,
Caught in the stubble of the world
Like a tender veil—
This stays me.
No strange move can I make
Without noise of tearing
I dare not.
If love loves,
There is no world
Nor word.
All is lost
Save thought of love
And place to dream.
You love me?

I love you.

You are, then, cold coward.

Aye; but, beloved—

From one view the world's "stubble" is the duty of responsible and respectable adulthood. But from the perspective of the scorned, the not-fully loved, a higher duty should call. Love is supposed to be "strong as death," the Song of Solomon (8:6) says, and a million romantic poems and plays concur. "Man's opinions, a thousand thickets, / my interwoven existence": these shouldn't matter too much. But they do to the coward, and love gets diluted, maybe poisoned.

Which brings us to the last of the cowardices of love, in the ending of it. A note on the nightstand, a phone call, not showing up at the altar, texting, emailing, changing one's relationship status on Facebook, paying a service such as idump4u.com ("$10 For a Basic Breakup; $25 For an Engagement Breakup; $50 for a Divorce Call"): if we can agree that the person with whom one shared sustained physical and emotional intimacy deserves more, these could all qualify as cowardly ways to end a romance. And then there are those too cowardly even for these cowardly ways, who fear ending it so much that they doom themselves and their partner to lovelessness until death do they part.

Moral cowardice can inhere not only in love but in laughter too. As fearfully blubbering clowns show—*The Wizard of Oz*'s cowardly lion, Charlie Chaplin, Stan Laurel (in contrast to Oliver Hardy), and many others—cowardice can be funny. Real life cowardice can sometimes be funny too—even in war. Consider Hooker DeLand telling a fellow soldier that "he thought it was too warm for him, that he did not want to get killed just then."[60] Such fearfulness may

strike us as shameful, but the candor wins our admiration—a humorous mix. Another court-martial case during the Civil War concerned private Mitchell Bernard who, as one witness reported, said
"he was going to lay down to avoid the next battle, or words to
that effect." When asked if there was "anything in his conduct or
manner about that time to induce you to believe he meant what
he said," the witnessed answered, "I rather believed him." And so do
we.[61] Who *does* want to die "just then"? If we laugh here (I know I
do), our laughter is as complicated as cowardice is. We laugh at and
with, contemptuously and condescendingly, sympathetically and
enviously, nervously.

If cowardice can be humorous, humor can also constitute
cowardice—its "most engaging form," according to Robert Frost.[62]
Frost held that "any form of humor shows fear and inferiority. Irony
is simply a kind of guardedness," an engaging form of disengage-
ment. Frost was writing especially of the irony of the poet; more
recent observers have seen irony as the pervasive and pernicious
tone of contemporary American discourse. Jedediah Purdy noted
that turn-of-the-millennium irony was comprised of a variety of
fears: "of betrayal, disappointment, and humiliation, and a suspicion that believing, hoping, or caring too much will open us to
these."[63] Those who give in to such fear refuse to acknowledge obligation, to commit to anything.

Sometimes irony makes the fear of danger comically huge, and
the possibilities of duty comically constrained. Irony can make
what passes for "honorable trial" (Dante's term) ludicrously trivial,
the contexts in which we might overcome cowardice becoming
more pathetic by the day until in the end we ask, with Prufrock,
"Do I dare to eat a peach?"[64] Yet moral cowardice is not as funny
as physical cowardice, perhaps because the former is less clear and

hits too close to home. We know the cowardly lion shouldn't be afraid of his tail, and so laugh at him as we are intended to, but we do not laugh at Prufrock. His fears are more nebulous—and more like our own. Is he worried about his dental work or staining his shirt? Is it a class thing? Is he self-conscious to the point of pathology?

Still, I would not want, in the name of avoiding cowardice, to forgo irony altogether. Irony can be a way of dealing with a brutal and stupid world that seems to have all the guns and numbers—a "counterforce," as Denis Donoghue called it, "to brainwashing: it brings to bear on a given system values antithetical to those in place; it holds out against the official blandishments."[65] And anyway, irony's opposite—earnestness, sincerity—can be morally cowardly too when it unthinkingly and abjectly stays the course, changing circumstance or new evidence be damned. This sort of cowardice is characterized by a fearful refusal to consider other possibilities, contingencies, and qualifications that may bring a salutary tentativeness to one's conduct. In this sense, the 9/11 terrorists or Boston Marathon bombers can indeed be called cowardly, guilty of what Olivier Roy calls the "holy ignorance" of those who fail to understand the fullness—the complexity and nuance—of their own theology and culture, not to mention the appalling cost of their violence. Fundamentalism of any kind runs the risk of cowardice when it clings, out of fear, to what it takes to be fundamental. It is possible to have the cowardice of one's convictions.

This is not to say that conviction or a bit of preaching (of the kind I find myself doing here, for instance) is necessarily cowardly. The fear of cowardice can in fact serve a spiritual end more appealing than Osama bin Laden's. In her last and perhaps most famous poem, Emily Brontë mounts her final testament to "Faith" upon a fierce rejection of cowardice. "No coward's soul is mine," the poem begins, "No trembler in the world's storm-troubled sphere."[66] Anchoring the poem in the depth of the contempt for cowardice enables Brontë to achieve spiritual height. "I see Heaven's glories shine, / And Faith shines equal, arming me from Fear." It was the lone poem read at the funeral service of Emily Dickinson.[67]

A similar note resounds through Ralph Waldo Emerson's "Self-Reliance," especially in the paragraph that begins, "Trust thyself: every heart vibrates to that iron string." Emerson goes on to say that "we are now men, and must accept in the highest mind the same transcendent destiny; and not minors and invalids in a protected corner, not cowards fleeing before a revolution, but guides, redeemers, and benefactors, obeying the Almighty effort, and advancing on Chaos and the Dark."[68] The transcendent gives us something to aim for, energy and validation to help us brave the dark and see the stars, but the fear of cowardice gets us out of the corner to begin with.

Rainer Maria Rilke, too, invokes cowardice to fortify the spirit:

We must assume our existence as *broadly* as we in any way can; everything, even the unheard-of, must be possible in it. That is at bottom the only courage that is demanded of us: to have courage for the most strange, the most singular and the most inexplicable that we may encounter. That mankind has in this sense been cowardly has done life endless harm; the experiences that are called "visions," the whole so-called "spirit-world," death, all those things that are so closely akin to us, have by daily parrying been so crowded out of life that the senses with which we could have grasped them are atrophied. To say nothing of God.

One does not have to be mystical or religious to feel the force of this lament about the narrowness of our lives, pinched by fear, distraction being a kind of escape, the coward's way out. Like Emerson, Rilke laments our settling in a protected corner, "for most people learn to know only a corner of their room, a place by the window, a strip of floor on which they walk up and down. Thus they have a certain security." [69]

That word again. Secure, comfortable in our corners, we are like that man in Franz Kafka's parable who sits before an open gate all his life, talking with a gatekeeper who refuses all his requests to let him in to "the law." And when with his dying breath the man asks why no one else has come, the gatekeeper says this gate was for the man only, and he closes it. The implication is that we squander our lives and souls when we await permission to go down a path that is ours for the taking.[70]

From a certain existentialist view, a view in which God's absence makes freedom and responsibility total, courage becomes the ultimate virtue, and cowardice the ultimate vice. And as one is one's own judge and jury, court is always in session. "I alone can absolve myself," wrote Jean-Paul Sartre[71]; and, man "can't start making excuses for himself. . . . There's no such thing as a cowardly constitution. . . . What the existentialist says is that the coward makes himself cowardly, that the hero makes himself heroic. What counts is total involvement."[72] Such extremity, such "dreadful freedom," places enormous pressure on the individual—the flip side, perhaps one of the causes, of the modern trend toward the therapeutic.

The most pervasive and profound cowardice may, in the final analysis, have to do with our awareness, with evasions so deep we are not aware of them. Classical thinking about courage connects it to knowing—knowing right from wrong, knowing, as Pericles put it in his famous funeral oration, "the meaning of what is sweet in life and of what is terrible, and then go[ing] out undeterred to meet what is to come."[73] Plato and through him Socrates also emphasized how important knowledge was to courage.[74] If the best courage is fully reflective, the worst cowardice utterly avoids reflection. Confucius may have been wrong to say that "to know what is right and not to do it is the worst cowardice," for it may be worse not to know, not even to try to know.[75] Acquainting yourself with a corner of your room isn't enough. Such a failure character- ized those negligent, oblivious Virginians whom Samuel Davies said labored under the curse of cowardice. It characterized those Germans who, as Levi put it, "had the possibility of knowing ev- erything but chose the more prudent path" of not knowing. It may characterize us. From our vantage point the cowardice of past ages is relatively easy to see, but what failures will future generations recognize in our present age, what duties did we fearfully shirk, and in so doing compromise ourselves, and bring harm to others, the planet, our descendants?

In studying moral blind spots, psychologists have noted how good we are at keeping ourselves unaware of inconvenient or threatening information, and how, when it comes time to choose and act, desire trumps duty.[76] We are good at not "acquiring infor- mation that would make vague fears specific enough to require decisive action," as one psychiatrist put it, and good at disregard- ing the demands of such fearful information that we do acquire.[77] Our ability to anesthetize ourselves is so powerful that just being aware of the ways we deceive ourselves is not enough to prevent self-deception, nor will all the good intentions in the world suffice to make us actually do the right thing. To "change the underlying dynamics," Robert Trivers writes in *The Folly of Fools: The Logic of Deceit and Self-Deception in Human Life*, "we need much deeper confrontations with ourselves and our inadequacies, ones often drenched in tears and humility."[78] The idea of cowardice, properly understood, can push us toward such deeper confrontations.

Our collective cowardices, and our individual ones as well, seemingly invisible to us now but threatening to haunt our death-bed recollections—the problems and possibilities avoided, the deadening habits, the talents buried, the longings dismissed, the duties we fail in fear, the fears we fail to confront: someone writing a book on cowardice begins to see them all everywhere. This chapter could go on for as long as the trail of neutrals Dante sees, for cowardice can inhere in so much that we do and fail to do. We have also seen the dangers of fearing cowardice too much and as a result acting wrongly, recklessly, violently. That chapter could go on forever too.

There are myriad other ways to understand failures in the face of fear. A disorder or phobia can explain why one did not defend the fort, climb the mountain, get on stage, or even try out for the part. Maybe one's background or environment explains dereliction of some dangerous duty. Explanation can excuse, or guide us to some other way to blame. Maybe John Marcher was egotistical, or maybe he was simply stupid. The politician genuinely feels he is the best man for the job; he tells himself that selling out in the short run will be good for his constituents in the long run. Arrogant, but probably not cowardly. Maybe you didn't climb the mountain because you were too lazy to train, did not try out for the part because memorizing the audition script was prohibitively difficult.

But—one last *but*—egotism, arrogance, stupidity, laziness, surrendering to difficulty ("prohibitively"—really?): these can all be
proximate causes. Cowardice may hide beneath each of them, as
universal as Mark Twain and Samuel Johnson say. Dante is amazed
at how many crying, moaning, undying dead there are. He never
thought death could have taken so many. Eliot takes up the image
in *The Waste Land*:

Unreal City,
Under the brown fog of a winter dawn,
A crowd flowed over London Bridge, so many,
I had not thought death had undone so many.
Sighs, short and infrequent, were exhaled,
And each man fixed his eyes before his feet.

Such are the main denizens of modern life—"hollow men," as
Eliot calls them elsewhere, "stuffed men"—shuffling along, spectators essentially, but refusing to look far beyond their toes.[79]

One critic of the "ante-Inferno" argues that having a sin so common it would apply to all mankind makes this particular part of
Dante's vision untenable.[80] How could an anteroom possibly hold
such multitudes? But maybe it is all too tenable. Maybe the numbers clinch the case.

The dangers of a thoughtless invocation of cowardice are abun-
dantly clear. We have seen, again and again, the horrors that the
fear of cowardice has wrought. It is also clear that letting the concept dissolve in the blood of its history would be a mistake. It still
has its uses. This is not to say that cowardice should be our only
consideration when facing a dangerous responsibility. Many other
factors obviously belong in our moral calculus. "Justice," the poet

William Stafford wrote, "will take us millions of intricate moves."[81] Yet if cowardice shouldn't be the first thing we think of when fear and duty conflict, neither should it always be the last. If it is a dangerous, harmful idea, it's a bracing one too. It pushes us to ponder seriously what we should do, how we should act, and what it is we're so afraid of.

Dante needs more than one reminder of the importance of overcoming cowardice to steel him to advance. He gets beyond the dark wood, away from the beasts that lurk there, is assured and reassured of safe passage, and Virgil scolds him repeatedly for his cowardly hesitations. Yet when he sees the gate and the inscription on it that ends, "Abandon all hope, ye who enter here," he hesitates again. The words' meaning is hard for him, he tells Virgil—hard to understand, and hard to take. He feels threatened. The souls damned for eternity need to abandon hope. But Dante's situation is different. He is undertaking an honorable trial, down and through the circles of hell, then upward through purgatory and beyond. Stop hesitating, Virgil tells him; "here you must put all cowardice to death."[82] Only then can he begin the journey that takes him, eventually, to paradise.

ACKNOWLEDGMENTS

A project that takes this long incurs generations of debt. I first explored the topic of "craven images" in American fiction with the guidance of Richard Fox, Saul Bellow, Peter Berger, and Marilyn Halter. Janis Freedman Bellow, Tom Denenberg, Carlos Ramos, Bruce Redford, and Jon Vogels were helpful too. Dennis Marnon read the entire manuscript with care and generosity. That was in the twentieth century. The next five years I left cowardice behind, though during the two of them I spent at the University of Ouagadougou, Richard Akresh, Amadou Bissiri, Jimmy Kolker, and Chris Palmer were indulgent when I couldn't help but talk or write about it.

When I returned to the subject in earnest, I greatly benefitted from working with such supportive colleagues at the College of Arts & Sciences Writing Program at Boston University. Within and outside of BU, many people have helped me in many ways: Allison Adair, Donald Altschiller, Josh Barkan, Marco Bracamante, Joe Bizup, Jeffrey Brown, Tomas Carbonell, Scott Challener, Jeff Cordell, Nathalie Favre-Gilly, Herb Friedman, Maria Gapotchenko, Billy Giraldi, Alyssa Hall, Raymond Herek, Jim Hopper, Karl

Iagnemma, P. J. Ivanhoe, Dan Ivey, Beverly and Thomas Lowry, Bill Marx, Askold Melnyczuk, Marisa Milanese, James L. Nelson, G. Dennis O'Brien, Stacey Peebles, Jason Prentice, Michael Prince, Brad Queen, Christopher Ricks, Clayton Robarchek, Jay Ryan, David Shawn, Nina Silber, Tom Underwood, and Frances Whistler. I am grateful to William Ian Miller not so much for leaving the field open as for opening it, clearing some thickets and flagging the swamps. This book owes more to *The Mystery of Courage* than is reflected in the footnotes; even the gesture of the first half of this sentence is borrowed from that book's acknowledgments, which pay tribute to Joanna Bourke, Paul Fussell, Richard Holmes, John Keegan, and Gerald Linderman, scholars whose work both surveys broad territory and shows how to dig in deeply. I thank them too, and add to their number Leo Braudy, Richard Gabriel, Christopher Hamner, Earl Hess, Ben Shephard, and Martin van Creveld. Among the many people who helped secure the images that appear in this book I'd like especially to thank Kaylie Jones; Laurie Kind, of the High Museum; Peer Ebbighausen, of NBC Universal, who dug into the archives for the shots from *The Execution of Private Slovik*; and Dr. Giovanni Perizzi and Marco Beck Peccoz, who allowed me to include Francesco Scaramuzza's depiction of the anteroom of Dante's *Inferno*.

Special mention is needed for those who read the whole manuscript in whatever state it was at the time: Janet Landman, Mo Lee, Lenore Myka, Stephanie Nelson, Bill Pierce, Jason Prentice, and Ricki Lee Silverman. Christopher Harris and Tony Wallace did this more than once. I am grateful to all these people for their generosity, and for remaining my friends even after they became members of this dubious club. Scott Hovey read it all at the very end, too, and I am grateful to him and Joe Lucas for their help over the years. Kate Canfield of Canfield Design is a great partner on and off the page.

The project also benefited from the attention of audiences at the United States Military Academy and annual conferences of the James Jones Literary Society; the Association of Literary Scholars, Critics, and Writers; and the Society of Civil War Historians. It benefited too from the camaraderie of my students who, over many years, heard me talk about the challenges I faced in writing, even as they were facing their own. I am particularly grateful to one of those students, captain Aaron W. Miller, a U.S. Army infantry officer and veteran of the recent American operations in Iraq and Afghanistan, who candidly and patiently discussed military matters with me. Faculty aides subsidized by the Harvard University Division of Continuing Education were also extraordinarily helpful: Marley Healy, Alex Kalish, Lisa Loren and, finally, Steven Richter.

Parts of this book have also been improved by seeing the light of day in different versions. Thanks to Susan Bianconi and J. D. McClatchy of the *Yale Review*; Lesley Gordon, Angela Riotto, and the anonymous readers of *Civil War History*; and Brian Doyle of *Portland Magazine*.

Funding from the Boston University College of Arts & Science, the Humanities Center at BU, and the Earhart Foundation also supported this enterprise. The staffs of the Howard Gotlieb Archival Research Center and Mugar Library at Boston University, as well as at Harvard University's Fine Arts Library, the Ransom Center of the University of Texas, and the University of Virginia, confirmed my long-standing belief that librarians are the most resourceful and helpful people in the world.

My editor Rob Tempio expressed interest in this project back in 2007, and has never, ever failed to be an encouraging and patient champion. The anonymous readers for Princeton University Press offered detailed, generous responses, critical in every good sense of that word. Thanks also to Ryan Mulligan and Debbie Tegarden for assisting with the endgame, to Dimitri Karetnikov for his beautiful work with the illustrations, and to Brian Bendlin for being such a deft and kind copy editor.

Expressing gratitude to all those above (and I'm sure I've forgotten a few) does not implicate them in my errors here, much less with any cowardly associations. Dedicating a book on this subject seemed like a bad idea. A study of a particular kind of wry warm humor could have been devoted to the memory of my father, Ed, even if he would have wanted the paragraphs to be shorter. An inquiry into graciousness and the cheerful fulfillment of the duties of a nurse and mother might have begun to pay due tribute to Kay Walsh. For my Tess, Calla, CeCe, and Malcolm: a book on rascal angels. I can't imagine—much less write—a book worthy of Mary, and certainly not this one.

NOTES

INTRODUCTION

1. Adam Smith, *The Theory of Moral Sentiments*, ed. Knud Haakonssen (Cambridge: Cambridge University Press, 2002), 287; Søren Kierkegaard, "Against Cowardice," in *Edifying Discourses*, trans. David F. Swenson and Lillian Marvin Swenson (Minneapolis: Augsburg, 1946), 4:83; Mikhail Bulgakov, *The Master and Margarita*, trans. Richard Pevear and Larissa Volokhonsky (New York: Penguin 1997), passim (305, 319, 329, 410n).

2. Samuel Johnson, *The Yale Edition of the Works of Samuel Johnson* (New Haven, CT: Yale University Press, 1958), 3:136.

3. Osama bin Laden, "Bin Laden's Fatwa," *PBS Newshour*, August 1996, www.pbs.org/newshour/terrorism/international/fatwa_1996.html.

4. William Safire, "Infamy: Words of the War on Terror," *New York Times Magazine*, September 23, 2001, 32. Susan Sontag, "Talk of the Town," *New Yorker*, September 24, 2001, 28. For an argument against calling the Boston Marathon bombers cowards, which makes some of the same points I raise here, see Philologos, "The Tsarnaev Brothers Are Many Things. But Cowards? Not So Much," *Jewish Daily Forward*, April 28, 2013, http://forward.com/articles/175399/the-tsarnaev-brothers-are-many-things-but-cowards/.

5. Dinesh D'Souza, interviewed by Bill Maher, *Politically Incorrect*, ABC, September 17, 2001; Celestine Bohlen, "Think Tank; In New War on Terrorism, Words are Weapons, Too," *New York Times*, Sept. 29, 2001, A11.

6. Bohlen, "Think Tank."

7. Noel Langley, Florence Ryerson, and Edgar Allan Woolf, *The Wizard of Oz: The Screenplay* (New York: Dell, 1989), 99.

8. Aristotle, *Nicomachean Ethics*, trans. Terence Irwin, 2nd ed. (Indianapolis: Hackett, 1999), 1115–17. See also James D. Wallace, "Cowardice and Courage," in *Studies in Ethics* (Oxford: Basil Blackwell, 1973), 97–108.

9. John Wilmot, Earl of Rochester, *The Complete Poems of John Wilmot, the Earl of Rochester*, ed. David M. Vieth (New Haven, CT: Yale University Press, 1968), 28.

10. Historically, attitudes toward suicide in the American military have been disdainful. The families of American soldiers who died in a combat zone received a letter of condolence from the president—unless the soldier died by suicide. This policy changed in July 2011. In announcing the change, president Barack Obama noted that soldiers who committed suicide in a combat zone "didn't die because they were weak." Leo Shane III, "White House to Send Condolence Letters after Military Suicides," *Stars and Stripes*, July 5, 2011, updated July 6, 2011, http://www.stripes.com/news/special-reports/sui cide-in-the-military/white-house-to-send-condolence-letters-after-military -suicides-1.148446.

11. Plutarch, *Plutarch's Lives*, trans. Bernadotte Perrin (New York: G. P. Putnam, 1916), 3:135.

12. *Manual for Courts-Martial United States* (2008 edition), IV-35, Article 99, 23d, http://www.loc.gov/rr/frd/Military_Law/pdf/MCM-2008.pdf.

13. See Douglas N. Walton, *Courage: A Philosophical Investigation* (Berkeley and Los Angeles: University of California Press, 1986), 89; see also Mary Mothersill, "Duty," *Encyclopedia of Philosophy*, ed. Paul Edwards (New York: Macmillan, 1967), 443.

14. Code of Federal Regulations, Title 32, 2, chap. 5, part 578, sec. 578.4, "Medal of Honor," http://edocket.access.gpo.gov/cfr_2002/julqtr/32cfr578.4 .htm.

15. *Encyclopedia of Ethics*, 2nd ed. (New York: Routledge, 2001), s.v. "courage" by Douglas N. Walton.

16. Plato, *Laches and Charmides*, trans. Rosamond Kent Sprague (Indianapolis: Bobbs-Merrill, 1973), 33, 47.

17. William Ian Miller, *The Mystery of Courage* (Cambridge, MA: Harvard University Press, 2000), 2.

18. There are good reasons to be careful about drawing general conclusions from Ngram graphs. As Claude S. Fischer, "Digital Humanities, Big Data, and Ngrams," *Boston Review*, June 20, 2013 (https://www.bostonreview. net/blog/digital-humanities-big-data-and-ngrams), notes, the nature of the Ngram corpus can be confounding. The decline in mentions of "cowardice" could reflect the fact that moralistic documents such as sermons made up a larger proportion of publications earlier in American history, and cowardice would naturally figure more prominently in such documents. The wider range of documents published in more recent times dilutes the sample. Also,

since the number of words in the English language has grown considerably, *cowardice* has more terms to compete with now than it did in 1800. It could further be argued that the decrease in mentions of cowardice shows that the idea has been so absorbed into common thinking, into what anthropologists call "cultural tone," that we no longer have even to say or write the words associated with it; it is in the air without being expressed, so pervasive that it does not need saying. Or it may be that other words serve to convey the concept of cowardice without using that term. And yet, I find the graph suggestive of the diminishing (though not vanishing) significance of the concept, and this book tells why.

19. Noah Webster, *An American Dictionary of the English language*, rev. Chauncey A. Goodrich and Noah Porter (Springfield, MA: G. and C. Merriam, 1864), s.v. "coward."

20. H. W. Fowler, *A Dictionary of Modern English Usage* (Oxford: Clarendon Press, 1926), s.v. "coward(ly)."

21. Generally, this book does not put quotation marks around terms for cowardice, trusting the reader to remember that my use of the terms does not necessarily indicate endorsement of them—nor, for that matter, do quotation marks always suggest skepticism.

22. William J. Hardee to Samuel Cooper, February 7, 1863, in *The War of the Rebellion: A Compilation of the Official Records of the Union and Confederate Armies*, series 1, 10, pt. 1., 570 (Washington, DC: Government Printing Office, 1884); Lesley Gordon, "Confederate Cowards," paper presented at the Southern Historical Association Annual Meeting, Atlanta, November 4, 2005.

23. S.L.A. Marshall, *Men against Fire: The Problem of Battle Command in Future War* (New York: William Morrow, 1947). Some of Marshall's methods for studying soldiers' behavior have been questioned, but his conclusions have largely withstood careful scrutiny; see Kelly C. Jordan, "Right for the Wrong Reasons: S.L.A. Marshall and the Ratio of Fire in Korea," *Journal of Military History* 66 (January 2002): 135–62. See also Dan Baum, "The Price of Valor," *New Yorker*, July 12, 2004, http://www.newyorker.com/archive/2004/07/12/040712fa_fact.

24. James M. McPherson, *For Cause and Comrades: Why Men Fought in the Civil War* (New York: Oxford University Press, 1997), 77.

25. Horace, *Odes* 3.2, lines 13–16, in *Odes and Epodes*, trans. Niall Rudd (Cambridge, MA: Harvard University Press, 2004), 144–45. Elsewhere Horace seems to admit to cowardly flight, and without much apparent shame. At the Battle of Philippi, he writes, he left his "little shield behind without much credit"; Horace, *Odes* 2.7, lines 9–12, in *Odes and Epodes*, 108–9. Exactly what Horace did or did not do at Philippi remains unclear. He may actually have

thrown down his shield, or he may have been simply evoking in the ode a common motif in Greek poetry. See the discussion in Jacques Perret, *Horace*, trans. Bertha Humez (New York: New York University Press, 1964), 20–22.

26. Dante, *Inferno*, trans. Henry Wadsworth Longfellow, ed. Matthew Pearl (New York: Modern Library, 2003), lines 22–43. For further examinations of this scene in the *Inferno*, see Wallace Fowlie, *A Reading of Dante's Inferno* (Chicago: University of Chicago Press, 1981), 31–35; Maria Picchio Simonelli, *Lectura Dantis Americana: Inferno III* (Philadelphia: University of Pennsylvania Press, 1993); and John Freccero, "Infernal Irony: The Gate of Hell," *Modern Language Notes* 98 (1983): 769–86.

27. As Maria Picchio Simonelli notes in *Lectura Dantis Americana: Inferno III*, 5, "There is no doubt that the sin punished in the ante-Inferno is cowardice."

28. Aristotle, *Nicomachean Ethics*, 1115a.

29. Miller, *Mystery of Courage*, 12.

30. Max Hastings, "Drawing the Wrong Lesson," *New York Review of Books*, March 11, 2010, http://www.nybooks.com/articles/archives/2010/mar/11/drawing-the-wrong-lesson/. Military historian Richard Gabriel, *No More Heroes: Madness and Psychiatry in War* (New York: Hill and Wang, 1987), 46, notes that "[a]ccounts of past battles seem so often to offer examples of individual heroism and courage and all too seldom report acts of cowardice and fear."

31. Stephen Walker, *Forgotten Soldiers: The Irishmen Shot at Dawn* (Dublin: Gill and Macmillan, 2007), viii.

32. J. Douglas Harvey, "Cowards," http://web.archive.org/web/20120423050939/http://www.shotatdawn.info/page7.html.

33. Dante, *Inferno*, trans. Longfellow, canto 3, lines 49–52.

34. Kierkegaard, "Against Cowardice," 86, 83.

35. "Heilmittel gegen Feigheit" [Cure for Cowardice], in *Deutsche-Wehr; die zeitschrift fur wehrmacht und wehrpolitik Wehr*, November 1942, 20; excerpt translated and with commentary by H. L. Ansbacher, reprinted in *Psychological Abstracts* 17 (1943): 2775.

36. "No Coward's Death Mars U.S. in France," *New York Times*, December 28, 1944, 1.

37. Miller, *Mystery of Courage*, 8.

38. Siegfried Sassoon, *The War Poems of Siegfried Sassoon* (London: Faber and Faber, 1983), 49.

39. Johnson, *Works*, 3:136.

40. J. E. Lendon, *Soldiers and Ghosts: A History of Battle in Classical Antiquity* (New Haven, CT: Yale University Press, 2005), 207. As Elizabeth Samet notes in *Soldier's Heart: Reading Literature through Peace and War at West Point* (New

York: Farrar, Straus and Giroux, 2007), 189, "There are few monuments to the prudent soldier, to the one who decided against making a bold but foolhardy charge."

41. Representative Joseph W. Bailey, *Congressional Record* 31, pt. 3, March 8, 1898, 2616; Kristin Hoganson, *Fighting for American Manhood: How Gender Politics Provoked the Spanish-American and Philippine-American Wars* (New Haven, CT: Yale University Press, 1998), 72.

42. Johnson, *Works*, 3:136.

43. Another example of the way incidents of cowardice give way to stories of courage appears in the novel and many film versions of A.E.W. Mason's *The Four Feathers*. These begin by depicting Harry Feversham suffering disgrace as a coward when he decides not to go to war, but most of his story is taken up with the courageous exploits through which he redeems himself. A.E.W. Mason, *The Four Feathers* (London: Macmillan, 1902).

44. Miller, *Mystery of Courage*, ix.

45. Relatively recent works that explicitly address cowardice include William Moore's *The Thin Yellow Line* (New York: St. Martin's, 1975), which presents a historically informed investigation of soldiers executed for desertion and cowardice by the British military in World War I. Elmar Dinter explores what makes some soldiers perform well and others badly in *Hero or Coward: Pressures Facing the Soldier in Battle* (London: Frank Cass, 1985). Gerald Linderman explores cowardice in the Civil War in *Embattled Courage: The Experience of Combat in the American Civil War* (New York: Macmillan, 1987), as does Lesley J. Gordon in *"I Never Was a Coward": Questions of Bravery in a Civil War Regiment* (Milwaukee: Marquette University Press, 2005). More recently, in *Heroes and Cowards: The Social Face of War* (Princeton, NJ: Princeton University Press, 2009), the economists Dora Costa and Matthew Kahn used the army, pension, and census records of 41,000 Union soldiers to examine, among other matters, how company makeup, particularly diversity or homogeneity in age, ethnicity, race, or occupation, affected the likelihood that soldiers in the Union Army would desert. They found that diversity increased the likelihood of desertion. Charles Glass's *The Deserters: A Hidden History of World War II* (New York: Penguin, 2012) tells the story of three soldiers who deserted, but Glass's project does not focus on cowardice except to show that the deserters were not guilty of it.

46. Anthony Babington, *For the Sake of Example: Capital Courts-Martial, 1914–1920*, rev. ed. (London: Penguin, 2001), xiii–xv.

47. Court-martial cases for the Continental Army in the Revolutionary War are indexed in James C. Neagles, *Summer Soldiers: A Survey and Index of Revolutionary War Courts-Martial* (Salt Lake City, UT: Ancestry Inc., 1986). Indexing of

Union court-martials during the Civil War is described in Thomas P. Lowry, "Research Note: New Access to a Civil War Resource." *Civil War History* 49, no. 1 (2003): 52–63.

48. Dante, *Inferno*, trans. Longfellow, canto 3, lines 44–46.

49. Curiously, *The Red Badge of Courage* never quite mentions the word that most concerns us. "They allus knew he was a—" says a soldier about a shirking officer in another company, and my guess is that "coward" will be the next word out of the soldier's mouth—but he is interrupted and never finishes the sentence. Still, the novel fairly obsesses over what it does not quite name. Stephen Crane, *The Red Badge of Courage: An Episode of the Civil War* (New York: Library of America, 2010), 29.

50. James Jones, interview by Nelson W. Aldrich Jr., in *Writers at Work: The "Paris Review" Interviews*, ed. George Plimpton, 3rd series (New York: Viking, 1967), 247.

51. See Alexis de Tocqueville, *Democracy in America*, trans. Harvey C. Mansfield and Delba Winthrop (Chicago: University of Chicago Press, 2000), 217–20, 617–18. Tocqueville was not the last to make this critique. As Niall Ferguson writes in *Colossus: The Price of American Empire* (New York: Penguin, 2004), 295, "Consuming on credit, reluctant to go to the front line, inclined to lose interest in protracted undertakings: if all this conjures up an image of America as a sedentary Colossus—to put it bluntly, a kind of strategic couch potato—then the image may be worth pondering."

52. Plato, *Laches*, 33. For a discussion about the *Laches* and whether one needs courage to pursue philosophy, see Charles L. Griswold Jr., "Philosophy, Education, and Courage in Plato's Laches," *Interpretation* 14 (1986): 177–93.

53. *The Divine Comedy of Dante Alighieri: Inferno: A Verse Translation*, trans. Allen Mandelbaum (New York: Bantam, 1980), canto 2, lines 45–48.

CHAPTER I
PROFILES IN COWARDICE

1. War was not formally declared until 1756. My account of this conflict draws on Fred Anderson, *Crucible of War: The Seven Years' War and the Fate of the Empire in British North America, 1754–1766* (New York: Vintage, 2000).

2. Warren M. Billings, John E. Selby, and Thad W. Tate, *Colonial Virginia: A History* (White Plains, NY: KTO, 1986), 265. On the difficulties of military recruiting in Virginia between 1754 and 1757, see John Ferling, "Soldiers for Virginia: Who Served in the French and Indian War?" *Virginia Magazine of History and Biography* 94 (1986): 307–28.

3. For more on the relationship of government to society in Virginia at this time, see Rhys Isaac, *The Transformation of Virginia* (Chapel Hill: University of North Carolina Press, 1982). Isaac describes this period as crucial to Virginia's "transformation" from loyal colony to hotbed of revolution and notes "the ill-defined outlines of [the] incomplete institutions" of colonial authority in Virginia (147, 153). Matthew C. Ward, *Breaking the Backcountry: The Seven Years' War in Virginia and Pennsylvania* (Pittsburgh: University of Pittsburgh Press, 2003), covers much of the same territory, emphasizing the conflicts between Virginians and "[t]he breakdown of civil society and civil authority in Virginia and Pennsylvania during the Seven Years' War ..." (90). For a more general account of colonial military affairs, see Alan Rogers, *Empire and Liberty: American Resistance to British Authority* (Berkeley and Los Angeles: University of California Press, 1974), esp. chaps. 3 and 4.

4. George William Pilcher, *Samuel Davies: Apostle of Dissent in Colonial Virginia* (Knoxville: University of Tennessee Press, 1971), 168.

5. Maria L. Ahearn, *The Rhetoric of War: Training Day, the Militia, and the Military Sermon* (New York: Greenwood, 1989). Ahearn notes that Davies's war rhetoric "proffered even more than the usual strident virulence against papists and Indians, quite likely fired by equal parts backwater circumstance and audience, New Light enthusiasm, and English whig animadversions against the French" (106). For a study of Davies's rhetorical techniques, see Barbara A. Larson, "Samuel Davies and the Rhetoric of the New Light," *Speech Monographs* 38, no. 3 (1971): 207–16. Sandra M Gustafson, *Eloquence Is Power: Oratory and Performance in Early America* (Chapel Hill: University of North Carolina Press, 2000), xxi, enumerates the qualities colonials looked for in preachers—authenticity, sincerity, and spiritual strength combined with some physical weakness. Davies had all these attributes.

6. John Holt Rice, "Memoir of the Rev. Samuel Davies," *Virginia Evangelical and Literary Magazines* 1 (1819): 359.

7. Hayes Baker-Crothers, *Virginia and the French and Indian War* (Chicago: University of Chicago Press, 1928), 24–26.

8. On Davies's family background, see Pilcher, *Samuel Davies*, 1–5. On Virginia's population at this time, see Baker-Crothers, *Virginia and the French and Indian War*, 24–26; and David Hackett Fischer and James C. Kelly, *Bound Away: Virginia and the Western Movement* (Charlottesville: University Press of Virginia, 2000).

9. Samuel Davies, A.M., *The Curse of Cowardice: Preached to the Militia of Hanover County, in Virginia, at a General Muster, May 8, 1758 With a View to raise a Company for Captain Samuel Meredith* (Woodbridge, NJ, and Boston: n.p., 1759 [1758]), 7.

10. Holt Rice, "Memoir of the Rev. Samuel Davies," 131.

11. Pilcher, *Samuel Davies*, 167.

12. Anderson, *Crucible of War*, 283, 281.

13. John Shy, *A People Numerous and Armed: Reflections on the Military Struggle for American Independence*, rev. ed. (Ann Arbor: University of Michigan Press, 1990), 129. See also Royster, *Revolutionary People*, 10.

14. Hiller B. Zobel, *The Boston Massacre* (New York: W. W. Norton, 1970), 186, 188.

15. John Ferling, *Almost a Miracle: The American Victory in the War of Independence.* (New York: Oxford University Press, 2007), 194.

16. Bertram Wyatt-Brown, *The Shaping of Southern Culture: Honor, Grace, and War 1760s–1890s* (Chapel Hill, University of North Carolina Press, 2001), 35–36.

17. Thomas J. Fleming, *Now We Are Enemies: The Story of Bunker Hill* (New York: St. Martin's, 1960), 337.

18. George Washington to Richard Henry Lee, August 29, 1775, in *The Papers of George Washington*, http://rotunda.upress.virginia.edu/founders/GEWN -03–01–02–0270.

19. Samuel Swett, *History of Bunker-Hill Battle. With a Plan*, 2d ed. (Boston: Munroe and Frances, 1825), 57–58.

20. Thomas Paine, *Collected Writings* (New York: Library of America, 1995), 91, 96–97.

21. Elizabeth R. Varon, *Disunion! The Coming of the American Civil War, 1789–1859* (Chapel Hill: University of North Carolina Press, 2008), 152.

22. *Morning Courier and New-York Enquirer*, May 27, 1856; John Russell Bartlett, *Dictionary of Americanisms: A glossary of words and phrases usually regarded as peculiar to the United States*, 4th ed. (Boston: Little, Brown, 1877), s.v. "slaveocracy."

23. *Montgomery Advertiser*, June 14, 1856; William W. Freehling, *The Road to Disunion*, vol. 2, *Secessionists Triumphant* (Oxford: Oxford University Press, 2007), 124.

24. Bertram Wyatt-Brown, *Yankee Saints and Southern Sinners* (Baton Rouge: Louisiana State University Press, 1986), 205–7.

25. Henry Jackson to Howell Cobb, December 19, 1860, Cobb Papers, Manuscripts Division, University of Georgia Library; Freehling, *Road to Disunion*, 2:412.

26. Frederick Douglass, "The Union and How to Save It," *Douglass' Monthly*, February 1861, University of Rochester Frederick Douglass Project http:// www.lib.rochester.edu/index.cfm?PAGE=4375.

27. Abraham Lincoln to George D. Prentice, October 29, 1860, in *Collected Works of Abraham Lincoln*, ed. Roy P. Basler (New Brunswick, NJ: Rutgers Uni-

versity Press, 1953), 4:134–35. David M. Potter, *The Impending Crisis, 1848–1861*, completed and ed. Don E. Fehrenbacher (New York: Harper Torchbooks, 1976), 558, notes that at this time Lincoln "seemed almost neurotically sensitive" to the suspicion that he was cowardly, weak, or timid. See also James McPherson, *Battle Cry of Freedom: The Civil War Era* (New York: Oxford University Press, 1988), 231.

28. Bell Irvin Wiley, *The Life of Billy the Yank: The Common Soldier of the Union*, updated ed. (Baton Rouge: Louisiana State University Press, 2008), 73.

29. Gerald Linderman, *Embattled Courage: The Experience of Combat in the American Civil War* (New York: Free Press, 1987), 25.

30. Henry Ward Beecher, quoted in George M. Fredrickson, *The Inner Civil War: Northern Intellectuals and the Crisis of the Union* (Urbana: University of Illinois Press, 1993), 153.

31. Bertram Wyatt-Brown, *Southern Honor: Ethics and Behavior in the Old South* (Oxford: Oxford University Press, 1982), 40.

32. Reid Mitchell, *Civil War Soldiers* (New York: Viking, 1988), 29–30.

33. Nina Silber, *The Romance of Reunion: Northerners and the South, 1865–1900* (Chapel Hill: University of North Carolina Press, 1993), 22; 18.

34. Mitchell, *Civil War Soldiers*, 29–31.

35. Phillips, *Diehard Rebels*, 72–73. A "characteristic jeer" in the South, according to William Freehling, was that "[c]owardly Northerners . . . would never fill more than a thimble with southern blood." Freehling, *The Road to Disunion*, 2:375.

36. These figures are emended slightly from the figures given in Thomas P. Lowry, "Research Note: New Access to a Civil War Resource," *Civil War History* 44, no. 1 (2003): 52–63.

37. David Herbert Donald, *Liberty and Union: The Crisis of Popular Government 1830–1890* (Boston: Little, Brown, 1978), 121, argues that "even while devising novel means for destroying each other, Northerners and Southerners showed themselves to be fundamentally similar, fundamentally part of the same great people." Pete Maslowski, "A Study of Morale in Civil War Soldiers," in *The Civil War Soldier: A Historical Reader*, ed. Michael Barton and Larry M. Logue (New York: New York University Press, 2002), 312–26, makes a similar point.

38. "From Knoxville, Tennessee," *Richmond Daily Dispatch*, June 7, 1861; Diane Miller Sommerville, "'A Burden Too Heavy to Bear': War Trauma, Suicide and Confederate Soldiers," *Civil War History* 59, no. 4 (2013), 488.

39. "Determined Suicide," *Richmond Daily Dispatch*, March 7, 1865; Sommerville, "'A Burden Too Heavy to Bear,'" 464.

40. As Harriet Beecher Stowe, "Introduction," in William C. Nell, *The Colored Patriots of the American Revolution* (New York: Arno, 1968 [1855]), 5,

noted, "The colored race have been generally considered by their enemies, and sometimes even by their friends, as deficient in energy and courage."

41. Joseph T. Glatthaar, *Forged in Battle: The Civil War Alliance of Black Soldiers and White Officers* (New York : Free Press, 1990), 153.

42. Ibid., 154. Court-martial cases for cowardice of black troops include those of private Jackson Henderson (file NN2812) and private John H. Johnson (file MM1833), both of the Twenty-Sixth Colored Regiment; National Archives, Washington DC, Record Group No. 153, Records of the Judge Advocate General's Office (Army). (All Civil War court-martial cases cited in this manuscript are from Record Group No. 153; hereafter, they will be cited by the name of the accused soldier and the file number. Some files contain more than one court-martial.) The belief in the cowardice of blacks and black soldiers persisted after the Civil War. In his account of his adventures in the Spanish-American war in *The Rough Riders: An Autobiography*, ed. Louis Auchincloss (New York: Library of America, 2004 [1899]), 117, Theodore Roosevelt reported an incident in which a mixture of black and white soldiers was facing heavy fire. Among them were "colored infantrymen" who had up to that point behaved well—though "of course," Roosevelt noted, such soldiers are "peculiarly dependent upon their white officers." He continued, "None of the white regulars or Rough Riders showed the slightest sign of weakening; but under the strain the colored infantrymen (who had none of their officers) began to get a little uneasy and to drift to the rear, either helping wounded men, or saying that they wished to find their own regiments."

Roosevelt pulled out his revolver and told the soldiers, "Now, I shall be very sorry to hurt you, and you don't know whether I will keep my word, but my men can tell you that I always do." His men confirmed as much. "This was the end of the trouble, for the 'smoked Yankees' as the Spanish called them." As late as the Korean War, white soldiers often thought of black soldiers as variations of the popular movie character Stepin Fetchit, who shirked duties at every turn. See William T. Bowers, William M. Hammond, and George L. MacGarrigle, *Black Soldier, White Army: The 24th Infantry Regiment in Korea* (Honolulu: University Press of the Pacific, 2005), 104.

Yet the legacy of this racial prejudice has an intriguing twist. The peculiar institution of slavery turned the moral order upside down in more ways than one. Running away, a paradigmatically cowardly act, was for the slave most courageous, as tales of the Underground Railroad show. But it would be difficult for white Southerners to consider it such—and yet neither could they be called cowardice. More plausible to them as an explanation of "this troublesome practice that many negroes have of running away" was the medical idea of "Drapetomania"; see Samuel Cartwright, "Diseases and Peculiarities of the Negro Race," *Debow's Review* 11 (1851): 64–69, 209–13, 331–37.

Perhaps knowing that running was not necessarily cowardly helped African Americans disconnect conventional associations of cowardice in their campaign for civil rights, which in its most prominent form (nonviolent civil disobedience) depended on the idea that *not* fighting was not cowardly.

43. On both sides, eagerness to end the war was sometimes seen as cowardly. A Southern preacher noted in August 1863 that a plea for peace was "the essence of cowardice." J.J.D. Renfroe, *"The Battle Is God's": A Sermon Preached before Wilcox's Brigade* (Richmond, VA: n.p., 1863), Confederate Imprints Microfilm Series 4186; Jason Phillips, *Diehard Rebels: The Confederate Culture of Invincibility* (Athens: University of Georgia Press, 2007), 27–28. In a fall 1864 pamphlet, New Yorker Charles Astor Bristed criticized the "Peace Democrats" who sought an accommodation with the secessionists: "What words can depict … those who … run away from battle when victory is hovering in their grasp?" His answer to this question came in the pamphlet's title: "The Cowards' Convention." *Union Pamphlets of the Civil War, 1861–1865*, ed. Frank Freidel (Cambridge, MA: Harvard University Press, 1967): 2:1140.

44. McPherson, *Battle Cry*, 824.

45. John Wilkes Booth to Mary Ann Holmes Booth, Philadelphia, November 1864 in *"Right or wrong, God Judge Me": The Writings of John Wilkes Booth*, ed. John Rhodehamel and Louise Taper (Urbana: University of Illinois Press, 1997), 130–31.

46. Sarah Grand, "The Man of the Moment," *North American Review* 158 (1894): 626, http://www.jstor.org/stable/25103334.

47. Theodore Roosevelt, *Theodore Roosevelt's History of the United States: His Own Words*, ed. Daniel Ruddy (New York: Smithsonian Institution Press, 2010), 283. Hoganson, *Fighting for American Manhood*, 88–106, explores "McKinley's backbone" at some length.

48. Theodore Roosevelt, *America at War* (New York: Charles Scribner's Sons, 1915), xi, 229.

49. Theodore Roosevelt to Archibald Bulloch Roosevelt, May 19, 1915, in *The Letters of Theodore Roosevelt*, 8, *The Days of Armageddon 1914–1919*, ed. Elting E. Morison (Cambridge, MA: Harvard University Press, 1954), 922.

50. "Two Placards of the Past Week," *Harvard Alumni Bulletin* 19, no. 21 (1917): 409.

51. Tocqueville, *Democracy in America*, 595.

52. Erich Maria Remarque, *All Quiet on the Western Front*, trans. A. W. Wheen (New York: Fawcett Crest, 1928), 15.

53. Ernest Hemingway, *A Farewell to Arms* (New York: Charles Scribner's Sons, 1929), 191, 129.

54. Robert A. Divine, *The Reluctant Belligerent: American Entry into World War II*, 2nd ed. (New York: John Wiley and Sons, 1979), 19.

55. Harry H. Semmes, *Portrait of Patton* (New York: Paperback Library, 1955), 155.

56. "Khaki in White House Better'n Pink," *New York Daily News*, October 10, 1952, 3; K. A. Cuordileone, *Manhood and Political Culture in the Cold War* (New York: Routledge, 2004), 89. Cuordileone, 88, notes that the 1952 presidential election may have seen the starkest "hard/soft dichotomy" in American history, with the Republicans and their allies in the press associating Stevenson's intellectualism with effeminacy and homosexuality.

57. Doris Kearns Goodwin, *Lyndon Johnson and the American Dream* (New York: St. Martin's Griffin, 1991), 253, 252.

58. U.S. Department of State, Office of the Historian, *Foreign Relations of the United States, 1964–1968*, 2, Vietnam, January–June 1965, Document 77, http://history.state.gov/historicaldocuments/frus1964–68v02/d77.

59. Kearns Goodwin, *Lyndon Johnson*, 253. Kearns Goodwin also explores how Johnson decided not to run for reelection in 1968 without condemning himself for cowardice (343–48).

60. United States v. Private First Class (E-3) Melvin Myers, CM 416318, United States Army Board of Review 38 C.M.R. [Court-Martial Reports] 587; 1967 CMR LEXIS 184.

61. Melvin Small, *Antiwarriors: The Vietnam War and the Battle for America's Hearts and Minds* (Lanham, MD: Rowman and Littlefield, 2002), 33.

62. Osama Bin Laden, "Bin Laden Tape: Text," http://news.bbc.co.uk/2/low/middle_east/2751019.stm.

63. "Saddam's Message of Friendship to President Bush," https://www.wikileaks.org/plusd/cables/90BAGHDAD4237_a.html.

64. Peter Beinart, "Time Out," *New Republic*, February 2003, http://www.tnr.com/article/time-out.

65. Elgin Medea Brunner, *Foreign Security Policy, Gender, and US Military Identity* (London: Palgrave Macmillan), 117, discusses the ways leaflets depict American enemies in Iraq and Afghanistan as "evil and brutal cowards." Instances of many military propaganda leaflets are available at http://www.psy-war.org.

66. Brian Blomquist, "Cowardly Lyin' Saddam: Bush Whacks Scaredy Rat for Crawling in Hole," *New York Post*, December 16, 2003, http://nypost.com/2003/12/16/cowardly-lyin-saddam-bush-whacks-scaredy-rat-for-crawling-in-hole/.

67. Gary Kamiya, "Obama's Call to Arms," *Salon*, January 27, 2009, http://www.salon.com/opinion/kamiya/2009/01/27/terror.

68. Samir Khan, "Blended Duality: Muslim and American?" *Inspire* 8 (2011): 3, 9, http://azelin.files.wordpress.com/2012/05/inspire-magazine-8.pdf.

69. The AQ Chef, "Make a Bomb in the Kitchen of Your Mom," *Inspire* 1 (1431 [2010]): 33–40, http://cryptome.org/2012/01/inspire/inspire-1.pdf. Kevin Johnson and Doug Stanglin, "Bomb Suspect Claims He, Brother Acted Alone," *USA Today*, April 23, 2013, http://www.usatoday.com/story/news/nation/2013/04/23/boston-bomber-foreign-motive-dzhokhar-tsarnaev-terrorist-groups/2105705/.

CHAPTER 2
OF ARMS AND MEN

1. Crane, *The Red Badge of Courage*, 47–48.

2. Charles Darwin, *The Descent of Man, and Selection in Relation to Sex* (Princeton, NJ: Princeton University Press, 1982 [1871]), 98.

3. In his 2009 novel *The Great Perhaps* (New York: W. W. Norton), 320, Joe Meno invents a scholarly article that argues that evolution favors cowardly conduct: "the less aggressive of the human species who chose flight over fight are now more likely to reproduce, resulting in . . . 'the heredity of cowardice.' . . . The longer human beings exist, it seems, the less likely we are to choose to be brave." Worry about the heritability of cowardice led one American colonel to propose, in the pages of a military medical journal in 1948, the sterilization of men who had faltered in the face of fear. Colonel Amos R. Koontz, "Psychiatry in the Next War: Shall We Again Waste Manpower?" *Military Surgeon*, 103, no. 3 (1948): 200; Joanna Bourke, *Fear: A Cultural History* (Emeryville, CA: Shoemaker Hoard, 2006), 219.

4. Thomas Gibson, *Sacrifice and Sharing in the Philippine Highlands: Religion and Society among the Buid of Mindoro* (London: Athlone, 1986), 107. See also Thomas Gibson, "Raiding, Trading, and Tribal Autonomy in Insular Southeast Asia," in *The Anthropology of War*, ed. Jonathan Haas (Cambridge: Cambridge University Press, 1990), 124–45.

5. Clayton A. Robarcheck, "Learning to Fear: A Case Study of Emotional Conditioning," *American Ethnologist* 6 (1979): 556, 557.

6. Richard W. Thorington Jr. and Katie E. Ferrell, *Squirrels: The Animal Answer Guide* (Baltimore, MD: Johns Hopkins, 2006), 63–65.

7. Frans de Waal, *Primates and Philosophers: How Morality Evolved* (Princeton, NJ: Princeton University Press, 2006); Richard Joyce, *The Evolution of*

Morality (Cambridge, MA: Bradford Books/MIT Press, 2006); and Lee Alan Dugatkin, *The Altruism Equation: Seven Scientists Search for the Origins of Goodness* (Princeton, NJ: Princeton University Press, 2006).

8. Darwin, *The Descent of Man*, 98.

9. Christopher Boehm, *Moral Origins: The Evolution of Virtue, Altruism, and Shame* (New York: Basic Books, 2012), 199.

10. Nathan Pike and Andrea Manica, "The Basis of Cowardice in Social Defenders," *Ecological Modeling* 196, nos. 3–4 (2006): 272–82.

11. As David Sloan Wilson, *Evolution for Everyone: How Darwin's Theory Can Change the Way We Think about Our Lives* (New York: Delacorte, 2007), 110–11, notes, "There is no single best ... [animal] personality, but rather a diversity of personalities maintained by natural selection." Daniel Smail discusses the way balanced selection heterogenizes individuals within a species in *On Deep History and the Brain* (Berkeley and Los Angeles: University of California Press, 2004), 125.

12. Jonathan Haidt and Craig Joseph, "Intuitive Ethics: How Innately Prepared Intuitions Generate Culturally Variable Virtues," *Daedalus* 133 (2004): 55–66.

13. E. O. Wilson, *The Social Conquest of Earth* (New York: Liveright, 2012), 290.

14. De Waal, *Primates and Philosophers*, 53–54. For a recent review of work on the evolution of morality that explores the importance of intergroup conflict, see Allen Buchanan and Russell Powell, "Beyond the Paleo," *Aeon*, December 12, 2013, http://aeon.co/magazine/living-together/morality-may-have-evolved -but-it-isnt-fixed/. Sarah Blaffer Hrdy's *Mothers and Others: The Evolutionary Origins of Mutual Understanding* (Cambridge, MA: Harvard University Press, 2009) gives an alternative view of the origins of morality. Instead of emphasizing competition and combat, Hrdy argues that morality comes first from the cooperation necessary to raise human children to breeding age. She also maintains that this cooperation—"the ability to participate with others in collaborative activities with shared goals and intentions"—distinguishes human beings from other species (9). Cowardice, in this view, would still be a serious moral failure. Hrdy does allow "(as book after book describing 'human nature and the origins of war' remind us) that 'a high level of fellow feeling makes us better able to unite to destroy outsiders'" (30)—cowardice being a fearful failure to make good on that fellow feeling.

15. George Washington, General Orders, July 7, 1775. *The Papers of George Washington*, digital ed., ed. Theodore J. Crackel (Charlottesville: University of Virginia Press/Rotunda, 2008), http://rotunda.upress.virginia.edu/founders/ GEWN-03-01-02-0040.

16. *Beowulf*, trans. Seamus Heaney (New York: Farrar, Straus and Giroux, 2000), lines 2887–91, 3152–54.

17. Michael B. Oren, "Fleeing Moment: A Cultural History of Desertion," *New Republic*, June 17, 2009, http://www.tnr.com/article/fleeing-moment.

18. Mahatma Gandhi, *The Essential Gandhi: An Anthology*, ed. Louis Fischer (New York: Random House, 1962), 156–57. Gandhi talked repeatedly of the difference between cowardice and nonviolence. See Mahatma Gandhi, *The Mind of Mahatma Gandhi*, ed. R. K. Prabhu and U. R. Rao (Ahmedabad, India: Navajivan, 1967), 119–20, 142–45, 149, 154.

19. Martin Luther King Jr., *A Testament of Hope: The Essential Writings and Speeches of Martin Luther King, Jr.*, ed. James Melvin Washington (San Francisco: HarperSanFrancisco, 1991), 360.

20. Donald Kagan, *On the Origins of War and the Preservation of Peace* (New York: Doubleday, 1995), 8.

21. Here is a short list of writing about honor: *Encyclopedia of the Social Sciences* (New York: Macmillan, 1932), s.v. "honor," by T. V. Smith; *International Encyclopedia of the Social Sciences* (New York: Macmillan, 1968), s.v. "honor," by Julian Pitt-Rivers; Peter L. Berger, "On the Obsolescence of the Concept of Honor," in Peter L. Berger, Brigitte Berger, and Hansfried Kellner, *The Homeless Mind: Modernization and Consciousness* (New York: Vintage, 1973), 83–96; Wyatt-Brown, *The Shaping of Southern Culture*; Wyatt-Brown, *Southern Honor*; James Bowman, *Honor: A History* (New York: Encounter, 2006); Paul Robinson, *Military Honour and the Conduct of War: From Ancient Greece to Iraq* (London: Routledge, 2006); and Kwame Anthony Appiah, *The Honor Code* (New York: W. W. Norton, 2010).

22. Glenn Tucker, *Hancock the Superb* (Indianapolis: Bobbs-Merrill, 1960), 122.

23. Herant A. Katchadourian, *Guilt: The Bite of Conscience* (Stanford, CA: Stanford University Press, 2010), 8, 25.

24. Martha C. Nussbaum, *Hiding from Humanity: Disgust, Shame, and the Law* (Princeton, NJ: Princeton University Press, 2004), 184, 183.

25. Crane, *The Red Badge of Courage*, 68, 87.

26. Erez Yoelia, Moshe Hoffman, David G. Rand, and Martin A Nowak, "Powering Up with Indirect Reciprocity in a Large-Scale Field Experiment," *Proceedings of the National Academy of Science* 110 (2013): 10424, http://www.pnas.org/content/early/2013/06/04/1301210110.

27. Henry Morford, *The Coward: A Novel of Society and the Field in 1863* (Philadelphia: T. B. Peterson, 1864), 171.

28. Alisdair C. McIntyre, *After Virtue: A Study in Moral Theory* (Notre Dame, IN: University of Notre Dame Press, 1981), 123.

29. Morford, *The Coward*, 52.

30. James M. McPherson, *For Cause and Comrades*, 80.

31. Mike Bunn and Clay Williams, *Battle for the Southern Frontier: The Creek War and the War of 1812* (Charleston, SC: History Press, 2008), 163.

32. George Cary Eggleston, *A Rebel's Recollections* (Bloomington: Indiana University Press, 1959 [1875]), 156; Linderman, *Embattled Courage*, 10.

33. Morford, *The Coward*, 99.

34. Wyatt-Brown, *Southern Honor*, xv, 22.

35. James I. Robertson, *Soldiers Blue and Gray* (Columbia: University of South Carolina Press, 1988), 133.

36. [Charles Jean-Jacques Joseph] Ardant du Picq, *Battle Studies: Ancient and Modern Battle*, trans. John N. Greely and Robert C. Cotton (New York: Macmillan, 1921), 116.

37. Tim O'Brien, *The Things They Carried* (New York: Penguin, 1990), 20–21.

38. Eugene B. Sledge, *With the Old Breed, at Peleliu and Okinawa* (Novato, CA: Presidio, 1981), 118.

39. Plutarch, *Plutarch's Moralia*, trans. Frank Cole Babbitt (Cambridge, MA: Harvard University Press, 1931), 3:451–72. In 1938, Virginia Woolf observed in *Three Guineas*, annotated by Jane Marcus (Orlando, FL: Harcourt, 2006), 215, that "a man still feels it a peculiar insult to be taunted with *cowardice* by a woman in much the same way that a woman feels it a peculiar insult to be taunted with *unchastity* by a man."

40. Elizabeth Fries Ellet, *Women of the American Revolution*, 6th ed. (New York: Charles Scribner's Sons, 1856), 3:166.

41. Mason, *The Four Feathers*. For an extended discussion of how *The Four Feathers* explores cowardice and courage in relation to sexuality, imperialism, and masculinity, see Nicoletta F. Gullace, "White Feathers and Wounded Men: Female Patriotism and the Memory of the Great War," *Journal of British Studies* 36 (1997): 178–206, esp. 188–91.

42. William Brooks, interviewed in Terry Cunningham, *14–18: The Final Word from the Trenches of the First World War* (London: Stagedoor, 1993), 43. When a war ends and the need or desire to prevent or punish cowardice diminishes, women may get a disproportionate amount of blame for being so effective in laying the charge of cowardice or inciting their men to guard against it. Feminist historians have noted how hostile the post–World War I British public was toward women for their part in shaming men to take part in a war that they now lamented. In retrospect, the white feathers represented to many an aggressive warmongering. There were plenty of other examples of warmongering—fierce conscription laws, the disenfranchisement of consci-

entious objectors, the execution of deserters and cowards. But these were all perpetrated by men, and so it was not jarring that such practices were decidedly unfeminine; see Gullace, "White Feathers and Wounded Men," 205–6.

43. Morford, *The Coward*, 46–47, 41, 58, 428.

44. [Wheeler Case,] *Poems, occasioned by several circumstances and occurrencies* [sic]*, in the present grand contest of America for liberty* (New Haven, CT: Thomas and Samuel Green, 1778), 6, Early American Imprints, series 1, no. 15754; Charles Royster, *A Revolutionary People at War: The Continental Army and American Character* (Chapel Hill: Institute of Early American History and Culture/University of North Carolina Press, 1979), 30; emphasis in the original.

45. As Leo Braudy, *From Chivalry to Terrorism: War and the Changing Nature of Masculinity* (New York: Alfred A. Knopf, 2003), 33, notes, "In a purely functional way, the animal [that puts its tail between its legs] is protecting its testicles, and by analogy the gesture specifies what unmanly shape the coward has taken on—another Latin word for tail being penis." The analogy would seem to break down when female animals are brought into the picture, for they lack testicles but put their tails between their legs.

46. Sexual potency in a coward evokes an incongruence that can be shameful or comical or both, as in Ken Saro-Wiwa's Biafran war novel, *Sozaboy: A Novel in Rotten English* (London: Longman, 1994), 37–38: "One day, when I meet Agnes for road," says the young narrator, Mene, "I tell her that I want to marry her." Agnes laughs at him and says, "You foolish man. All your friends are making soza [becoming soldiers], you want to stay here and marry with your thing standing like snake wey no get house." Mene had been uncertain about joining the military, but not after this exchange. "I will show that Agnes that I am not a coward man. I can defend her anytime. Oh yes. I will show her proper."

47. Plutarch, *Plutarch's Moralia*, 461.

48. Crane, *The Red Badge of Courage*, 6–7.

49. Morford, *The Coward*, 67–68.

50. Homer, *The Iliad*, 4:462–66.

51. Michel de Montaigne, "Of the Punishment of Cowardice," in *The Complete Essays of Montaigne*, trans. Donald Frame (Stanford, CA: Stanford University Press, 1958), 48–49.

52. Samuel Stouffer et al., *The American Soldier: Combat and Its Aftermath*, Studies in Social Psychology in World War II, vol. 2 (Princeton, NJ: Princeton University Press, 1949), 132–33.

53. Kevin Powers, *Yellow Birds* (New York: Little, Brown, 2012), 145.

54. Kingsley R. Browne, "Women at War: An Evolutionary Perspective." *Buffalo Law Review* 49 (2001), 132. See also Mary B. Harris, "How Provoking! What Makes Men and Women Angry?" *Aggressive Behavior* 19 (1993): 199–211. Harris reports that not one person in a study of college students in Georgia "thought that being called a coward was the 'worst thing' that one could say to a woman; only males, apparently, can be seriously insulted by being called a wimp" (208).

55. Emma Dunham Kelly-Hawkins, *Four Girls at Cottage City* (New York, Oxford: Oxford University Press, 1988 [1895]), 43.

56. Lotte Thomsen, Willem E. Frankenhuis, McCaila Ingold-Smith, and Susan Carey, "Big and Mighty: Preverbal Infants Mentally Represent Social Dominance," *Science* 331, no. 6016 (2011): 477–80.

57. Jeffrey Alan Gray, *The Psychology of Fear and Stress*, 2nd ed. (Cambridge: Cambridge University Press, 1987), 113.

58. In a Civil War novel written by a veteran of that war, a soldier says to a woman, "We are as much afraid as you are, only we are more afraid to show it." The woman responds, "If you were as much afraid as I should be, you wouldn't have to show it; it would show itself in spite of you." John Kirkland, *The Captain of Company K* (Chicago: Dibble, 1891), 42.

59. Court-Martial of Private Edward Hughes, National Archives, Washington DC, Record Group No. 153, file NN 3470.

60. Judith Kay Nelson, *Seeing through Tears: Crying and Attachment* (New York: Routledge, 2005), 138–39. Ashley Montague, "Natural Selection and the Origin and Evolution of Weeping in Man," *Journal of the American Medical Association* 174 (1960), 134, notes that we may see fewer of men's tears because their wider nasal passages channel them inside, away from the face. See also Michael Trimble, *Why Humans Like to Cry: Tragedy, Evolution, and the Brain* (Oxford: Oxford University Press, 2012), 30.

61. Andrew J. Huebner, *The Warrior Image: Soldiers in American Culture from the Second World War to the Vietnam Era* (Chapel Hill: University of North Carolina, 2008), 278–80, explores the acceptance of soldiers crying as a symptom of the "rising prominence of sensitive soldiers" (279) since World War II. Joshua S. Goldstein, *War and Gender: How Gender Shapes the War System and Vice Versa* (Cambridge: Cambridge University Press, 2001), 268, notes that "crying seems to be a central taboo among hardened men."

62. Miller, *Mystery of Courage*, 252. My research indicates that no American woman has ever been charged with cowardly conduct. This has been confirmed by Fred Borch, formerly of the Judge Advocate General's Office

(telephone conversation, August 5, 2008) and in John Kang, "The Burdens of Manliness," *Harvard Journal of Law and Gender*, 33, no. 2 (2010): 495.

63. Donna Hart and Robert W. Sussman, *Man the Hunted: Primates, Predators, and Human Evolution* (New York: Westview, 2005), 247.

64. Hannah J. Bailey, "Gleanings," undated pamphlet, reel 69.2, Hannah Johnston Bailey Collection, Swarthmore College Peace Collection, Swarthmore, Pennsylvania; Hoganson, *Fighting for American Manhood*, 178.

65. More recently, in 2003, Liberian women went on a "sex strike" to help bring an end to the civil war there. The strike leader, Leymah Gbowee, said that it had "little or no practical effect, but it was extremely valuable in getting . . . media attention." L. V. Anderson, "Do Sex Strikes Ever Work? 'Lysistratic nonaction' can be surprisingly effective," *Slate*, August 27, 2012, http://www.slate.com/articles/news_and_politics/explainer/2012/08/sex_strike_in_togo_do_sex_strikes_ever_work_.html.

66. Kayla Williams, *Love My Rifle More Than You: Young and Female in the U.S. Army*. (New York: W. W. Norton, 2005), 62.

67. Sledge, *With the Old Breed*, 56.

68. *New Dictionary of American Slang*, ed. Robert L. Chapman (New York: Harper and Row, 1986), s.vv. "shitless" and "shit one's pants."

69. Aristophanes, *Plays*, vol. 1, *Acharnians, Knights, Peace, Lysistrata*, trans. Kenneth McLeish (London: Methuen Drama, 1993), 183.

70. Thomas P. Lowry, *Tarnished Eagles: The Court-Martial of Fifty Union Colonels and Lieutenant Colonels* (Mechanicsburg, PA: Stackpole, 1997), 138.

71. John Ellis, *The Sharp End of War: The Fighting Man in World War II* (North Pomfret, VT: David and Charles, 1980), 103.

72. Frank MacShane, *Into Eternity: The Life of James Jones, American Writer* (Boston: Houghton Mifflin, 1985), 199.

73. Philip Larkin, *Collected Poems* (New York: Farrar, Straus and Giroux, 1988), 197.

74. Ernst Becker, *The Denial of Death* (New York: Free Press, 1973), 33.

75. Rush W. Dozier Jr., *Fear Itself: The Origin and Nature of the Powerful Emotion That Shapes Our Lives and World* (New York: St. Martin's, 1998), 37.

76. Stouffer et al., *The American Soldier*, 201.

77. Remarque, *All Quiet on the Western Front*, 60.

78. Laura Hillenbrand, *Unbroken: A World War II Story of Survival, Resilience, and Redemption* (New York: Random House, 2010), 82. Barry Broadfoot, *Six War Years 1939–1945: Memories of Canadians at Home and Abroad* (Garden City, N.Y. : Doubleday, 1974), 234, gives another instance of incontinence

being claimed as a badge of honor. Upon hearing his sergeant swear while his unit was being shelled during World War II, a Canadian soldier asked him if he was injured. The sergeant "sort of smiled and said no, he had just pissed his pants. He always pissed them, he said, just when things started and then he was okay. He wasn't making any apologies either, and then I realized something wasn't quite right with me either. . . . I told the sarge, I said, 'Sarge, I've pissed too,' . . . and he grinned and said, 'Welcome to the war.'"

79. Homer, *The Iliad*, 6:572-73.

80. Louis Simpson, "The Heroes," *Collected Poems* (New York: Paragon House, 1988), 54.

81. In a legion judged cowardly under Roman law, those who were injured were exempted from punishment. C. E. Brand, *Roman Military Law* (Austin: University of Texas Press, 1968), 157.

82. This image appears in Mark E. Neely and Harold Holzer, *The Union Image: Popular Prints of the Civil War* (Chapel Hill: University of North Carolina Press, 2000), 102. The man—"Adam Cowherd"—whose finger has just been cut off yells, "Oh Lord! Oh Lord! how it hurts." The other man, who has already had a finger amputated says, "Twont hurt but a minute and then you can get one of these"—a document certifying that he cut off the finger "while digging post holes." For more on self-injury to avoid military service during the Civil War, see Eugene Converse Murdock, *One Million Men: The Civil War Draft in the North* (Madison: State Historical Society of Wisconsin, 1971), 145–46; as Murdock notes, "Self-mutilation achieved only indifferent success in winning exemption. Occasionally the men got off, but as a rule, where the wound was obviously a fresh one, the man was held" (146).

83. Civil War court-martial cases for cowardice involving self-injury include those of privates Wilford Tucker and Lorin F. Johnston of the Thirty-First Regiment Maine Volunteers, found guilty of maiming themselves and cowardice, and sentenced to three years' hard labor. Tucker shot off the middle finger of his left hand, and Johnston his right thumb (both cases File NN2015). See also the cases of private John Barron of the Third Regiment Maryland Infantry (file MM2121) and private Thomas Baker of the Seventeenth Vermont Infantry (file NN2359), who both shot themselves in the foot. Private Robert Risley of the Indiana Seventh Infantry apparently shot himself in the arm and was found guilty of "habitual cowardice and general worthlessness" and sentenced to hard labor with a ball and chain until the end of the war (file LL447).

84. Morford, *The Coward*, 478.

85. John H. Burnham to Sarah B. Burnham, October 4, 1862, John H. Burnham Papers, Connecticut State Library; Lesley J. Gordon, *"I Never Was a*

Coward": Questions of Bravery in a Civil War Regiment (Milwaukee: Marquette University Press, 2005), 17.

86. John Dooley, *John Dooley, Confederate Soldier: His War Journal*, ed. Joseph T. Durkin (Washington, DC: Georgetown University Press, 1945), 46–47; Miller, *The Mystery of Courage*, 99.

87. Tyrtaeus, "To the Soldiers, after a Defeat," in *Greek Lyrics*, trans. Richmond Lattimore (Chicago: University of Chicago Press, 1960), 15.

88. Dave Grossman, *On Killing: The Psychological Cost of Learning to Kill in War and Society*, rev. ed. (New York: Little, Brown, 2009), 127–28.

89. Tyrtaeus, "To the Soldiers," 15.

90. Stephen Crane to John Northern Hilliard [1897?], in *The Correspondence of Stephen Crane*, ed. Stanley Wertheim and Paul Sorrentino (New York: Columbia University Press, 1988), 1:322.

91. Crane, *The Red Badge of Courage*, 55.

92. James Jones, "A Book Report on *The Red Badge of Courage*," in *The James Jones Reader: Outstanding Selections from His War Writings*, ed. James R. Giles and J. Michael Lennon (Secaucus, NJ: Carol, 1991), 387–93.

93. James Jones, *The Thin Red Line* (New York: Delta, 1998 [1962]), 48. Jones himself had been "wounded in the head by a random mortar shell," as he put it, at Guadalcanal; he had a bad ankle too, and he was often ill with tropical diseases. When he was sent back to the States on a hospital ship, he observed the injured and their terrible injuries very closely and saw little that struck him as heroic. MacShane, *Into Eternity*, 54, 60.

94. Jones interview in *Writers at Work*, 246–47.

95. Miller, *The Mystery of Courage*, 191, notes, "We hold some deeply primitive belief that the paradigmatic test of courage" takes place not simply in war, but in "hand-to-hand fighting, a pitting of the unmediated strength of one human being against another. . . ."

96. Jones, *The Thin Red Line*, 172–73, 175. William Manchester, *Goodbye, Darkness: A Memoir of the Pacific War* (New York: Viking, 1979), 7, recalls an incident strikingly similar to the one Jones depicts here. After killing a man at close quarters, Manchester writes, "I began to tremble, and next to shake, all over. I sobbed, in a voice still grainy with fear: 'I'm Sorry.' Then I threw up all over myself." Then he urinated on himself. "I knew I had become a thing of tears and twitchings and dirtied pants. I remember wondering dumbly, *Is this what they mean by 'conspicuous gallantry'?*"

97. Jones, *The Thin Red Line*, 510. In a 1975 book of history and memoir, *WWII: A Chronicle of Soldiering* (New York: Grosset and Dunlap, 1975), 16, Jones lamented that the lessons of war that pain teaches are quickly forgotten: "Thus

we old men can in all good conscience sit over our beers at the American Legion on Friday nights and recall with affection moments of terror thirty years before. Thus we are able to tell the youngsters that it wasn't all really so bad."

98. Joshua Goldstein, *Winning the War on War: The Decline of Armed Conflict Worldwide* (New York: Dutton, 2011); Steven Pinker, *The Better Angels of Our Nature: Why Violence Has Declined* (New York: Viking, 2011); John Horgan, *The End of War* (San Francisco: McSweeney's, 2012).

99. Crane, *The Red Badge of Courage*, 5, 16, 26, 134.

100. Stephen Crane, "The Veteran," in *Tales of War*, ed. Fredson Bowers (Charlottesville: University Press of Virginia, 1970), 82–83, 86.

CHAPTER 3

THE WAYS OF EXCESSIVE FEAR

1. Raymond J. Herek, *These Men Have Seen Hard Service: The First Michigan Sharpshooters in the Civil War* (Detroit: Wayne State University Press, 1998), 173, 193.

2. Court-Martial of Lieutenant Moses Powell, Record Group No. 153, file NN 2032.

3. Miller, *The Mystery of Courage*, 130, notes that until 1800 or so there was "a near universal taboo" against documenting one's own fear, except in stories where one conquered that fear.

4. Linderman, *Embattled Courage*, 18.

5. Gray, *The Psychology of Fear and Stress*, 56.

6. Dozier, *Fear Itself*, 4–6, 44–45.

7. Joshua M. Susskind, Daniel H. Lee, Andrée Cusi, Roman Feiman, Wojtek Grabski, and Adam K. Anderson, "Expressing Fear Enhances Sensory Acquisition," *Nature Neuroscience* 11 (2008): 847.

8. U.S. War Department, *Army Life*, Pamphlet 21–13 (Washington, DC: Government Printing Office, 1944), 159.

9. Stouffer et al., *The American Soldier*, 196.

10. U.S. War Department, *Army Life*, 8.

11. Martin van Creveld, *The Culture of War* (New York: Ballantine, 2008), 163.

12. Charles Moran, *The Anatomy of Courage*, 2nd ed. (London: Constable, 1966), 30.

13. John Keegan, *The Face of Battle* (New York: Viking, 1976), 307–12.

14. For discussion of advances in military technology after World War I, see Williamson Murray and Allan R. Millett, eds., *Military Innovations in the Interwar Period* (Cambridge: Cambridge University Press, 1996).

15. Keegan, *The Face of Battle*, 313, 323. Keegan also notes that weapons since World War II have become even nastier, that "rounds fired by anti-tank guns are designed to fill the interior of armored vehicles with showers of metal splinters or streams of molten metal, so disabling the tank and killing its crew" (323). For more on the development of "more ruthless" military practices, see Stanton A. Coblentz, *From Arrow to Atom Bomb: The Psychological History of War* (New York: Beechhurst, 1953), 431.

16. *Oxford English Dictionary*, s.v. "overkill."

17. Meirion and Susie Harries, *Soldiers of the Sun: The Rise and Fall of the Japanese Imperial Army* (New York: Random House, 1991), 325; for more on the Japanese fighting spirit, see esp. 317–25.

18. Harries and Harries, *Soldiers of the Sun*, 461, vii.

19. Russell Braddon, *Japan against the World 1941–2041: The 100-Year War for Supremacy* (New York: Stein and Day, 1983), 128.

20. Linderman, *Embattled Courage*, 166.

21. Stouffer et al., *The American Soldier*, 197.

22. Bourke, *Fear: A Cultural History*, 214–15.

23. Costa and Kahn, *Heroes and Cowards*, 107.

24. For a careful review of the current knowledge about mirror neurons, see J. M. Kilner and R. N. Lemon, "What We Know Currently about Mirror Neurons," *Current Biology* 23, no. 23 (2013): R1057–62.

25. Court-Martial of Lieutenant John King, Record Group No. 153, file LL294. In a 1944 survey about "extreme fear breakdown," 49 percent of almost two thousand American combat veterans in Italy agreed with the statement that "seeing a man's nerves 'crack up' made me nervous, jittery, or feel like cracking up myself." Stouffer et al., *The American Soldier*, 209.

26. In an exploration of running and cowardice that informs my discussion, Miller, *The Mystery of Courage*, 94, deemed running to be cowardice in its "purest form." Running is not always cowardly, of course—not even running in fear. Samuel Davies, *The Curse of Cowardice*, 13, tells his audience of Virginia militiamen in 1758 that they should not fear battle but rather "Jehovah's curse." From that, the men are well advised to run: "fly from it by venturing your lives for your country." Davies may be echoing the beginning of John Bunyan, *The Pilgrim's Progress* (Boston: Houghton Mifflin, 1969), 94: Christian is stuck in the City of Destruction until The Evangelist tells him, "Fly from the wrath to come." Only then does he begin his pilgrimage, fear of his fellow mortals leading him astray and fear of God driving him on. On Bunyan's "complex" view of fear, see David Mills, "The Dreams of Bunyan and Langland," in *The Pilgrim's Progress: Critical and Historical Views*, ed. Vincent Newey (Totowa, NJ: Barnes and Noble, 1980): 154–81, esp. 167–70.

Courage is fear running in the right direction—a formulation that strikes me as proverbial, as something I've heard before, but the closest expression of it I could find comes in Patrick White, *The Twyborn Affair: A Novel* (New York: Viking, 1980), 138: "Courage is often despair running in the right direction."

27. Crane, *The Red Badge of Courage*, 9, 41, 42.

28. Paul E. Griffiths, *What Emotions Really Are: The Problem of Psychological Categories* (Chicago: University of Chicago Press, 1997), 81.

29. Ambrose Bierce, *The Unabridged Devil's Dictionary*, ed. David E. Schultz and S.T. Joshi (Athens: University of Georgia Press, 2000), 44.

30. Brand, *Roman Military Law*, 159. See also Victor Davis Hanson, *The Western Way of War: Infantry Battle in Classical Greece*, 2nd ed. (Berkeley and Los Angeles: University of California Press, 1989); and Miller, *The Mystery of Courage*, 98.

31. Crane, *The Red Badge of Courage*, 87.

32. Plato, *Plato's Symposium*, trans. Seth Benardete (Chicago: University of Chicago Press, 2001), 221b. See also Miller, *The Mystery of Courage*, 104.

33. David A. Clary, *George Washington's First War: His Early Military Adventures* (New York: Simon and Schuster, 2011), 164.

34. Crane, *The Red Badge of Courage*, 104.

35. Randall Collins, *Violence: A Micro-sociological Theory* (Princeton, NJ: Princeton University Press, 2008), 83–133.

36. Louis-Ferdinand Céline, *Journey to the End of the Night*, trans. Ralph Manheim (New York: New Directions, 1983 [1928]), 9 (emphasis added), 28.

37. Jones, *The Thin Red Line*, 70.

38. Ibid, 305–6.

39. Lawrence Rothfield, *Vital Signs: Medical Realism in Nineteenth-Century Fiction* (Princeton, NJ: Princeton University Press, 1992).

40. Jones, *The Thin Red Line*, 306.

41. Amy F. T. Arnsten, "Stress Signalling Pathways That Impair Prefrontal Cortex Structure and Function," *Nature Reviews Neuroscience* 10 (2009): 410–22.

42. Crane, *The Red Badge of Courage*, 42.

43. Richard Gabriel and Karen S. Metz, *A Short History of War: The Evolution of Warfare and Weapons* (Carlisle Barracks, PA: Strategic Studies Institute, U.S. Army War College, 1992), 83–85.

44. Coblentz, *From Arrow to Atom Bomb*, 434. See also Alfred W. Crosby, *Throwing Fire: Projectile Technology throughout History* (Cambridge: Cambridge University Press, 2002).

45. James Jones, *World War II: A Chronicle of Soldiering* (New York: Grosset and Dunlap, 1975), 31.

46. Allan R. Millett and Peter Maslowski, *For the Common Defense: A Military History of the United States of America*, 2d ed. (New York: Free Press, 1994), 70. The Continental Army's use of guerrilla tactics became a part of the lore of the Revolutionary War. How accurately this lore reflects the actual tactics of the Revolutionary War has been the subject of some debate. George Washington was called an American Fabius, after the Roman general who refused to engage Hannibal directly, but Ferling, *Almost a Miracle*, 137, 564, writes that "the rebels' fabled Fabian warfare has become the stuff of legend" and "the Americans actually remained amazingly—perhaps injudiciously—faithful to the European manners of war."

47. James Fenimore Cooper, *The Spy: A Tale of the Neutral Ground* (New York: Heritage, 1963), 29.

48. Royster, *A Revolutionary People*, 12.

49. Cooper, *The Spy*, 29.

50. Dave McTiernan, "The Novel as 'Neutral Ground': Genre and Ideology in Cooper's *The Spy*." *Studies in American Fiction* 25, no. 1 (1997): 8. As Bruce A. Rosenberg, "James Fenimore Cooper's *The Spy* and the Neutral Ground," *American Transcendental Quarterly*, n.s., 6, no. 1 (1992): 11, notes, "Spying was a dirty business for Cooper's audience, even though a number of them had spied during the Revolution."

51. Keegan, *The Face of Battle*, 179.

52. Earl J. Hess, *The Union Soldier in Battle: Enduring the Ordeal of Combat* (Lawrence: University Press of Kansas, 1997), 82. Frances Clarke, *War Stories: Suffering and Sacrifice in the Civil War North* (Chicago: University of Chicago Press, 2011), 201, observes something similar: "Soldiers may have come to accept that adopting defensive cover was no cause for shame, but," she adds, "the officer who 'coolly' exposed himself to enemy fire remained the beau ideal of heroism, as popular in the war's last year as in its first."

53. Lowry, *Tarnished Eagles*, 186–88; Court-martial of colonel David H. Williams, Record Group No. 153, file KK81.

54. In the case of colonel David H. Williams, the court saw fit to chastise the men who had taunted him as a coward for their "mutinous spirit and want of harmony"; Lowry, *Tarnished Eagles*, 187. That a charge as serious as cowardice should come, even informally, from enlisted men seemed to outweigh the actual evidence of cowardly conduct on the part of the officer. Rank in this case had its privileges.

55. Court-Martial of Lieutenant Ferdinand Ornesi, Record Group No. 153, file KK5.

56. Mark E. Neely Jr. and Harold Holzer, *The Union Image: Popular Prints of the Civil War North* (Chapel Hill: University of North Carolina Press, 2000), 150; see also Linderman, *Embattled Courage*, 134–55.

57. Crane, *The Red Badge of Courage*, 39, 186.

58. Guy Hartcup, *Camouflage: A History of Concealment and Deception in War* (New York: Charles Scribner's Sons, 1980), 11–12.

59. Hartcup, *Camouflage*, 7, 11.

60. Marius Broekmeyer, *Stalin, the Russians, and Their War*, trans. Rosalind Buck (Madison: University of Wisconsin Press, 2004), 219.

61. Carlo D'Este, *Patton: A Genius for War* (New York: HarperCollins, 1995), 257, 506.

62. Jones, *The Thin Red Line*, 145, 100.

63. Alexander Cavalié Mercer, *Journal of the Waterloo Campaign* (London: Greenhill, 1985 [1870]), 165; Keegan, *The Face of Battle*, 180.

64. Van Creveld, *The Culture of War*, 21. Recent studies of the display of pride and shame offer further insight into why cowering can seem cowardly. While the proud human or animal (studies have been done on chimpanzees, crayfish, salamanders, and elephants, among others) expands itself to assert dominance and attract attention, shame is expressed "through slumped shoulders and narrowed chest," cringing, and lowered posture. Zoologists speculate that such behavior is meant to indicate the shamed creature's submission to the order of the group. One study suggests that "these expressions . . . may be biologically innate behavioral responses to success and failure." Jessica L. Tracy and David Matsumoto, "The Spontaneous Expression of Pride and Shame: Evidence for Biologically Innate Nonverbal Displays," *Proceedings of the National Academy of Science* 105, no. 33 (2008): 11655.

65. Donald Kagan, *On the Origins of War and the Preservation of Peace* (New York: Doubleday, 1995), 514.

66. Christopher H. Hamner, *Enduring Battle: American Soldiers in Three Wars, 1776–1945* (Lawrence: University Press of Kansas, 2011), 98, 122, 142, 205.

67. Christopher Coker, "The Unhappy Warrior," *Historically Speaking* 7, no. 4 (2006): 35.

68. See P. W. Singer, *Wired for War: the Robotics Revolution and Conflict in the Twenty-First Century* (New York: Penguin, 2009); see also Elliot Abrams and Andrew J. Bacevich, "A Symposium on Citizenship and Military Service," *Parameters* 31, no. 2 (2001): 18.

69. As Coker, "The Unhappy Warrior," 40, notes, "By 2035, the Pentagon tells us, the U.S. will be fielding robots that look, think, and fight like today's soldiers."

70. Singer, *Wired for War*, 367.

71. The question of drone strikes and cowardice is a vexed one. The strikes are often perceived as cowardly, but then, historically, advances in weaponry

or tactics often are. Sixteenth-century French observer Blaise de Monluc, in *The Habsburg-Valois Wars and the French Wars of Religion*, trans. Charles Cotton [1674], ed. Ian Roy (London: Longman, 1971 [1592]), 41, lamented the invention of the arquebus, a predecessor to the musket, for "so many valiant men [have] been slain for the most part by the most pitiful fellows and the greatest cowards; poltroons that had not dared to look those men in the face at close hand, which at a distance they laid dead with their confounded bullets." Drones, one might say, are simply extraordinarily confounded bullets. But differences in degree eventually become differences in kind, and surely the latest weapon in development—"autonomous drones" that can "hunt, identify and kill the enemy based on calculations made by software, not decisions made by humans"—is a different kind of weapon; Peter Finn, "A Future for Drones: Automated Killing," *Washington Post*, September 19, 2011, http://articles.wash ingtonpost.com/2011–09–19/national/35273383_1_drones-human-target -military-base. Perhaps it is more accurate to say that drones take cowardice out of the combat equation, for they take fear out of the equation and lead to a recklessness born of technology that can make us more aggressive than is prudent. But to say the drone operators feel no fear does not mean they avoid experiencing trauma. See Elisabeth Bumiller, "Air Force Drone Operators Report High Levels of Stress," *New York Times*, December 18, 2011, http:// www.nytimes.com/2011/12/19/world/asia/air-force-drone-operators-show -high-levels-of-stress.html.

72. Susan B. Carter, Scott Sigmund Gartner, Michael R. Haines, Alan L. Olmstead, Richard Sutch, and Gavin Wright, eds., *Historical Statistics of the United States: Earliest Times to the Present*, millennial ed. (New York: Cambridge University Press, 2006),1:440–41. Figure for 2008 drawn from U.S. Census table 104, "Expectation of Life at Birth, 1970 to 2008, and Projections, 2010 to 2020," http://www.census.gov/compendia/statab/2012/tables/12s0104.pdf.

73. William James, *Principles of Psychology* (New York: Henry Holt, 1890), 2:415.

74. Herek, *These Men Have Seen Hard Service*, 197. Court-Martial of Lieutenant Hooker DeLand, Record Group No. 153, file NN2032.

75. Miller, *The Mystery of Courage*, 95.

76. Private Slovik's statement reads:

I Pvt Eddie D. Slovik #36896415 confess to the Desertion of the United States Army. At the time of my desertion we were in Albuff in France. I come to Albuff as a replacement. They were shilling the town and we were told to dig in for the night. The flowing morning they were shilling us again. I was so scared nerves and trembling that at the time the other replacements moved out I couldn't move. I stayed their in my fox hole till it was quite and I was able to move. I then walked in town. Not seeing any of our troops so I stayed over night at a French hospital. The next morning I turned myself over to the Canadian Provost Corp. After being with them six weeks I was turned over to American M.P. They turned me lose. I told my commanding officer my story. I said that if I had to go out their again Id run away. He said there was nothing he could do for me so I ran away again AND ILL RUN AWAY AGAIN IF I HAVE TO GO OUT Their.

Signed Pvt. Eddie D. Slovik

A.S.N. 3689641

77. William Bradford Huie, *The Execution of Private Slovik* (New York: Duell, Sloan and Pierce, 1954), 142, 129–30, 19.

78. Davies, *The Curse of Cowardice*, 5–6.

79. As an example of *security* being used to mean "culpable absence of anxiety, carelessness," the *Oxford English Dictionary* cites a spell being cast on Shakespeare's Macbeth:

> He shall spurn fate, scorn death, and bear
> He hopes 'bove wisdom, grace and fear:
> And you all know, security
> Is mortals' chiefest enemy. (*Macbeth*, act 3, scene 5, verse 32)

Macbeth has already decided that he is too deep in blood to turn back, but fear's instruction might have slowed him, might even have pointed a way to some redemption. He might at least have elected not to have Macduff's wife and children murdered, for instance, and this might have spared him Macduff's vengeance. But Macbeth is above fear; the spell of security stupefies him and slicks the path to his final doom.

80. Benjamin Franklin, *Selections from Poor Richard's Almanack* (New York: Century, 1898), 128. This was a reformulation of a 1748 entry—"He that's secure is not safe"—which, as with many of Franklin's sayings, was itself a reformulation of folk wisdom. See Robert Howard Newcomb, "The Sources of Benjamin Franklin's Sayings of Poor Richard," (PhD diss., University of Maryland, 1957).

81. Davies, *The Curse of Cowardice*, 7, 6.

82. Billings, Selby, and Tate, *Colonial Virginia*, 202. These authors also speak of the relative ease and peace of the "generation born after 1720" (275). Ward, *Breaking the Backcountry*, 92, notes that "there had been little warfare in the region" since 1677. Richard H. Steckel suggests that in the late colonial period

men in America grew significantly taller than men raised in Britain, probably as a result of better health and nutrition, and that wealth was distributed more equally in America than in Europe. Richard H. Steckel, "Stature and the Standard of Living," *Journal of Economic Literature* 33 (1995): 1903–40; on height, 1919–21; on economic equality, 1925–26.

83. William Shakespeare, *Cymbeline*, act 3, scene 6, verse 21; the line continues, "hardness ever of hardiness is mother."

84. Theodore Roosevelt, "The Strenuous Life," in *The Strenuous Life: Essays and Addresses* (New York: Century, 1904), 1, 2.

85. "President Says 'It is a Moment of Truth' for UN," press release, February 9, 2003, http://georgewbush-whitehouse.archives.gov/news/releases/2003/02/20030209–1.html.

86. "President Discusses the Future of Iraq," press release, February 26, 2003, http://georgewbush-whitehouse.archives.gov/news/releases/2003/02/2003 0226–11.html.

87. Davies, *The Curse of Cowardice*, 5–6.

88. Andrew J. Bacevich, "The Cult of National Security," *Commonweal*, January 27, 2006, 7–8.

89. Zygmunt Bauman, *Liquid Fear* (Cambridge: Polity, 2006), 4.

90. See Richard Hofstadter, "The Paranoid Style in American Politics," in *The Paranoid Style in American Politics and Other Essays* (Cambridge: Harvard University Press, 1963), 3–40. For a more recent exploration of the theme of American paranoia, see Michael Barkun, *A Culture of Conspiracy: Apocalyptic Visions in Contemporary America* (Berkeley and Los Angeles: University of California Press, 2003).

CHAPTER 4

DUTY-BOUND

1. Davies, *The Curse of Cowardice*, 4.

2. *Encyclopedia Britannica*, 11th ed., s.v. "duty."

3. Winthrop, *Military Law and Precedents* (New York: Arno, 1979[1920]), 623.

4. Aristotle, *Nicomachean Ethics*, 1116b.

5. For more on phalanx formation and tactics, see John Lazenby, "The Killing Zone," in *Hoplites: The Classical Greek Battle Experience*, ed. Victor Davis Hanson (London: Routledge, 1991), 87–109.

6. The phalanx discussion draws from Hanson, *The Western Way of War*, 97–101, 104.

7. Tyrtaeus, quoted in Hanson, *The Western Way of War*, 119.

8. Homer, *The Iliad*, 4:321; Lendon, *Soldiers and Ghosts*, 29. See also Hanson, *The Western Way of War*, 104.

9. Crane, *The Red Badge of Courage*, 34.

10. Jones, *The Thin Red Line*, 403. The 1998 movie version of *The Thin Red Line*, directed by Terence Malick, gestures to *The Red Badge of Courage* when a soldier says, "You're in a box . . . a moving box!"

11. Joseph Gould, *The Story of the Forty-Eighth* (Philadelphia: Regimental Association, 1908), 177–78.

12. Plato, *Laws*, 12.944e; Miller, *Mystery of Courage*, 16.

13. "Heilmittel gegen Feigheit," 2775.

14. Polybius, *The Histories of Polybius*, trans. Evelyn S. Shuckburgh (Bloomington: Indiana University Press, 1962), 1:490.

15. Antony Beevor, *Stalingrad* (New York: Penguin, 1999), 117.

16. Dudley Pope, *At Twelve Mr. Byng Was Shot* (Philadelphia: J. B. Lippincott, 1962), 287. The text of the 1749 Articles of War appears in Markus Eder, *Crime and Punishment in the Royal Navy of the Seven Years' War* (Aldershot, England: Ashgate, 2004), 158–73 (quotation on 161).

17. Pope, *At Twelve*, 188.

18. *Bungiana, or an assemblage of what-d'ye-call-em's, . . . relative to the conduct of a Certain naval commander, now first collected; in order to perpetuate the MEMORY of his Wonderful Atchievements* [sic] (London: J. Doughty, 1756), 24.

19. "A Rueful Story, Admiral B——g's Glory, or Who Run Away First," in *Naval Songs and Ballads*, ed. C. H. Firth (London: Naval Records Society, 1908), 210.

20. John Byng, *The trial of the Honourable Admiral John Byng: at a court-martial . . . To which is added, an account of Admiral Byng's behaviour in his last moments . . .* (New York: J. Parker and W. Weyman, 1757), 27.

21. On King George's belief that Byng was a coward, see Pope, *At Twelve*, 303. For evidence of the enduring belief that, despite the actual verdict, Byng was executed for cowardice, see Winston Churchill, *A History of the English-Speaking Peoples: The Age of Revolution* (New York: Dodd, Mead, 1958), 3:138, which notes, "By one of the most scandalous evasions of responsibility that an English Government has ever perpetrated Byng was shot for cowardice. . . ." A recent attempt to persuade parliament to grant Byng a posthumous pardon failed; Stephen Bates and Richard Norton-Taylor, "No Pardon for Admiral Byng," *Guardian*, March 15, 2007, http://www.guardian.co.uk/uk/2007/mar/15/military.immigrationpolicy. The *Dictionary of National Biography*, s.v. "John Byng," by Daniel A. Baugh, has an excellent overview of the controversy.

22. Brian Tunstall, *Admiral Byng and the Battle for Minorca* (London: Philip Allan, 1928), 280, 283.

23. Pope, *At Twelve*, 287.

24. Sylvia M. Frey, "Courts and Cats: British Military Justice in the Eighteenth Century," *Military Affairs* 43 (1979): 8.

25. Arthur N. Gilbert, "British Military Justice during the American Revolution," *Eighteenth Century: Theory and Interpretation* 20, no. 1 (1979): 24–38. See also Arthur N. Gilbert, "The Changing Face of British Military Justice, 1757–1783," *Military Affairs* 49, no. 2 (1985): 80–84.

26. Moore, *The Thin Yellow Line*, 30.

27. Robert Southey, *Life of Nelson* (New York: Thomas Y. Crowell, 1901), 327, 337.

28. Voltaire, *Candide*, trans. Daniel Gordon (Boston: Bedford/St. Martin's, 1999), 99.

29. Walter Millis, *Arms and Men: A Study in Military History* (New York: G. P. Putnam's Sons, 1956), 21; Stephen Brumwell, *Redcoats: The British Soldier and War in the Americas: 1755–1763* (New York: Cambridge University Press, 2002), 100. Brumwell also notes that harsh discipline was not the only motivator of regulars' conduct, and that British soldiers were "quick to protest when they considered that their traditional 'rights'" or when the terms of their enlistment "had been flouted" (127–28).

30. Millis, *Arms and Men*, 21.

31. Davies, *The Curse of Cowardice*, 22.

32. Brumwell, *Redcoats*, 63.

33. James Titus, *The Old Dominion at War: Society, Politics and Warfare in Late Colonial Virginia* (Columbia: University of South Carolina Press, 1991), 145. In Europe, where firearms were more expensive and not as necessary to contend with native peoples or hunt wild game, the general population was not so well armed. "The colonists in America," writes Charles Winthrop Sawyer, in *Firearms in American History*, vol. 1, The Colonial Period (Boston: Author, c. 1910–20), 1, "were the greatest weapon-using people of that epoch in the world." The extent of gun ownership in colonial America has been a matter of some scholarly controversy, but it appears to have exceeded that of Great Britain.

34. John Richard Alden, *Robert Dinwiddie: Servant of the Crown* (Williamsburg, Virginia: Colonial Williamsburg Foundation, 1973), 64.

35. Titus, *The Old Dominion at War*, 64. Dinwiddie was far from alone in his attitude toward the colonists. Albert H. Tillson Jr. describes the antagonism that "common folk," accustomed to a localized and relatively unhierarchical political style, felt toward the attempts of the gentry to lord over militia

members; see Albert H. Tillson Jr., "The Militia and Popular Political Culture in the Upper Valley of Virginia," *Virginia Magazine of History and Biography* 94, no. 3 (1986): 285–306. See also Douglas Edward Leach, *Roots of Conflict: British Armed Forces and Colonial Americans, 1677–1763* (Chapel Hill: University of North Carolina Press, 1986), 86–97.

36. *A Dictionary of Philosophy*, 2nd ed. (Routledge: New York, 1986), s.v. "Duty," by A. R. Lacey, 166–67.

37. For a broad consideration of the militia in the context of colonial society, see Millett and Maslowski, *For the Common Defense*, 1–14. Lawrence Delbert Cress examines the militia in prerevolutionary America in *Citizens in Arms: The Army and the Militia in American Society to the War of 1812* (Chapel Hill: University of North Carolina Press, 1982), 3–50. For a more general account of colonial military affairs, see Alan Rogers, *Empire and Liberty: American Resistance to British Authority* (Berkeley and Los Angeles: University of California Press, 1974); and John Ferling, *A Wilderness of Miseries: War and Warriors in Early America* (Westport, CT: Greenwood, 1980).

38. James Wolfe to Lord George Sackville, August 7, 1758, in *Life and Letters of James Wolfe*, ed. Beckles Wilson (London: W. Heinemann, 1909), 392; Leach, *Roots of Conflict*, 131.

39. John Forbes to William Pitt, May 1, 1758, in *Writings of General John Forbes Relating to His Service in North America*, ed. Alfred Procter James (Menasha, Wisconsin: Collegiate, 1938), 77.

40. The men's souls and Davies's own pastoral work were at stake in Davies's recruiting efforts, too. Free will, to Davies—a champion of Presbyterian dissent and an important figure in the Great Awakening—was central not only to his religious and moral beliefs but also to his case for religious toleration. Davies's successful recruiting would also confirm in a dramatic way his loyalty to the Crown and help him achieve his main goal of working through official government channels to extend religious toleration to the colonies. For biographical material on Davies, see Holt Rice, "Memoir," *The Virginia Evangelical and Literary Magazines* 1 (1819): 112–19, 186–88, 201–17, 329–35, 353–63, 474–79, 560–67; Richard M. Gummere, "Samuel Davies: A Voice for Religious Freedom," in *Seven Wise Men of Colonial America* (Cambridge, MA, 1967), 41–49; Pilcher, *Samuel Davies*; and Rhys Isaac, "Religion and Authority," *William and Mary Quarterly*, 3rd ser., 30, no. 1 (1973): 3–36.

41. Davies, *The Curse of Cowardice*, 3.

42. Ibid., 4.

43. To be sure, the existence of contracts does not guarantee an emphasis on voluntarism; the British regulars had contracts, too. They had often been

pressed into service, however, or joined out of economic desperation, and they enlisted for life, or for at least three years or the duration of the war. See Brumwell, *Redcoats*, 59. Compared to the regulars, the colonists Davies was trying to recruit were on the whole at greater liberty to accept or reject the terms of enlistment.

44. Davies, *The Curse of Cowardice*, 8–9.

45. Ibid, 11.

46. Tocqueville, *Democracy in America*, 501. Walter A. McDougall, *Freedom Just Around the Corner: A New American History, 1585–1828* (New York: Harper Collins, 2004), 5, argues that the feature that most distinguishes American history is the freedom Americans have had to "hustle." Ambrose Bierce, *The Unabridged Devil's Dictionary* (Athens: University of Georgia Press, 2000 [1911]), 25, caricatures the self-concerned American sense of duty as a mask for selfish materialism: "Duty, n. That which sternly impels us in the direction of profit, along the line of desire."

47. Linderman, *Embattled Courage*, 10–11, discusses the questions of obligation and freedom that Civil War soldiers brought to their sense of duty.

48. Davies, *The Curse of Cowardice*, 17.

49. Had Davies lived longer, he probably would have taken the side of fellow Virginians such as Patrick Henry and Thomas Jefferson when the American Revolution came, and he certainly influenced the revolution-minded. Indeed, Henry may have been in the audience when Davies delivered *The Curse of Cowardice*, for he lived right next to the Hanover muster grounds at the time, and was brother-in-law to captain Samuel Meredith, for whom Davies's sermon aimed to "raise a company." See Henry Mayer, *A Son of Thunder: Patrick Henry and the American Revolution* (New York: Grove, 1986), 36–37, 42, 47–48, 267; see also Pilcher, *Samuel Davies*, 83–85, 120. For more on Davies's influence on the American Revolution see Cedric B. Cowing, T*he Great Awakening and the American Revolution: Colonial Thought in the 18th Century* (Chicago: Rand McNally, 1971), esp. 204–5.

50. Paine, *Paine: Political Writings*, 52. As Wyatt-Brown, *The Shaping of Southern Culture*, 35, points out, "Tract writers sought to animate manly instincts by portrayals of Tory or neutral citizens as gutless cowards."

51. Baron Von Steuben to Baron von der Golts, n.d., in John M. Palmer, *Baron von Steuben* (New Haven, CT: Yale University Press, 1937), 157; George F. Scheer and Hugh F. Rankin, *Rebels and Redcoats: The American Revolution Through the Eyes of Those Who Fought and Lived It* (Cleveland: World, 1957), 307.

52. The limit of thirty-nine stayed just below the biblical maximum of forty lashes asserted in Deuteronomy 25:1–3. Paul reports receiving thirty-nine

lashes five times in 2 Corinthians 11:24. Caroline Cox, *A Proper Sense of Honor: Service and Sacrifice in George Washington's Army* (Chapel Hill: University of North Carolina Press, 2004), 83, 102.

53. Some officers got around this limit by assessing one hundred lashes per offense. Cox, *A Proper Sense of Honor*, 94–95.

54. George Washington, General Orders, September 20, 1776, *The Papers of George Washington*, digital ed., http://rotunda.upress.virginia.edu/founders/GEWN-03-06-02-0274.

55. George Washington, General Orders, September 15, 1777, *The Papers of George Washington*, digital ed., http://rotunda.upress.virginia.edu/founders/GEWN-03-11-02-0227.

56. Official records are indexed in Neagles, *Summer Soldiers*.

57. Edmund Burke, "Conciliation with America," in *Pre-Revolutionary Writings*, ed. Ian Harris (Cambridge: Cambridge University Press, 1993), 266. For an exploration of ways Americans perceived obedience after independence, see Elizabeth D. Samet, *Willing Obedience: Citizens, Soldiers, and the Progress of Consent in America, 1776–1898* (Stanford, CA: Stanford University Press, 2004). Discipline in the Continental Army is examined in Cox, *A Proper Sense of Honor*, and in Harry M. Ward, *George Washington's Enforcers: Policing the Continental Army* (Carbondale: Southern Illinois University Press, 2006).

58. George Washington, General Orders, March 1, 1778, *The Papers of George Washington*, digital ed., http://rotunda.upress.virginia.edu/founders/GEWN-03-14-02-0001z . See also Ward, *George Washington's Enforcers*, 31.

59. Soldiers came from farms and cities, "[b]y-products of an unsophisticated age," as James Robertson puts it, "possessed of an individualism spawned in the land they inhabited." Robertson, *Soldiers Blue and Gray*, 4.

60. McPherson, *For Cause and Comrades*, 168–69.

61. Charles A. Graves, *The Forged Letter of General Robert E. Lee* (Richmond, VA: Richmond Press, 1914), 2, 4. Though the letter was forged, it did accurately reflect Lee's belief in the importance of duty. As John M. Taylor, *Duty Faithfully Performed: Robert E. Lee and His Critics* (Washington, DC: Brassey's, 1999), 238, notes, "At the core of Lee's personality, as many writers have noted, was a sense of duty." See also Elizabeth Brown Pryor, *Reading the Man: A Portrait of Robert E. Lee through His Private Letters* (New York: Viking, 2007), 234.

62. McPherson, *For Cause and Comrades*, 169.

63. Herek, *These Men Have Seen Hard Service*, 195; Court-Martial of Hooker DeLand, Record Group No. 153, file NN 2032.

64. Dwight D. Eisenhower, *Crusade in Europe* (Garden City, NY: Doubleday, 1948), 314.

65. Hamner, *Enduring Battle*, 199–200. The French soldier and military theorist Ardant du Picq noticed that soldiers were dispersed on the battlefield in the 1800s, and pondered its relation to cowardice. He wrote in a manuscript published after his death in 1870, "Unity is no longer insured by mutual surveillance. A man falls, and disappears. Who knows whether it was a bullet or the fear of advancing further that struck him!" Du Picq, *Battle Studies*, 116.

66. Titus, *The Old Dominion at War*, 145.

67. Keegan, *The Face of Battle*, 325.

68. Robert Jackall, introduction to *Propaganda* (New York: New York University Press, 1995) 1–13. See also *Propaganda and Communication in World History*, ed. Harold D. Lasswell, Daniel Lerner, and Hans Speier, 2 vols. (Honolulu: University Press of Hawaii, 1979–1980).

69. Thomas A. Palmer, "Why We Fight: A Study of Indoctrination Activities in the Armed Forces," in *The Military in America, From the Colonial Era to the Present*, new rev. edition, ed. Peter Karsten (New York: Free Press, 1986), 383. Palmer notes that the Korean conflict, especially the perceived success of communist "brainwashing" of American prisoners of war, led American authorities to strengthen indoctrination programs (383).

70. Jones, *The Thin Red Line*, 198, 223, 82.

71. Joseph Heller, *Catch-22* (New York: Simon and Schuster, 1995), 131.

72. "Where a white flag appears on a house," as Heinrich Himmler put it in an order issued just a month before the end of hostilities in Europe, "all the male persons are to be shot." Richard Bessel, *Nazism and War* (New York: Modern Library 2006), 176–77.

73. "Order No. 227 by the People's Commissar of Defence of the USSR," Wikisource, //en.wikisource.org/w/index.php?title=Order_No._227_by_the_People%27s_Commissar_of_Defence_of_the_USSR&oldid=2977000.

74. Max Hastings, *Inferno: The World at War, 1939–1945* (New York: Alfred A. Knopf, 2011), 148, puts the number of official executions for cowardice and desertion at 168,000 and notes that many more soldiers were shot summarily, without trial.

75. Norman Davies, *No Simple Victory: World War II in Europe, 1939–1945* (New York: Penguin, 2008), 266. Zhukov's comment is often attributed to Stalin.

76. Huie, *The Execution of Private Slovik*, 194.

77. In Huie's book, the chaplain says, "Give him another volley if you like it so much!" Ibid., 234.

78. Rebecca Woodham, "William Bradford Huie," *Encyclopedia of Alabama*, http://www.encyclopediaofalabama.org/face/Article.jsp?id=h-1547. Donald R.

Noble, "Introduction," in William Bradford Huie, *Mud on the Stars* (Tuscaloosa: University of Alabama Press, 1996), xxi.

79. Richard Levinson and William Link, *Stay Tuned: An Inside Look at the Making of Prime-Time Television* (New York: St. Martin's, 1981), 167.

80. Captain William Wilders to James F. Wilders, in Richard R. Moser, *The New Winter Soldiers: GI and Veteran Dissent during the Vietnam Era* (New Brunswick, NJ: Rutgers University Press, 1996), 45.

81. As Moser, *The New Winter Soldiers*, 50, puts it, "Whether actually used or not, the threat of fragging was a means by which soldiers tried to discipline their commanders."

82. The Vietnam era was not the first to see troops killing their superiors, but it occurred among American troops in Vietnam twice as often as it did in World Wars I or II or in the Korean War. Moser, *The New Winter Soldiers*, 48.

83. O'Brien, *The Things They Carried*, 63. O'Brien's earlier novel *Going After Cacciato* also explores the theme of cowardice and duty through the story of a squad of soldiers whose mission is to bring back a deserter, Cacciato, who lures them further and further from the front lines—until they themselves desert, following him all the way to Paris. As one character puts it, "The war's not over. We left the bloody war—walked away, ran. . . . No more crap about duty and mission. I'm out of it." Tim O'Brien, *Going After Cacciato: A Novel* (New York: Delacorte Press/S. Lawrence, 1978), 174. Compare this to Frederic Henry in Hemingway, *A Farewell to Arms*, 248: "I was through. I wished them all the luck. There were the good ones, and the brave ones, and the calm ones and the sensible ones, and they deserved it. But it was not my show any more." One hears the same resignation in both cases—detached in Hemingway's, more strident and impudent in O'Brien's.

84. John Dos Passos, *Three Soldiers* (New York: Modern Library, 1932 [1921]), 221. The Nietzschean overtones are underscored later in the text with talk of the "psychology of slavery" and of the "Human; all too Human!" (372, 303).

85. Jones, *The Thin Red Line*, 225.

86. Huie, *The Execution of Private Slovik*, 11.

CHAPTER 5

THE RISE OF THE DIAGNOSTIC

1. Homer, *The Iliad*, 12:279–80.

2. Aristotle, *Nicomachean Ethics*, 1115b.

3. Ibid., 1110a25.

4. See Elizabeth D. Leonard, *Lincoln's Forgotten Ally: Judge Advocate General Joseph Holt of Kentucky* (Chapel Hill: University of North Carolina Press, 2011).

5. Mary Bernard Allen, "Joseph Holt, Judge Advocate General (1862–1875): A Study in the Treatment of Political Prisoners by the United States Government during the Civil War" (PhD diss., University of Chicago, 1927), 67.

6. Thomas P. Lowry, "Research Note: New Access to a Civil War Resource," *Civil War History* 49, no. 1 (2003): 59.

7. After his prison term ended, Hooker DeLand had a long but very difficult life. There is record of him playing in a Fourth of July all-star baseball game in Michigan in 1866 (Peter Morris, *Baseball Fever: Early Baseball in Michigan* [Ann Arbor: University of Michigan Press, 2003], 115), but he moved away from Michigan not long after, married, divorced, moved, and moved again. He had intermittent fever, a bad knee, and rotten teeth. Like many other Civil War soldiers, he seems to have suffered from what would today be called posttraumatic stress disorder. None of his numerous appeals were granted by the government, which refused to give a pension to someone who had been cashiered from service. The last item in his file came after DeLand's death in 1931. The government capped a sixty-five-year series of bureaucratic humiliations by refusing to reimburse his family for funeral expenses. "If ever a man was haunted by past deeds," writes the historian of DeLand's regiment, "that man was Hooker Ashton DeLand." See Herek, *These Men Have Seen Hard Service*, 200, 380.

8. Court-Martial of Private Henry Barker, Record Group No. 153, file MM437.

9. Samuel Clements, Thirty-Second Maine Regiment, Adjutant General, Civil War Soldier's Cards, Maine State Archives, Augusta.

10. Court-Martial of Private Samuel Clements, Record Group No. 153, file LL3119.

11. Clements's name does not appear on the "List of U.S. Soldiers Executed by United States Military Authorities during the Late War" published in 1885, but a Portland, Maine, newspaper, the *Eastern Argus*, reported on February 13, 1865, 2, that Clements had been executed on February 10, 1865.

12. The soldier who first spotted Clements and his fellow soldiers in hiding was worried that they might be "guerrillas," but when he "asked the major for four or five men" to help him arrest them, the major told him "he did not believe there were any guerrillas there." He and one other man took Clements and two others prisoner without encountering resistance; Court-Martial of

Private Samuel Clements, Record Group No. 153, file LL3119. Other than noting the final record of Clements—that he deserted, was tried and convicted and was "executed in the presence of the regiment"—the history of the Maine Thirty-Second makes no mention of Clements or of marauding. Henry C. Houston, *The Thirty-Second Maine Regiment of Infantry Volunteers: An Historical Sketch* (Portland, ME: Southworth Brothers, 1903), 509.

13. Linderman, *Embattled Courage*, 25.

14. Court-Martial of Private Simon Snyder, Record Group No. 153, file MM441.

15. Winthrop, *Military Law and Precedents*, 440–41. On ancient practices, see C. P. Jones, "Stigma: Tattooing and Branding in Graeco-Roman Antiquity," *Journal of Roman Studies* 77 (1987): 139–55.

16. Court-Martial of Private Joseph C. Waldron, Record Group No. 153, file NN2699; Court-Martial of Private Andrew Whack, Record Group No. 153, file NN 2699. See also the case of Private Daniel J. Webber, Record Group No. 153, file LL663. "C" might have gained poetically punitive weight from the government practice of branding that letter "on all public property when sold or condemned." See Article XLI of United States War Department, *Revised Regulations for the Army of the United States, 1861* (Philadelphia: J. B. Lippincott, 1861), 1016. Branding of deserters also smacked of the punishment of slaves, an insult on top of injury that might have been especially galling to Confederate soldiers. Drew Gilpin Faust, "Christian Soldiers: The Meaning of Revivalism in the Confederate Army," in *The Civil War Soldier: A Historical Reader*, ed. Michael Barton and Larry M. Logue (New York: New York University Press, 2002): 336.

17. Steven J. Ramold, *Baring the Iron Hand: Discipline in the Union Army* (DeKalb: Northern Illinois University Press, 2011), 366. Convicted cowards were sentenced to be branded as late as January 1865, but, as noted, it is often difficult to tell if the sentences were carried out. See the court-martial cases of privates Benjamin Erway and Charles Shuter of New York, Record Group No. 153, file NN3420.

18. Court-Martial of Private Andrew Cronan, Record Group No. 153, file LL151.

19. Judge advocate general Joseph Holt, quoted in William Winthrop, *Military Law and Precedents*, 440–41. See also Robert O. Rollman, "Of Crimes, Courts-Martial and Punishment—A Short History of Military Justice," *JAG Law Review*, 11, no. 2 (1969): 212–22. In 1862 private John Clark of the Ninety-Fifth New York Volunteers was found guilty of deserting upon hearing the sound of battle and sentenced "to be branded with the letter 'C' on the

right cheek and the letter 'D' on the forehead." Clark's sentence was returned to the court "for reconsideration, the sentence being unusual and unmilitary." The branding was remitted. Though the revised sentence included confinement and hard labor, Clark apparently saw combat at Gettysburg in 1863; the last document in his file is an 1864 letter from his superior officer to president Abraham Lincoln requesting the remittance of Clark's entire sentence. Court-Martial of Private John Clark, Record Group No. 153, file LL262.

20. Allen, "Joseph Holt," 100.

21. Linderman, *Embattled Courage*, 167.

22. Eric T. Dean Jr., *Shook over Hell: Post-Traumatic Stress, Vietnam, and the Civil War* (Cambridge, MA: Harvard University Press, 1997), 116–17.

23. The "constitutional" defense also figures in Henry Morford's novel *The Coward*, when Carlton Brand realizes what his problem had been all along. Since childhood, the sight of blood made him faint, and he thought that "if he should ever be brought into conflict among deadly weapons, this horror of blood would make him run away like a poltroon, disgracing himself forever.... High cultivation of the imaginative faculty... and a constitutional predisposition in that direction, had made him painfully *nervous*—a weakness which to him, and eventually to others, assumed the shape of cowardice." Morford even goes to far as to diagnose Brand's "sense of honor" as "painfully delicate—his love of approbation [and, correspondingly, his hatred of disdain] so strong as to be little less than a disease." Morford, *The Coward*, 508. Cowardice was not Brand's problem; fear of cowardice was.

24. Court-Martial of Lieutenant Moses Powell, Record Group No. 153, file NN2032.

25. Dean, *Shook over Hell*, 116, 131.

26. Frances Clarke, "So Lonesome I Could Die: Nostalgia and Debates over Emotional Control in the Civil War North," *Journal of Social History* 41, no. 2 (2007): 254. David K. Kentsmith, "Principles of Battlefield Psychiatry," *Military Medicine* 151 (1986): 90. The term *nostalgia* was coined in 1688 by Swiss physician Johannes Hofer; Fred Davis, *Yearning for Yesterday: A Sociology of Nostalgia* (New York: Free Press, 1979), 1. The first definition of *nostalgia* in the *Oxford English Dictionary* is "Path. A Form of melancholia caused by prolonged absence from one's home or country; home-sickness." Entries for this meaning date from 1770. For a summary of the old usage (and an attempt to revive it for medical use), see Charles A. A. Zwingmann, "'Heimweh' or 'Nostalgic Reaction': A Conceptual Analysis and Interpretation of a Medico-Psychological Phenomenon" (PhD diss., Stanford University, 1959). See also Donald Lee Anderson and Godfrey Tryggve Anderson, "Nostalgia and Malingering in the

Military during the Civil War," *Perspectives in Biology and Medicine* 28, no. 1 (1984): 156–66.

27. Charles Smart, *The Medical and Surgical History of the War of the Rebellion*, part 3, vol. 1. (Washington, DC: Government Printing Office, 1888), 885.

28. Mary Ashton Rice Livermore, *My Story of the War* (New York: Arno, 1972 [c. 1889]), 559.

29. Other cases in which medical conditions did not serve to mitigate either the judgment of cowardice or sentencing include that of private Frank A. Schmeisser of the Sixth Regiment Connecticut Volunteers. At his 1862 court-martial for cowardice a surgeon testified that Schmeisser had "heart palpitations" and "nervous debility," but he was found guilty of cowardice (having left his company five minutes before battle commenced) and sentenced to have his head shaved and be drummed out. Court-Martial of Private Frank A. Schmeisser, Record Group No. 153, file KK347. Private Archibald Gilchrist of the 105th Pennsylvania Infantry told a court-martial that he had "a disease of the heart and cannot keep up on long marches. I am a drafted man. . . ." But he was found guilty of cowardice and straggling in late 1864 and, in addition to a financial penalty, was sentenced to parade two hours a day for ten days while wearing a placard that read "Coward." Court-Martial of Private Archibald Gilchrist, Record Group No. 153, File LL3020.

30. Smart, *The Medical and Surgical History*, 886. The anonymous report Smart quotes is undated, but it seems to have been written during the latter part of the Civil War.

31. Mike W. Martin, *From Morality to Mental Health: Virtue and Vice in a Therapeutic Culture* (New York: Oxford University Press, 2006).

32. Michel Foucault, *Discipline and Punish: The Birth of the Prison*, trans. Alan Sheridan (New York: Vintage, 1995 [1975]), 17–18, 19.

33. Thomas Salmon, quoted in Edward A. Strecker, "Military Psychiatry: World War I 1917–1918," in American Psychological Association, *One Hundred Years of American Psychiatry* (New York: Columbia University Press, 1944), 385.

34. Ben Shephard, *A War of Nerves* (London: Jonathan Cape, 2000), 2.

35. "Nervous Manifestations Due to the Winds of High Explosives," *Lancet* 2 (1915): 348.

36. Shephard, *A War of Nerves*, 2–31.

37. Theodore Bogacz, "Shell Shock," in *The United States in the First World War: An Encyclopedia*, ed. Ann Cipriano Venzon (New York: Garland, 1995), 545–48.

38. Strecker, "Military Psychiatry: World War I 1917–1918," 412.

39. Shephard, *A War of Nerves*, 28.

40. Caroline Cox, "Invisible Wounds: The American Legion, Shell-Shocked Veterans, and American Society, 1919–1924," in *Traumatic Pasts: History, Psy-*

chiatry, and Trauma in the Modern Age, 1870–1930, ed. Mark S. Micale and Paul Lerner (Cambridge: Cambridge University Press, 2001), 280–306.

41. Bogacz, "Shell Shock," 548.

42. Stouffer et al., *The American Soldier*, 198–99.

43. Ernest Hemingway to Charles Scribner, April 11–12, 1951, in *Ernest Hemingway, Selected Letters 1917–1961*, ed. Carlos Baker (New York: Charles Scribner's Sons, 1981), 725. After going AWOL three times, Jones was admitted to a psychiatric ward, where, after some politicking by friends, he was ultimately diagnosed with psychoneurosis and in 1944 given an honorable discharge. George Garrett, *James Jones* (San Diego: Harcourt Brace Jovanovich, 1984), 72.

44. D'Este, *Patton*, 533–34.

45. Fred Ayer Jr., *Before the Colors Fade* (Boston: Houghton Mifflin, 1964), 138–39.

46. Rick Atkinson, *The Day of Battle: The War in Sicily and Italy, 1943–1944* (New York: Henry Holt, 2007), 171.

47. Martin Blumenson, ed., *The Patton Papers* (Boston: Houghton Mifflin, 1972–74), 2:413.

48. D'Este, *Patton*, 553.

49. George S. Patton, quoted in H[erbert]. Essame, *Patton: A Study in Command* (New York: Charles Scribner's Sons, 1974), 105.

50. "A Matter of Rank," *Richmond News Leader*, May 30, 1970, 14; D'Este, *Patton*, 538–39.

51. George S. Patton to George Patton IV, May 19, 1944, in Blumenson, ed., *Patton Papers*, 2:458.

52. "A Matter of Rank," 14.

53. Dean, *Shook over Hell*, 40.

54. Jones and Wessely, *Shell Shock to PTSD*, 191. This book provides an overview of British and American syndromes in the twentieth century, esp. chap. 9, "War Syndromes."

55. Bryan Bender, "Veterans Forsake Studies of Stress: Stigma Impedes Search for Remedies," *Boston Globe*, August 24, 2009, http://www.boston.com/news/nation/washington/articles/2009/08/24/few_iraq_afghanistan_veterans_willing_to_take_part_in_boston_vas_studies_on_post_traumatic_stress/.

56. Joseph Shapiro, "A Wounded Soldier Struggles to Adapt," *Morning Edition*, National Public Radio, November 29, 2005, http://www.npr.org/templates/story/story.php?storyId=5030571.

57. Amy Goodman, "Memorial Day Special . . . Winter Soldier on the Hill: War Vets Testify before Congress," http://www.democracynow.org/2009/5/25/memorial_day_specialwinter_soldier_on_the_hill.

58. Appeals: United States v. Thomas H. King, Lance Corporal (E-3), U.S. Marine Corps NMCCA 200401338, United States Navy–Marine Corps Court of Criminal Appeals 2006, CCA Lexis 299. If considering and then dismissing medical explanations can fortify a conviction of cowardice, considering and then dismissing a suspicion of cowardice can fortify a medical explanation. In *The Caine Mutiny*, the elimination of cowardice as a possibility is used to confirm the diagnosis of a psychological problem. In his effort to defend men for mutiny against Captain Queeg, the defense lawyer argues that Queeg was mentally ill and unfit for command. Stipulating that Queeg is not a coward because "no commander of a naval ship can possibly be a coward," the lawyer asserts that the explanation for any "questionable acts . . . must be elsewhere"—namely, in Queeg's mental state. This man is no coward, the logic goes; therefore he's simply and sadly crazy; therefore the alleged mutineers acted properly. When Queeg, played by Humphrey Bogart, breaks down in the dramatic court-martial scene, rolling metal balls in his hands in an unsuccessful attempt to calm himself, the defense can pretty much rest. Edward Dmytryk, dir., *The Caine Mutiny*, 1954.

59. Field Marshal Richard Michael Power Carver (Lord Carver), quoted in Wendy Holden, *Shell Shock* (London: Channel 4, 1998), 180.

60. Paul R. McHugh and Glenn Treisman, "PTSD: A Problematic Diagnostic Category," *Journal of Anxiety Disorders* 21(2007): 216.

61. U.S. Department of Veterans Affairs, "VA Simplifies Access to Health Care and Benefits for Veterans with PTSD," press release, July 12, 2010, http://www1.va.gov/opa/pressrel/pressrelease.cfm?id=1922.

62. Allen G. Breed, "In Tide of PTSD Cases, Fear of Fraud Growing," *Army Times*, May 2, 2010, http://www.armytimes.com/news/2010/05/ap_military_ptsd_fraud_050210/.

63. Ben Fenton, "Pardoned: The 306 Soldiers Shot at Dawn for 'Cowardice,'" *Telegraph*, August 16, 2006, http://www.telegraph.co.uk/news/1526437/Pardoned-the-306-soldiers-shot-at-dawn-for-cowardice.html. Details of Farr's case are described in Simon Wessely, "The Life and Death of Private Harry Farr," *Journal of the Royal Society of Medicine* 99, no. 9 (2006): 440–43.

64. Stephanie Condron, "Haig's Son Attacks Pardoning of 306 Soldiers Shot for Cowardice," *Telegraph*, September 5, 2006, http://www.telegraph.co.uk/news/1528044/Haigs-son-attacks-pardoning-of-306-soldiers-shot-for-cowardice.html.

65. William Sheehan, Richard J. Roberts, Steven Thurber, and Mary Ann Roberts, "Shell Shocked and Confused: A Reconsideration of Captain Myers's Case Reports of Shell-Shock in World War One," *Priory Psychiatry* 2 (2009), http://priory.com/psychiatry/ptsdshellshock.htm. For further recent

information about the physiological basis of shell shock, see Rebecca Anderson, "Shell Shock: An Old Injury with New Weapons," *Molecular Interventions* 8, no. 5 (2008): 204–18; Emily Singer, "Brain Trauma in Iraq," *Technology Review*, May–June 2008, http://m.technologyreview.com/biomedicine/20571/; and Sharon B. Shively and Daniel P. Perl, "Traumatic Brain Injury, Shell Shock, and Posttraumatic Stress Disorder in the Military—Past, Present, and Future," *Journal of Head Trauma Rehabilitation* 27 (2012): 234–39.

66. "Tribute to WWI 'Cowards,'" *BBC News*, June 21, 2001, http//news.bbc .co.uk/2/hi/uk_news/1399983.

67. Julian Putkowski, "Joined at 16, Shot at 17," http://web.archive.org/ web/20110618042624/http://www.shotatdawn.info/page20.html.

68. "Shot at Dawn, Pardoned 90 Years On," *BBC News*, August 16, 2006, http://news.bbc.co.uk/2/hi/uk_news/england/4798025.stm.

69. A list of memorials to deserters in Germany is available at http://www .desertuer-denkmal.de.

70. Mark R. Hatlie, "Memorial to Deserters in Ulm," http://sites-of-memory .de/main/ulmdeserters.html.

71. Stephen R. Welch, "Commemorating 'Heroes of a Special Kind': Deserter Monuments in Germany," *Journal of Contemporary History* 47, no. 2 (2012): 394, notes that the Stuttgart sculpture depicts "the deserter as an individual figure who has escaped the stifling bonds of social conformity."

72. Rudyard Kipling, *Complete Verse, Definitive Edition* (New York: Anchor, 1989), 385.

73. James J. Sheehan, *Where Have All the Soldiers Gone? The Transformation of Modern Europe* (Boston: Houghton Mifflin, 2008), 3. "Non-war community" is a phrase coined by Ole Wæver, Sheehan notes (223).

74. Michael B. Oren, "Fleeing Moment: A Cultural History of Desertion," *New Republic*, June 17, 2009, http://www.tnr.com/article/fleeing-moment.

75. Barack Obama, "Nobel Prize Acceptance Speech," http://www.white house.gov/the-press-office/remarks-president-acceptance-nobel-peace-prize.

76. Singer, *Wired for War*, 318. See also James Wright, *Those Who Have Borne the Battle: A History of America's Wars and Those Who Fought Them* (New York: Public Affairs, 2012).

77. James, "The Moral Equivalent of War," *The Heart of William James*, ed. Robert Richardson (Cambridge, MA: Belknap Press of Harvard University Press, 2010), 303.

78. Ken McCracken, "You Haven't Earned the Right to Be 'War-Weary,'" September 8, 2007, http://www.willisms.com/archives/2007/09/you_havent_ earn.html. See also http://www.chuckhawks.com/america_not_at_war.htm.

79. On "the generic use of heroism to describe all who serve," see Wright, *Those Who Have Borne the Battle*, 271.

80. Jeanne Marie Laskas, "The Coward," *GQ*, July 2004, 106–12, 159–61.

81. Georg-Andreas Pogany Collection, AFC/2001/001/34120, Veterans History Project, American Folklife Center, Library of Congress.

82. Laskas, "The Coward," 159; Laskas also notes that "the team sergeant who first called [Pogany] a coward . . . was killed in Iraq by a roadside bomb" and that Pogany attended his memorial service (161).

83. "In Focus: Cowards in War," *Paula Zahn Now*, CNN, November 6, 2003.

84. Pauline Arrillaga, "One-Man Army Fights War's Stresses," *USA Today*, April 18, 2010, http://usatoday30.usatoday.com/news/military/2010-04-18-pogany-army-ptsd-veteran_N.htm.

85. Daniel Glick, "Branded," *Salon*, June 9, 2004, http://www.salon.com/2004/06/09/georg_pogany/.

86. Arrilaga, "One-Man Army."

87. Ibid.

88. Daniel Zwerdling, "Former Soldier Helps Others Fight Army for Help," *Weekend Edition Saturday*, National Public Radio, July 7, 2007, http://www.npr.org/templates/story/story.php?storyId=11782535.

CHAPTER 6
SO LONG A FILE

1. James, "The Moral Equivalent of War," 308.

2. Shephard, *A War of Nerves*, 376.

3. Richard J. McNally, "Conceptual Problems with the DSM IV Criteria," in *Posttraumatic Stress Disorder: Issues and Controversies*, ed. Gerald M. Rosen (Sussex, England: John Wiley and Sons, 2004), 3–4.

4. Critics of the *DSM-5*'s PTSD criteria include James Coyne, "But It's Not PTSD! Bad Research Distorts Our Understanding of a Serious Disorder," http://blogs.plos.org/mindthebrain/2013/07/23/but-its-not-ptsd-bad-research-distorts-our-understanding-of-a-serious-disorder/; and Allen Frances, MD, "DSM5 in Distress," http://www.psychologytoday.com/blog/dsm5-in-distress. Elspeth Cameron Ritchie celebrates the new criteria in "An Easier PTSD Diagnosis," *Time*, May 14, 2013, http://nation.time.com/2013/05/14/an-easier-ptsd-diagnosis/#ixzz2f5nnH8tW.

5. Christina Hoff Sommers and Sally Satel, *One Nation under Therapy: How the Helping Culture Is Eroding Self-Reliance* (New York: St. Martin's, 2005), 5.

6. Ben Shephard, "Risk Factors and PTSD: A Historian's Perspective," in Rosen, ed., *Posttraumatic Stress Disorder*, 57–58. See also McHugh and Treisman, "PTSD: A Problematic Diagnostic Category," 211–22.

7. James Bowman, "The Field of Honor," *New Criterion* 24, no. 5 (2006): 64. Christopher Lasch makes the more general argument that not just cowardice, or insult, but shame itself "survives, nowadays, only in the attenuated form of damaged self-esteem." *A Companion to American Thought*, ed. Richard Wightman Fox and James T. Kloppenberg (Malden, MA: Blackwell, 1998), s.v. "shame."

8. Theophrastus, *Characters and Observations: An Eighteenth Century Manuscript* (London: J. Murray, 1930), 43.

9. Jeffrey R. Snyder, "A Nation of Cowards," *Public Interest* 113 (993): 42. Kierkegaard, "Against Cowardice," 83, notes that the term "had completely disappeared from use" in 1840s Denmark.

10. John R. Ellement, "Attack Leaves Voter, 73, in Pain and Fear," *Boston Globe*, September 18, 2008, B1.

11. If bullies really were cowards, one might expect to find evidence of inner weakness—the vulnerability for which they were trying to overcompensate by bullying, but a recent study found that among a group of Canadian sixth graders, "bullies were psychologically strongest and enjoyed high social standing among their classmates." Jaana Juvonen, Sandra Graham, and Mark A. Schuster, "Bullying among Young Adolescents: The Strong, the Weak and the Troubled," *Pediatrics* 112, no. 6 (2003): 1231.

12. Tony Parker, *The Violence of Our Lives: Interviews with American Murderers* (New York: Henry Holt, 1995), 167.

13. Fyodor Dostoevsky, *Crime and Punishment*, trans. Richard Pevear and Larissa Volokhonsky (New York: Vintage, 1993), 3–4.

14. Ibid, 65–66.

15. James Gilligan, *Preventing Violence* (New York: Thames and Hudson, 2001), 57.

16. Truman Capote, *In Cold Blood: A True Account of Multiple Murder and Its Consequences* (New York: Random House, 1965), 244.

17. Anthony Petrosino, Carolyn Turpin-Petrosino, and John Buehler, "'Scared Straight' and Other Juvenile Awareness Programs for Preventing Juvenile Delinquency: A Systematic Review of the Randomized Experimental Evidence," *Annals of the American Academy of Political and Social Science* 589 (2003): 41–62.

18. Richard Maxwell Brown, *No Duty to Retreat: Violence and Values in American History and Society* (Oxford: Oxford University Press, 1991), 5. Brown's claims about how "no duty to retreat" has helped make American

society exceptionally violent were questioned and largely dismissed by historians, but his history of the absence or removal of a duty to retreat has stood. See Pieter Spierenburg, "Masculinity, Violence, and Honor: An Introduction," in *Men and Violence: Gender, Honor, and Rituals in Modern Europe and America*, ed. Pieter Spierenburg (Columbus: Ohio State University Press, 1998), 1–29.

19. Arian Campo-Flores, "Shooting Draws U.S. Probe: Teenager's Death Spotlights Laws Lowering Bar for Citizens' Use of Lethal Force," *Wall Street Journal*, March 21, 2012, A3.

20. Wheeler v. State, 175 S.E. 540, 541–542 (Ga. 1934); John Kang, "The Burdens of Manliness," *Harvard Journal of Law and Gender* 33, no. 2 (2010): 478–507.

21. Snyder, "A Nation of Cowards," 40, 42.

22. Paddy Chayefsky, *The Americanization of Emily: Shooting Script*. Electronic ed. (Alexandria, VA: Alexander Street Press, 2009), 41–42. As James Wolcott, "From Fear to Eternity," *Vanity Fair*, March 2005, 227–28, points out, *The Americanization of Emily* was "the first major Hollywood production to portray an American serviceman proudly professing the virtues of cowardice." The movie, however, was not a popular success, and many reviewers were shocked and angered by the celebration of cowardice.

23. James Boswell, *The Life of Johnson* (New York: E. P. Dutton, 1960) 2:233.

24. Mark Twain, "The United States of Lyncherdom," in *Prospects: An Annual of American Cultural Studies*, 25, ed. Jack Salzman (New York: Cambridge University Press, 2000), 142. In exploring why Twain did not publish this essay during his lifetime, L. Terry Oggel asks, "was he guilty of exactly what he had accused the majority of people in the lynch mobs of—cowardice?" Oggel does not offer a definitive answer to the question, noting that Twain actually planned a book on the subject of lynching, and may have delayed publication of the essay because he contemplated using it as an introduction for the book, or publishing it as a kind of advertisement when the book came out. Twain also may have thought that lynchings were only going to become more common, and so the essay would become even more timely if he waited to publish it. (Actually, lynchings seem to have peaked around this time.) Twain's worry that if he published a book about lynching he "shouldn't have even half a friend left" in the South may smack of that "aversion to being unpleasantly conspicuous, pointed at, shunned" that he calls moral cowardice. An uncharitable judgment, but one to which Twain might readily assent. L. Terry Oggel, "Speaking Out about Race: 'The United States of Lyncherdom' Clemens Really Wrote," in Salzman, ed., *Prospects*, 129.

25. Carl Andrew Castro, "Military Courage," in *Military Life: The Psychology of Serving in Peace and Combat*, ed. Thomas W. Britt, Carl Andrew Castro, and Amy B. Adler (Westport, CT: Praeger, 2005), 4:68.

26. James Fitzjames Stephen, "Courage," in *Essays by a Barrister* (London: Smith, Elder, 1862), 176.

27. Miller, *The Mystery of Courage*, 258, 263. See also Stephen, "Courage."

28. William Shakespeare, *Henry the Fourth, Part 1*, act 5, scene 4, verse 115. Falstaff's actual words are, "The better part of valour is discretion, in the which better part I have saved my life." To make playing dead look even discretely valorous is hard, so after saying this Falstaff stabs Hotspur's corpse. Hotspur might be playing dead himself, after all.

29. Twain, "The United States of Lyncherdom," 142.

30. T. S. Eliot, *Selected Prose of T. S. Eliot*, ed. Frank Kermode (New York: Harcourt Brace Jovanovich, 1975), 236.

31. John S. Carroll, *Exiles of Eternity: An Exposition of Dante's Inferno* (Port Washington, NY: Kennikat, 1971), 53, 55.

32. Eugenio N. Frongia, "Canto III: The Gate of Hell," in *Lectura Dantis: Inferno*, ed. Allen Mandelbaum, Anthony Oldcorn, and Charles Ross (Berkeley and Los Angeles: University of California Press, 1998), 41.

33. Jane Goodall, *In the Shadow of Man* (Boston: Houghton Mifflin, 1971), 275, fig. 4b.

34. David Bygott, personal communication with the author, October 17, 2013.

35. Primo Levi, *The Drowned and the Saved*, trans. Raymond Rosenthal (New York: Summit, 1988), 15.

36. Daniel Goldhagen, *Hitler's Willing Executioners: Ordinary Germans and the Holocaust* (New York: Alfred A. Knopf, 1996).

37. Hannah Arendt, *Responsibility and Judgment* (New York: Schocken, 2003), 111.

38. Taylor Branch, *At Canaan's Edge: America in the King Years, 1965–68* (New York: Simon and Schuster, 2006), 107.

39. Martin Luther King Jr., "Why I Am Opposed to the War in Vietnam," sermon at Riverside Church, New York, April 30, 1967, http://www.lib.berke ley.edu/MRC/pacificaviet/riversidetranscript.html.

40. Mark Twain, *Mark Twain in Eruption: Hitherto Unpublished Pages about Men and Events*, ed. Bernard DeVoto (New York: Grosset and Dunlap, 1940), xxix.

41. Mark Twain, *Collected Tales, Sketches, Speeches, and Essays 1852–1890* (New York: Library of America, 1992), 881.

42. Mark Twain, *Mark Twain's Notebook*, ed. Albert Paine (New York: Harper and Brothers, 1935), 126.

246 — NOTES TO PAGES 179–186

43. Crane, *The Red Badge of Courage*, 87.

44. Lendon, *Soldiers and Ghosts*, 52.

45. Henry David Thoreau, *Walden: A Fully Annotated Edition*, ed. Jeffrey S. Cramer (New Haven, CT: Yale University Press, 2004), 317.

46. Henry David Thoreau, *The Writings of Henry David Thoreau*, ed. Elizabeth Hall Witherell, 6, *Journal, 1853* (Princeton, NJ: Princeton University Press, 2000), 126.

47. Miller, *Mystery of Courage*, 12.

48. Johnson, *Works*, 4:323. In a later edition, Johnson replaced "the mean and cowardly dereliction of ourselves" with "against the folly of presupposing impossibilities, and anticipating frustration."

49. Dante scholars note that he was here dramatizing what Aquinas would call "pusillanimity," which "causes one to fall short of his capability when he refuses to extend himself to achieve an aim commensurate with his powers." Frongia, "Canto III: The Gate of Hell," 41.

50. Dante, *Inferno*, trans. Anthony Esolen (New York: Modern Library, 2002), canto 2, lines 41–42.

51. William Shakespeare, *Hamlet*, act 3, scene 1, line 83.

52. Kierkegaard, "Against Cowardice," 86–87.

53. Ibid., 88.

54. Henry James, "The Beast in the Jungle," in *Complete Stories, 1898–1910* (New York: Library of America, 1996), 503, 516.

55. Ibid., 539, 540.

56. Ibid., 528.

57. Readings of Marcher as a coward are rare, and none connect him to Dante's cowards. Clifton Fadiman comes close in saying that "Marcher stands for un-Faust, for man the coward, not the hero, of experience" in *Party of One: The Selected Writings of Clifton Fadiman* (Cleveland: World, 1955), 166. A psychological diagnosis is offered in Winslow Hunt, "The Diffident Narcissist: A Character-Type Illustrated in *The Beast in the Jungle* by Henry James," *International Journal of Psychoanalysis* 76 (1995): 1257–67.

58. James, "The Beast in the Jungle," 510.

59. Junot Diaz, *This is How You Lose Her* (New York: Riverhead, 2012), 216.

60. Court-Martial of Lieutenant Hooker DeLand, Record Group No. 153, file NN2032.

61. Court-Martial of Private Mitchell Bernard, Record Group No. 153, file MM444.

62. Robert Frost to Louis Untermeyer, March 10, 1924, in *Collected Poems, Prose and Plays* (New York: Library of America, 1995), 703.

63. Jedediah Purdy, *For Common Things: Irony, Trust, and Commitment in America Today* (New York: Alfred A. Knopf, 1999), xi–xii. Purdy also notes, "The point of irony is a quiet refusal to believe in the depth of relationships, the sincerity of motivation, or the truth of speech—especially earnest speech. In place of the romantic idea that each of us harbors a true self struggling for expression, the ironist offers the suspicion that we are just quantum selves—all spin, all the way down" (10).

64. T. S. Eliot, "The Love Song of J. Alfred Prufrock," *Collected Poems 1909–1962* (New York: Harcourt, Brace and World, 1962), 7.

65. Denis Donoghue, *The Practice of Reading* (New Haven, CT: Yale University Press, 1998), 183.

66. Emily Brontë, *Selected Brontë Poems*, ed. Edward Chitham and Tom Winnifrith (Oxford: Basil Blackwell, 1985), 172–73.

67. Richard B. Sewall, *The Life of Emily Dickinson* (New York: Farrar, Straus and Giroux, 1974), 667.

68. Ralph Waldo Emerson, *Complete Essays and Other Writings of Ralph Waldo Emerson*, ed. Brooks Atkinson (New York: Modern Library, 1950), 146–47.

69. Rainer Maria Rilke, *Letters to a Young Poet*, rev. ed., trans. M. D. Herter Norton (New York: W. W. Norton, 1954), 67–68.

70. The parable appears in Franz Kafka, *The Trial*, trans. Mike Mitchell (New York: Oxford University Press, 2009), 153–55.

71. Jean-Paul Sartre, *The Devil and the Good Lord*, from *The Devil and the Good Lord and Two Other Plays*, trans. Kitty Black (New York: Vintage, 1962), 141.

72. Jean-Paul Sartre, *Existentialism and Human Emotions*, trans. Bernard Frechtman (New York: Citadel, 1985 [1957]), 22, 34, 35.

73. Thucydides, *History of the Peloponnesian War*, trans. Rex Warner (New York: Penguin, 1986 [1954]), 147.

74. Miller, *The Mystery of Courage*, 39, 176, 290.

75. Chichung Huang offers a more precise translation of Confucius's statement: "To see something you ought to do and not to do it is want of courage"; *The Analects of Confucius (Lun Yu): A Literal Translation with an Introduction and Notes*, trans. Chichung Huang (Oxford: Oxford University Press, 1997), 57. But if a Google search is any indication, the looser translation, "to know what is right and not to do it is the worst cowardice," is by far the most popular.

76. Max H. Bazerman and Ann E. Tenbrunsel, *Blind Spots: Why We Fail to Do What's Right and What to Do about It* (Princeton, NJ: Princeton University Press, 2011), 153, note that we have blind spots in the moment of action or inaction, and also prospectively and retrospectively: "We tend to predict that

we will behave as we think we should behave, but at the time of the decision, we behave how we want to behave." Then "when we reflect back on the decision, we tend to believe that we acted as we thought we should behave."

77. Lester Grinspoon, quoted in Daniel Goleman, *Vital Lies, Simple Truths: The Psychology of Self-Deception* (New York: Simon and Schuster, 1985), 19–20.

78. Robert Trivers, *The Folly of Fools: The Logic of Deceit and Self-Deception in Human Life* (New York: Basic Books, 2011), 332.

79. T. S. Eliot, *Collected Poems*, 61.

80. Frongia, "Canto III: The Gate of Hell," 49.

81. William Stafford, "Thinking for Berky," in *Stories That Could Be True: New and Collected Poems* (New York: Harper and Row, 1977), 64.

82. Dante, *Inferno*, trans. Esolen, canto 3, lines 14–15.

BIBLIOGRAPHY

Abrams, Elliot, and Andrew J. Bacevich. "A Symposium on Citizenship and Military Service." *Parameters* 31, no. 2 (2001): 18–22.

Ahearn, Maria L. *The Rhetoric of War: Training Day, the Militia, and the Military Sermon*. New York: Greenwood, 1989.

Alden, John Richard. *Robert Dinwiddie: Servant of the Crown*. Williamsburg, VA: Colonial Williamsburg Foundation, 1973.

Allen, Mary Bernard. "Joseph Holt, Judge Advocate General (1862–1875): A Study in the Treatment of Political Prisoners by the United States Government during the Civil War." PhD diss., University of Chicago, 1927.

Anderson, Donald Lee, and Godfrey Tryggve Anderson. "Nostalgia and Malingering in the Military during the Civil War." *Perspectives in Biology and Medicine* 28, no. 1 (1984): 156–66.

Anderson, Fred. *Crucible of War: The Seven Years' War and the Fate of the Empire in British North America, 1754–1766*. New York: Alfred A. Knopf, 2000.

Anderson, L. V. "Do Sex Strikes Ever Work? 'Lysistratic Nonaction' Can Be Surprisingly Effective." *Slate*, August 27, 2012, http://www.slate.com/articles/news_and_politics/explainer/2012/08/sex_strike_in_togo_do_sex_strikes_ever_work_.html.

Anderson, Rebecca. "Shell Shock: An Old Injury with New Weapons." *Molecular Interventions* 8, no. 5 (2008): 204–18.

Appiah, Kwame Anthony. *The Honor Code*. New York: W. W. Norton, 2010.

The AQ Chef. "Make a Bomb in the Kitchen of Your Mom." *Inspire* 1 (1431/2010): 33–40, http://cryptome.org/2012/01/inspire/inspire-1.pdf.

Arendt, Hannah. *Responsibility and Judgment*. New York: Schocken, 2003.

Aristophanes. *Lysistrata*. Translated by Douglass Parker. New York: Mentor, 1964.

———. *Peace*. Translated by Kenneth McLeish. London: Methuen Drama, 1993.

Aristotle. *Nicomachean Ethics*. Translated by Terence Irwin. 2nd ed. Indianapolis: Hackett, 1999.

Arnsten, Amy F. T. "Stress Signalling Pathways That Impair Prefrontal Cortex Structure and Function." *Nature Reviews Neuroscience* 10 (2009): 410–22.

Arrillaga, Pauline. "One-Man Army Fights War's Stresses." *USA Today*, April 18, 2010, http://usatoday30.usatoday.com/news/military/2010–04–18-pog any-army-ptsd-veteran_N.htm.

Atkinson, Rick. *The Day of Battle: The War in Sicily and Italy, 1943–1944*. New York: Henry Holt, 2007.

Ayer, Fred, Jr. *Before the Colors Fade*. Boston: Houghton Mifflin, 1964.

Babington, Anthony. *For the Sake of Example: Capital Courts-Martial, 1914–1920*. Rev. ed. London: Penguin, 2001.

Bacevich, Andrew. "The Cult of National Security." *Commonweal*, January 27, 2006, 7–8.

Baker-Crothers, Hayes. *Virginia and the French and Indian War*. Chicago: University of Chicago Press, 1928.

Barkun, Michael. *A Culture of Conspiracy: Apocalyptic Visions in Contemporary America*. Berkeley and Los Angeles: University of California Press, 2003.

Bartlett, John Russell. *Dictionary of Americanisms: A glossary of words and phrases usually regarded as peculiar to the United States*. 4th ed. Boston: Little, Brown, 1877.

Bates, Stephen, and Richard Norton-Taylor. "No Pardon for Admiral Byng." *Guardian*, March 15, 2007, http://www.guardian.co.uk/uk/2007/mar/15/military.immigrationpolicy.

Baugh, Daniel A. "John Byng." *Dictionary of National Biography*, http://www.oxforddnb.com/view/article/4263.

Bauman, Zygmunt. *Liquid Fear*. Cambridge: Polity, 2006.

Bazerman, Max H., and Ann E. Tenbrunsel. *Blind Spots: Why We Fail to Do What's Right and What to Do About It*. Princeton, NJ: Princeton University Press, 2011.

Becker, Ernst. *The Denial of Death*. New York: Free Press, 1973.

Beevor, Antony. *Stalingrad*. New York: Penguin, 1999.

Beinart, Peter. "Time Out." *New Republic*, February 10, 2003, http://www.tnr.com/article/time-out.

Bender, Bryan. "Veterans Forsake Studies of Stress: Stigma Impedes Search for Remedies." *Boston Globe*, August 24, 2009, http://www.boston.com/news/nation/washington/articles/2009/08/24/few_iraq_afghanistan_veterans_willing_to_take_part_in_boston_vas_studies_on_post_traumatic_stress/.

Beowulf. Translated by Seamus Heaney. New York: Farrar, Straus and Giroux, 2000.

Berger, Peter L. "Excursus: On the Obsolescence of the Concept of Honor." In Peter L. Berger, Brigitte Berger, and Hansfried Kellner, *The Homeless Mind: Modernization and Consciousness*, 83–96. New York: Vintage, 1973.

Bessel, Richard. *Nazism and War*. New York: Modern Library, 2006.

Bierce, Ambrose. *The Unabridged Devil's Dictionary*. Edited by David E. Schultz and S. T. Joshi. Athens: University of Georgia Press, 2000.

Billings, Warren M., John E. Selby, and Thad W. Tate. *Colonial Virginia: A History*. White Plains, NY: KTO, 1986.

Bin Laden, Osama. "Bin Laden's Fatwa." *PBS Newshour*, August 1996, http://www.pbs.org/newshour/terrorism/international/fatwa_1996.html.

———. Bin Laden Tape: Text. BBC News World Edition, February 12, 2003, http://news.bbc.co.uk/2/low/middle_east/2751019.stm.

Blomquist, Brian. "Cowardly Lyin' Saddam: Bush Whacks Scaredy Rat for Crawling in Hole." *New York Post*, December 16, 2003, http://nypost.com/2003/12/16/cowardly-lyin-saddam-bush-whacks-scaredy-rat-for-crawling-in-hole/.

Blumenson, Martin. *The Patton Papers*. Vol. 2. Boston: Houghton Mifflin, 1974.

Boehm, Christopher. *Moral Origins: The Evolution of Virtue, Altruism, and Shame.* New York: Basic Books, 2012.

Bogacz, Theodore. "Shell Shock." In *The United States in the First World War: An Encyclopedia*, edited by Ann Cipriano Venzon, 545–48. New York: Garland, 1995.

Bohlen, Celestine. "Think Tank; In New War on Terrorism, Words are Weapons, Too." *New York Times*, September 29, 2001, A11.

Booth, John Wilkes. *"Right or Wrong, God Judge Me": The Writings of John Wilkes Booth*. Edited by John Rhodehamel and Louise Taper. Urbana: University of Illinois Press, 1997.

Boswell, James. *The Life of Johnson*. Vol. 2. New York: E. P. Dutton, 1960.

Bourke, Joanna. *Fear: A Cultural History*. Emeryville, CA: Shoemaker Hoard, 2006.

Bowers, William T., William M. Hammond, and George L. MacGarrigle. *Black Soldier, White Army: The 24th Infantry Regiment in Korea*. Honolulu: University Press of the Pacific, 2005.

Bowman, James. *Honor: A History*. New York: Encounter, 2006.

Braddon, Russell. *Japan against the World 1941–2041: The 100-Year War for Supremacy*. New York: Stein and Day, 1983.

Branch, Taylor. *At Canaan's Edge: America in the King Years, 1965–68*. New York: Simon and Schuster, 2006.

Brand, C. E. *Roman Military Law*. Austin: University of Texas Press, 1968.

Braudy, Leo. *From Chivalry to Terrorism: War and the Changing Nature of Masculinity*. New York: Alfred A. Knopf, 2003.

Breed, Allen G. "In Tide of PTSD Cases, Fear of Fraud Growing." *Army Times*, May 2, 2010, http://www.armytimes.com/news/2010/05/ap_military_ptsd _fraud_050210/.

Bristed, Charles Astor. "The Cowards' Convention." In *Union Pamphlets of the Civil War, 1861–1865*, edited by Frank Freidel, 2:1135–45. Cambridge, MA: Belknap Press of Harvard University Press, 1967.

Broadfoot, Barry. *Six War Years 1939–1945: Memories of Canadians at Home and Abroad*. Garden City, NY: Doubleday, 1974.

Broekmeyer, Marius. *Stalin, the Russians, and Their War*. Translated by Rosalind Buck. Madison: University of Wisconsin Press, 2004.

Brontë, Emily. *Selected Brontë Poems*. Edited by Edward Chitham and Tom Winnifrith. Oxford: Basil Blackwell, 1985.

Brown, Richard Maxwell. *No Duty to Retreat: Violence and Values in American History and Society*. Oxford: Oxford University Press, 1991.

Browne, Kingsley R. "Women at War: An Evolutionary Perspective." *Buffalo Law Review* 49 (2001): 53–142.

Brumwell, Stephen. *Redcoats: The British Soldier and War in the Americas, 1755– 1763*. New York: Cambridge University Press, 2002.

Brunner, Elgin Medea. *Foreign Security Policy, Gender, and US Military Identity*. New York: Palgrave Macmillan.

Buchanan, Allen, and Russell Powell. "Beyond the Paleo." *Aeon*, December 12, 2013, http://aeon.co/magazine/living-together/morality-may-have-evolved -but-it-isnt-fixed/.

Bulgakov, Mikhail. *The Master and Margarita*. Translated by Richard Pevear and Larissa Volokhonsky. New York: Penguin 1997.

Bumiller, Elisabeth. "Air Force Drone Operators Report High Levels of Stress." *New York Times*, December 18, 2011, http://www.nytimes.com/2011/12/19/ world/asia/air-force-drone-operators-show-high-levels-of-stress.html.

Bumiller, Elisabeth, and Thom Shanker. "War Evolves with Drones, Some Tiny as Bugs." *New York Times*, June 19, 2011, http://www.nytimes.com /2011/06/20/world/20drones.html.

Bungiana, or an assemblage of what-d'ye-call-em's, in Prose and verse That have occasionally appeared relative to the conduct of a Certain naval commander, now first collected; in order to perpetuate the MEMORY of his Wonderful Atchievements [sic]. London: J. Doughty, 1756.

Bunn, Mike, and Clay Williams. *Battle for the Southern Frontier: The Creek War and the War of 1812*. Charleston, SC: History Press, 2008.

Bunyan, John. *The Pilgrim's Progress*. Boston: Houghton Mifflin, 1969.

Burke, Edmund. *Pre-Revolutionary Writings*. Edited by Ian Harris. Cambridge: Cambridge University Press, 1993.

Bush, George W. "President Discusses the Future of Iraq." Press release, February 26, 2003, http://georgewbush-whitehouse.archives.gov/news/releases/2003/02/20030226–11.html.

——. "President Says 'It is a Moment of Truth' for UN." Press release, February 9, 2003, http://georgewbush-whitehouse.archives.gov/news/releases/2003/02/20030209–1.html.

Byng, John. *The trial of the Honourable Admiral John Byng: at a court-martial, as taken by Mr. Charles Ferne, judge-advocate of His Majesty's fleet. Published by order of the Right Honourable the Lords Commissioners of the Admiralty, at the desire of the court-martial. To which is added, an account of Admiral Byng's behaviour in his last moments. Also, a copy of a paper delivered by him to William Brough, Esq; marshal of the High Court of Admiralty, immediately before his death.* New York: J. Parker and W. Weyman, 1757.

Campo-Flores, Arian. "Shooting Draws U.S. Probe: Teenager's Death Spotlights Laws Lowering Bar for Citizens' Use of Lethal Force." *Wall Street Journal*, March 21, 2012, A3.

Capote, Truman. *In Cold Blood: A True Account of Multiple Murder and Its Consequences.* New York: Random House, 1965.

Carroll, John S. *Exiles of Eternity: An Exposition of Dante's Inferno.* Port Washington, NY: Kennikat, 1971.

Carter, Susan B., Scott Sigmund Gartner, Michael R. Haines, Alan L. Olmstead, Richard Sutch, and Gavin Wright, eds., *Historical Statistics of the United States: Earliest Times to the Present.* Millennial ed. New York: Cambridge University Press, 2006.

Cartwright, Samuel. "Diseases and Peculiarities of the Negro Race." *Debow's Review* 11 (1851): 64–69, 209–13, 331–37.

Castro, Carl Andrew. "Military Courage." In *Military Life: The Psychology of Serving in Peace and Combat*, edited by Thomas Britt, Carl Andrew Castro, and Amy B. Adler, 60–79. Westport, CT: Praeger Security International, 2006.

[Case, Wheeler.] *Poems, occasioned by several circumstances and occurrences* [sic], *in the present grand contest of America for liberty.* New Haven, CT: Thomas and Samuel Green, 1778.

Céline, Louis-Ferdinand. *Journey to the End of the Night.* Translated by Ralph Manheim. New York: New Directions, 1983.

Chapman, Robert L. *New Dictionary of American Slang.* New York: Harper and Row, 1986.

Characters and Observations: An Eighteenth Century Manuscript. London: J. Murray, 1930.

Chayefsky, Paddy. *The Americanization of Emily: Shooting Script.* Electronic Edition. Alexandria, VA: Alexander Street Press, 2009.

Churchill, Winston. *A History of the English-Speaking Peoples*. Volume 3, *The Age of Revolution*. New York: Dodd, Mead, 1958.

Clarke, Frances. "So Lonesome I Could Die: Nostalgia and Debates over Emotional Control in the Civil War North." *Journal of Social History* 41, no. 2 (2007): 253–82.

———. *War Stories: Suffering and Sacrifice in the Civil War North*. Chicago: University of Chicago Press, 2011.

Clary, David A. *George Washington's First War: His Early Military Adventures*. New York: Simon and Schuster, 2011.

Coblentz, Stanton A. *From Arrow to Atom Bomb: The Psychological History of War*. New York: Beechhurst, 1953.

Coker, Christopher. "The Unhappy Warrior." *Historically Speaking* 7, no. 4 (2006): 34–47.

Collins, Randall. *Violence: A Micro-sociological Theory*. Princeton, NJ: Princeton University Press, 2008.

Colon, Alicia. "Heroes and Cowards." *New York Sun*, February 20, 2007, http://www.nysun.com/new-york/heroes-and-cowards/48926/.

Condron, Stephanie. "Haig's Son Attacks Pardoning of 306 Soldiers Shot for Cowardice." *Telegraph*, September 5, 2006, http://www.telegraph.co.uk/news/1528044/Haigs-son-attacks-pardoning-of-306-soldiers-shot-for-cowardice.html.

Confucius. *The Analects of Confucius (Lun Yu): A Literal Translation with an Introduction and Notes*. Translated by Chichung Huang. Oxford: Oxford University Press, 1997.

Conrad, Joseph. *Lord Jim: A Tale*. Edited by J. H. Stape and Ernest W. Sullivan II. New York: Cambridge University Press, 2011.

Cooper, James Fenimore. *The Spy: A Tale of the Neutral Ground*. New York: Heritage, 1963.

Costa, Dora L., and Matthew E. Kahn. *Heroes and Cowards: The Social Face of War*. Princeton, NJ: Princeton University Press, 2009.

Cowing, Cedric B. *The Great Awakening and the American Revolution: Colonial Thought in the 18th Century*. Chicago: Rand McNally, 1971.

Cox, Caroline. "Invisible Wounds: The American Legion, Shell-Shocked Veterans, and American Society, 1919–1924." In *Traumatic Pasts: History, Psychiatry, and Trauma in the Modern Age, 1870–1930*, edited by Mark S. Micale and Paul Lerner, 280–306. Cambridge: Cambridge University Press, 2001.

———. *A Proper Sense of Honor: Service and Sacrifice in George Washington's Army*. Chapel Hill: University of North Carolina Press.

Coyne, James. "But It's Not PTSD! Bad Research Distorts Our Understanding of a Serious Disorder." http://blogs.plos.org/mindthebrain/2013/07/23/but-its-not-ptsd-bad-research-distorts-our-understanding-of-a-serious-disorder/.

Crane, Stephen. *The Correspondence of Stephen Crane*. 2 vols. Edited by Stanley Wertheim and Paul Sorrentino. New York: Columbia University Press, 1988.

———. *The Red Badge of Courage: An Episode of the Civil War* (New York: Library of America, 2000).

———. "The Veteran." In *Tales of War*, edited by Fredson Bowers, 82–86. Charlottesville: University Press of Virginia, 1970.

Cress, Lawrence Delbert. *Citizens in Arms: The Army and the Militia in American Society to the War of 1812*. Chapel Hill: University of North Carolina Press, 1982.

Crosby, Alfred W. *Throwing Fire: Projectile Technology throughout History*. Cambridge: Cambridge University Press, 2002.

Cuordileone, K. A. *Manhood and Political Culture in the Cold War*. New York: Routledge, 2004.

Cunliffe, Marcus. *Soldiers and Civilians: The Martial Spirit in America, 1775–1865*. Boston: Little, Brown, 1968.

Cunningham, Terry. *14–18: The Final Word From The Trenches Of The First World War*. London: Stagedoor, 1993.

Dante. *The Divine Comedy of Dante Alighieri: Inferno*. Translated by Anthony Esolen. New York: Modern Library, 2005.

———. *The Divine Comedy of Dante Alighieri: Inferno: A Verse Translation*. Translated by Allen Mandelbaum. New York: Bantam, 1980.

Darwin, Charles. *The Descent of Man, and Selection in Relation to Sex* (1871). Reprint, Princeton, NJ: Princeton University Press, 1982.

Davies, Norman. *No Simple Victory: World War II in Europe, 1939–1945*. Penguin: New York, 2008.

Davies, Samuel. *Collected Poems of Samuel Davies*. Gainesville, FL: Scholars' Facsimiles and Reprints, 1968.

———. *The Curse of Cowardice: Preached to the Militia of Hanover County, in Virginia, at a General Muster, May 8, 1758 With a View to raise a Company for Captain Samuel Meredith*. London: Printed for J. Buckland, in Pater-Noster Row; J. Ward, in Cornhill, and T. Field, Cheapside, 1758.

Davis, Fred. *Yearning for Yesterday: A Sociology of Nostalgia*. New York: Free Press, 1979.

Dean, Eric T., Jr. *Shook over Hell: Post-Traumatic Stress, Vietnam, and the Civil War*. Cambridge, MA: Harvard University Press, 1997.

De Forest, John William. *Miss Ravenel's Conversion from Secession to Loyalty.* New York: Harper and Brothers, 1867.

D'Este, Carlo. *Patton: A Genius for War.* New York: HarperCollins, 1995.

De Waal, Frans. *Primates and Philosophers: How Morality Evolved.* Princeton, NJ: Princeton University Press, 2006.

Diaz, Junot. *This is How You Lose Her.* New York: Riverhead, 2012.

Dinter, Elmar. *Hero or Coward: Pressures Facing the Soldier in Battle.* London: Frank Cass, 1985.

Dinwiddie, Robert. *The Official Records of Robert Dinwiddie, Lieutenant-Governor of Virginia, 1751–1758.* 2 vols. Edited by R. A. Brock. New York: AMS, 1971 (1883–84).

Divine, Robert A. *The Reluctant Belligerent: American Entry Into World War II.* 2nd ed. New York: John Wiley and Sons, 1979.

Donald, David Herbert. *Liberty and Union: The Crisis of Popular Government 1830–1890.* Boston: Little, Brown, 1978.

Donoghue, Denis. *The Practice of Reading.* New Haven, CT: Yale University Press, 1998.

Dooley, John. *John Dooley, Confederate Soldier: His War Journal.* Edited by Joseph T. Durkin. Washington DC: Georgetown University Press, 1945.

Dos Passos, John. *Three Soldiers.* New York: Modern Library, 1932 (1921).

Dostoevsky, Fyodor. *Crime and Punishment.* Translated by Richard Pevear and Larissa Volokhonsky. New York: Vintage, 1993.

Douglass, Frederick. "The Union and How to Save It." *Douglass' Monthly,* February 1861. University of Rochester Frederick Douglass Project, http://www.lib.rochester.edu/index.cfm?PAGE=4375.

Dozier, Rush W. Jr. *Fear Itself: The Origin and Nature of the Powerful Emotion That Shapes Our Lives and Our World.* New York: St. Martin's, 1998.

D'Souza, Dinesh. Interview by Bill Maher, *Politically Incorrect,* ABC, September 17, 2001.

Dugatkin, Lee Alan. *The Altruism Equation: Seven Scientists Search for the Origins of Goodness.* Princeton, NJ: Princeton University Press, 2006.

Du Picq Ardant. *Battle Studies: Ancient and Modern Battle.* Translated by John N. Greely and Robert C. Cotton. New York: Macmillan, 1921.

Eder, Markus. *Crime and Punishment in the Royal Navy of the Seven Years' War.* Aldershot, England: Ashgate, 2004.

Eggleston, George Cary. *A Rebel's Recollections.* Cambridge, MA: Riverside, 1875.

Eisenhower, Dwight D. *Crusade in Europe.* Garden City, NY: Doubleday, 1948.

Eliot, T. S. *Collected Poems 1909–1962.* New York: Harcourt, Brace and World, 1962.

————. *Selected Prose of T. S. Eliot*. Edited by Frank Kermode. New York: Harcourt Brace Jovanovich, 1975.

Ellement, John R. "Attack Leaves Voter, 73, in Pain and Fear." *Boston Globe*, September 18, 2008, B1.

Ellet, Elizabeth Fries. *Women of the American Revolution*. 6th edition. 3 vols. New York: Charles Scribner's Sons, 1856.

Ellis, John. *The Sharp End of War: The Fighting Man in World War II*. North Pomfret, VT: David and Charles, 1980.

Emerson, Ralph Waldo. *Complete Essays and Other Writings of Ralph Waldo Emerson*. Edited by Brooks Atkinson. New York: Modern Library, 1950.

Empson, William. *The Complete Poems*. New York: Penguin Modern Classics, 2001.

Essame, H[erbert]. *Patton: A Study in Command*. New York: Charles Scribner's Sons, 1974.

Euripides, *Andromache*. Translated by Michael Lloyd. Warminster, England: Aris and Phillips, 1994.

Fadiman, Clifton. *Party of One: The Selected Writings of Clifton Fadiman*. Cleveland: World, 1955.

Faust, Drew Gilpin. "Christian Soldiers: The Meaning of Revivalism in the Confederate Army." In *The Civil War Soldier: A Historical Reader*, edited by Michael Barton and Larry M. Logue, 327–53. New York: New York University Press, 2002.

Fenton, Ben. "Pardoned: The 306 Soldiers Shot at Dawn for 'Cowardice.'" *Telegraph*, August 16, 2006, http://www.telegraph.co.uk/news/1526437/Pardoned-the-306-soldiers-shot-at-dawn-for-cowardice.html.

Ferling, John. *Almost a Miracle: The American Victory in the War of Independence*. New York : Oxford University Press, 2007.

————. "Soldiers for Virginia: Who Served in the French and Indian War?" *Virginia Magazine of History and Biography* 94 (1986): 307–28.

————. *A Wilderness of Miseries*: *War and Warriors in Early America*. Westport, CT: Greenwood, 1980.

Finn, Peter. "A Future for Drones: Automated Killing." *Washington Post*, September 19, 2011, http://articles.washingtonpost.com/2011–09–19/national/35273383_1_drones-human-target-military-base.

Firth, C. H., ed. *Naval Songs and Ballads*. London: Naval Records Society, 1908.

Fischer, Claude S. "Digital Humanities, Big Data, and Ngrams." *Boston Review*, June 20, 2013, https://www.bostonreview.net/blog/digital-humanities-big-data-and-ngrams.

Fischer, David Hackett and James C. Kelly. *Bound Away: Virginia and the Western Movement*. Charlottesville: University Press of Virginia, 2000.

Fleming, Thomas J. *Now We Are Enemies: The Story of Bunker Hill*. New York: St. Martin's, 1960.

Forbes, John. *Writings of General John Forbes Relating to His Service in North America*. Edited by Alfred Procter James. Menasha, Wisconsin: Collegiate, 1938.

Foucault, Michel. *Discipline and Punish: The Birth of the Prison*. Translated by Alan Sheridan. New York: Vintage, 1995 (1975).

Fowler, H. W. *A Dictionary of Modern English Usage*. Oxford: Clarendon Press, 1926.

Fowlie, Wallace. *A Reading of Dante's Inferno*. Chicago: University of Chicago Press, 1981.

Fox, Richard Wightman, and James T. Kloppenberg, eds. *A Companion to American Thought*. Malden, MA: Blackwell, 1998.

Frances, Allen, MD. "DSM5 in Distress," http://www.psychologytoday.com/blog/dsm5-in-distress.

Franklin, Benjamin. *Selections from Poor Richard's Almanack*. New York: Century, 1898.

Freccero, John. "Infernal Irony: The Gate of Hell." *Modern Language Notes* 98 (1983): 769–86.

Fredrickson, George M. *The Inner Civil War: Northern Intellectuals and the Crisis of the Union*. Urbana: University of Illinois Press, 1993.

Freehling, William W. *The Road to Disunion*. Vol. 2, *Secessionists Triumphant*. Oxford: Oxford University Press, 2007.

Frey, Sylvia M. "Courts and Cats: British Military Justice in the Eighteenth Century." *Military Affairs* 43 (1979): 5–11.

Frongia, Eugenio N. "Canto III: The Gate of Hell." In *Lectura Dantis: Inferno*, edited by Allen Mandelbaum, Anthony Oldcorn, and Charles Ross, 36–49. Berkeley and Los Angeles: University of California Press, 1998.

Frost, Robert. *Collected Poems, Prose and Plays*. New York: Library of America, 1995.

Gabriel, Richard. *No More Heroes: Madness and Psychiatry in War*. New York: Hill and Wang, 1987.

Gabriel, Richard A., and Karen Metz. *A Short History of War: The Evolution of Warfare and Weapons*. Professional Readings in Military Strategy No. 5. Carlisle Barracks, Pennsylvania: Strategic Studies Institute, U.S. Army War College, 1992.

Gandhi, Mahatma. *The Essential Gandhi: An Anthology*. Edited by Louis Fischer. New York: Random House, 1962.

———. *The Mind of Mahatma Gandhi*. Edited by R. K. Prabhu and U. R. Rao. Ahmedabad, India: Navajivan, 1967.

Garrett, George. *James Jones*. San Diego: Harcourt Brace Jovanovich, 1984.

Gibson, Thomas. "Raiding, Trading, and Tribal Autonomy in Insular Southeast Asia." In *The Anthropology of War*, edited by Jonathan Haas, 124–45. Cambridge: Cambridge University Press, 1990.

———. *Sacrifice and Sharing in the Philippine Highlands: Religion and Society among the Buid of Mindoro*. London: Athlone, 1986.

Gilbert, Arthur N. "British Military Justice during the American Revolution." *Eighteenth Century: Theory and Interpretation* 20, no. 1 (1979): 24–38.

———. "The Changing Face of British Military Justice, 1757–1783." *Military Affairs* 49, no. 2 (1985): 80–84.

Gilligan, James. *Preventing Violence*. New York: Thames and Hudson, 2001.

Glass, Charles. *The Deserters: A Hidden History of World War II*. New York: Penguin, 2012.

Glassner, Barry. *The Culture of Fear: Why Americans Are Afraid of the Wrong Things*. New York: Basic, 2009.

Glatthaar, Joseph T. *Forged in Battle: The Civil War Alliance of Black Soldiers and White Officers*. New York: Free Press, 1990.

Glick, Daniel. "Branded." *Salon*, June 9, 2004, http://www.salon.com/2004/06/09/georg_pogany/.

Goffman, Erving. *Stigma: Notes on the Management of Spoiled Identity*. Englewood Cliffs, NJ: Prentice-Hall, 1963.

Goldhagen, Daniel. *Hitler's Willing Executioners: Ordinary Germans and the Holocaust.* New York: Alfred A. Knopf, 1996.

Goldstein, Joshua S. *War and Gender: How Gender Shapes the War System and Vice Versa*. Cambridge: Cambridge University Press, 2001.

———. *Winning the War on War: The Decline of Armed Conflict Worldwide*. New York: Dutton, 2011.

Goleman, Daniel. *Vital Lies, Simple Truths: The Psychology of Self-Deception*. New York: Simon and Schuster, 1985.

Goodman, Amy. "Memorial Day Special . . . Winter Soldier on the Hill: War Vets Testify before Congress." May 25, 2009, http://www.democracynow.org/2009/5/25/memorial_day_specialwinter_soldier_on_the.

Goodwin, Doris Kearns. *Lyndon Johnson and the American Dream*. New York: Harper and Row, 1976.

Gordon, Lesley. "Confederate Cowards." Paper presented at the Annual Meeting of the Southern Historical Association, Atlanta, November 2005.

———. *"I Never Was a Coward": Questions of Bravery in a Civil War Regiment.* Milwaukee: Marquette University Press, 2005.

Gould, Joseph. *The Story of the Forty-Eighth.* Philadelphia: Regimental Association, 1908.

Grand, Sarah. "The Man of the Moment." *North American Review* 158 (1894): 620–27, http://www.jstor.org/stable/25103334.

Graves, Charles A. *The Forged Letter of General Robert E. Lee.* Richmond, VA: Richmond Press, 1914.

Gray, Jeffrey Alan. *The Psychology of Fear and Stress.* 2nd ed. Cambridge: Cambridge University Press, 1987.

Griffiths, Paul E. *What Emotions Really Are: The Problem of Psychological Categories.* Chicago: University of Chicago Press, 1997.

Grinker, Roy B., and John P. Spiegel. *War Neuroses.* Philadelphia: Blakiston, 1945.

Grossman, Dave. *On Killing: The Psychological Cost of Learning to Kill in War and Society.* Rev. ed. New York: Little, Brown, 2009.

Gullace, Nicoletta F. "White Feathers and Wounded Men: Female Patriotism and the Memory of the Great War." *Journal of British Studies* 36 (1997): 178–206.

Gummere, Richard M. "Samuel Davies: A Voice for Religious Freedom." In *Seven Wise Men of Colonial Virginia,* 41–49. Cambridge, MA: Harvard University Press, 1967.

Gustafson, Sandra M. *Eloquence Is Power: Oratory and Performance in Early America.* Chapel Hill: University of North Carolina Press, 1999.

Haidt, Jonathan. *The Righteous Mind: Why Good People Are Divided by Politics and Religion.* New York: Pantheon, 2012.

Haidt, Jonathan, and Craig Joseph. "Intuitive Ethics: How Innately Prepared Intuitions Generate Culturally Variable Virtues." *Daedalus* 133 (2004): 55–66.

Hamner, Christopher H. *Enduring Battle: American Soldiers in Three Wars, 1776–1945.* Lawrence: University Press of Kansas, 2011.

Hanson, Victor Davis. *The Western Way of War: Infantry Battle in Classical Greece.* 2nd ed. Berkeley and Los Angeles: University of California Press, 1989.

Harries, Meirion and Susie. *Soldiers of the Sun: The Rise and Fall of the Japanese Imperial Army.* New York: Random House, 1991.

Harris, Mary B. "How Provoking! What Makes Men and Women Angry?" *Aggressive Behavior* 19, no. 3 (1993): 199–211.

Hart, Donna, and Robert W. Sussman. *Man the Hunted: Primates, Predators, and Human Evolution.* New York: Westview, 2005.

Hartcup, Guy. *Camouflage: A History of Concealment and Deception in War.* New York: Charles Scribner's Sons, 1980.

Harvey, Douglas J. "Cowards." October 18, 2011, http://web.archive.org/web/20120423050939/http://www.shotatdawn.info/page7.html.

Hastings, Max. *Inferno: The World at War, 1939–1945.* New York: Alfred A. Knopf, 2011.

Hatlie, Mark R. "Memorial to Deserters in Ulm." http://sites-of-memory.de/main/ulmdeserters.html.

"Heilmittel gegen Feigheit" [Cures for Cowardice], excerpt translated and with commentary by H. L. Ansbacher. *Deutsche-Wehr; die zeitschrift fur wehrmacht und wehrpolitik Wehr,* November 1942, 20.

Heller, Joseph. *Catch-22.* New York: Simon and Schuster, 2011 (1961).

Hemingway, Ernest. *A Farewell to Arms.* New York: Charles Scribner's Sons, 1929.

———. *For Whom the Bell Tolls.* New York: Charles Scribner's Sons, 1940.

———. *Selected Letters 1917–1961.* Edited by Carlos Baker. New York: Charles Scribner's Sons, 1981.

Herek, Raymond J. *These Men Have Seen Hard Service: The First Michigan Sharpshooters in the Civil War.* Detroit: Wayne State University Press, 1998.

Hess, Earl J. *The Union Soldier in Battle: Enduring the Ordeal of Combat.* Lawrence: University Press of Kansas, 1997.

Hillenbrand, Laura. *Unbroken: A World War II Story of Survival, Resilience, and Redemption.* New York: Random House, 2010.

Hofstadter, Richard. *The Paranoid Style in American Politics and Other Essays.* Cambridge, MA: Harvard University Press, 1963.

Hoganson, Kristin. *Fighting for American Manhood: How Gender Politics Provoked the Spanish-American and Philippine-American Wars.* New Haven, CT: Yale University Press, 1998.

Holden, Wendy. *Shell Shock.* London: Channel 4, 1998.

Holmes, Richard. *Acts of War: The Behavior of Men in Battle.* New York: Free Press, 1986.

Homer. *The Iliad.* Translated by Stanley Lombardo. Indianapolis: Hackett, 1997.

Horace. *The Complete Odes and Epodes with the Centennial Hymn.* Translated by W. G. Shepherd. New York: Penguin, 1983.

Horgan, John. *The End of War.* San Francisco: McSweeney's, 2012.

Houston, Henry C. *The Thirty-Second Maine Regiment of Infantry Volunteers: A Historical Sketch.* Portland, ME: Southworth Brothers, 1903.

Hrdy, Sarah Blaffer. *Mothers and Others.* Cambridge, MA: Harvard University Press, 2009.

Huebner, Andrew J. *The Warrior Image: Soldiers in American Culture from the Second World War to the Vietnam Era.* Chapel Hill: University of North Carolina Press, 2008.

Huie, William Bradford. *The Execution of Private Eddie Slovik.* New York: Duell Sloan and Pierce, 1954.

Hunt, Winslow. "The Diffident Narcissist: A Character-Type Illustrated in *The Beast in the Jungle* by Henry James." *International Journal of Psychoanalysis* 76 (1995): 1257–67.

Isaac, Rhys. *The Transformation of Virginia.* Chapel Hill: University of North Carolina Press, 1982.

Jackall, Robert, ed. *Propaganda.* New York: New York University Press, 1995.

James, Henry. "The Beast in the Jungle." In *Complete Stories, 1898–1910,* 496–541. New York: Library of America, 1996.

James, William. "The Moral Equivalent of War." In *The Heart of William James,* edited by Robert Richardson, 301–14. Cambridge, MA: Belknap Press of Harvard University Press, 2010.

———. *Principles of Psychology.* Vol. 2. New York: Henry Holt, 1890.

Johnson, Samuel. *The Yale Edition of the Works of Samuel Johnson.* Volumes 3–4, *The Rambler.* New Haven, CT: Yale University Press, 1958.

Jones, C. P. "Stigma: Tattooing and Branding in Graeco-Roman Antiquity." *Journal of Roman Studies* 77 (1987): 139–55.

Jones, Edgar, and Simon Wessely. *Shell Shock to PTSD: Military Psychiatry from 1900 to the Gulf War.* London: Psychology Press, 2005.

Jones, James. "A Book Report on The Red Badge of Courage." In *The James Jones Reader: Outstanding Selections from His War Writings,* edited by James R. Giles and J. Michael Lennon, 387–93. Secaucus, NJ: Carol, 1991.

———. Interview by Nelson W. Aldrich Jr. In *Writers at Work: The "Paris Review" Interviews,* edited by George Plimpton, 231–250. Third Series. New York: Viking, 1967.

———. *To Reach Eternity: The Letters of James Jones.* Edited by George Hendrick. New York: Random House, 1989.

———. *The Thin Red Line.* New York: Delta, 1962.

———. *World War II: A Chronicle of Soldiering.* New York: Grosset and Dunlap, 1975.

Josephus, Flavius. *Antiquities of the Jews.* Translated by William Whiston. Hertfordshire, England: Wordsworth Classics, 1997.

Joyce, Richard. *The Evolution of Morality.* Cambridge: Bradford/MIT Press, 2006.

Juvonen, Jaana, Sandra Graham, and Mark A. Schuster. "Bullying among Young Adolescents: The Strong, the Weak and the Troubled." *Pediatrics* 112, no. 6 (2003): 1231–37.

Kafka, Franz. *The Trial*. Translated by Mike Mitchell. New York: Oxford University Press, 2009.

Kagan, Donald. *On the Origins of War and the Preservation of Peace*. New York: Doubleday, 1995.

Kamiya, Gary. "Obama's Call to Arms." *Salon*, January 27, 2009, http://www.salon.com/opinion/kamiya/2009/01/27/terror_2/.

Kang, John. "The Burdens of Manliness." *Harvard Journal of Law and Gender* 33, no. 2 (2010): 478–507.

Katchadourian, Herant A. *Guilt: The Bite of Conscience*. Stanford, CA: Stanford University Press, 2010.

Keegan, John. *The Face of Battle*. New York: Viking, 1976.

———. *A History of Warfare*. New York: Alfred A. Knopf, 1993.

Kelly-Hawkins, Emma Dunham. *Four Girls at Cottage City*. New York: Oxford University Press, 1988 (1895).

Kennedy, David. *Freedom from Fear: The American People in Depression and War, 1929–1945*. New York: Oxford University Press, 1999.

Kentsmith, David K. "Principles of Battlefield Psychiatry." *Military Medicine* 151 (1986): 89–95.

"Khaki in White House Better'n Pink." *New York Daily News*, October 10, 1952, 3.

Khan, Samir. "Blended Duality: Muslim and American?" *Inspire* 8 (1432/2011): 3, 9, http://azelin.files.wordpress.com/2012/05/inspire-magazine-8.pdf.

Kierkegaard, Søren. "Against Cowardice." In *Edifying Discourses*. Vol. 4, translated by David F. Swenson and Lillian Marvin Swenson, 75–111. Minneapolis: Augsburg, 1946.

King, Martin Luther, Jr. *A Testament of Hope: The Essential Writings and Speeches of Martin Luther King, Jr*. Edited by James Melvin Washington. San Francisco: HarperSanFrancisco, 1991.

———. "Why I Am Opposed to the War in Vietnam." Sermon at the Riverside Church, New York, April 30, 1967, http://www.lib.berkeley.edu/MRC/pacificaviet/riversidetranscript.html.

Kipling, Rudyard. *Complete Verse, Definitive Edition*. New York: Anchor, 1989.

Kirkland, John. *The Captain of Company K*. Chicago: Dibble, 1891.

Koontz, Colonel Amos R. "Psychiatry in the Next War: Shall We Again Waste Manpower?" *Military Surgeon* 103, no. 3 (1948): 197–202.

Lacey, A. R. *A Dictionary of Philosophy*. 2nd ed. London: Routledge, 1986.

Langley, Noel, Florence Ryerson, and Edgar Allan Woolf. *The Wizard of Oz: The Screenplay*. New York: Dell, 1989.

Larkin, Phillip. *Collected Poems*. New York: Farrar, Straus and Giroux, 1988.

Larson, Barbara A. "Samuel Davies and the Rhetoric of the New Light." *Speech Monographs* 38, no. 3 (1971): 207–16.

Laskas, Jeanne Marie. "The Coward." *GQ*, July 2004, 106–12, 159–61.

Lasswell, Harold D., Daniel Lerner, and Hans Speier, eds. *Propaganda and Communication in World History*. 2 vols. Honolulu: University Press of Hawaii, 1979–1980.

Lazenby, John F. "The Killing Zone." In *Hoplites: The Classical Greek Battle Experience*, edited by Victor Davis Hanson, 87–109. London: Routledge, 1991.

Leach, Douglas Edward. *Roots of Conflict: British Armed Forces and Colonial Americans, 1677–1763*. Chapel Hill: University of North Carolina Press, 1986.

Lendon, J. E. *Soldiers and Ghosts: A History of Battle in Classical Antiquity*. New Haven, CT: Yale University Press, 2005.

Leonard, Elizabeth D. *Lincoln's Avengers: Justice, Revenge, and Reunion after the Civil War*. New York: W. W. Norton, 2004.

Levi, Primo. *The Drowned and the Saved*. Translated by Raymond Rosenthal. New York: Summit, 1988.

Levinson, Richard, and William Link. *Stay Tuned: An Inside Look at the Making of Prime-Time Television*. New York: St. Martin's, 1981.

Lincoln, Abraham. *Collected Works of Abraham Lincoln*. Vol. 4, edited by Roy P. Basler. New Brunswick, NJ: Rutgers University Press, 1953.

Linderman, Gerald. *Embattled Courage: The Experience of Combat in the American Civil War*. New York: Macmillan, 1987.

Livermore, Mary Ashton Rice. *My Story of the War*. New York: Arno, 1972 (1889).

Lowry, Thomas P. "Research Note: New Access to a Civil War Resource." *Civil War History* 49, no. 1 (2003): 52–63.

———. *Tarnished Eagles: The Courts-Martial of Fifty Union Colonels and Lieutenant Colonels*. Mechanicsburg, PA: Stackpole, 1997.

MacShane, Frank. *Into Eternity: The Life of James Jones, American Writer*. Boston: Houghton Mifflin, 1985.

Manchester, William. *Goodbye, Darkness: A Memoir of the Pacific War*. New York: Viking, 1979.

Manning, Chandra. *What This Cruel War Was Over: Soldiers, Slavery, and the Civil War*. New York: Alfred A. Knopf, 2007.

Manual for Courts-Martial United States. 2008 ed. http://www.loc.gov/rr/frd/Military_Law/pdf/MCM-2008.pdf.

Marshall, S.L.A. *Men against Fire: The Problem of Battle Command in Future War*. New York: William Morrow, 1947.

Martin, Mike W. *From Morality to Mental Health: Virtue and Vice in a Therapeutic Culture*. New York: Oxford University Press, 2006.

Maslowski, Pete. "A Study of Morale in Civil War Soldiers." In *The Civil War Soldier: A Historical Reader*, edited by Michael Barton and Larry M. Logue, 312–326. New York: New York University Press, 2002.

Mason, A.E.W. *The Four Feathers*. London: John Murray, 1960.

"A Matter of Rank." *Richmond News Leader*, May 30, 1970, 14.

Mayer, Henry. *A Son of Thunder: Patrick Henry and the American Revolution*. New York: Grove, 1986.

McCracken, Ken. "You Haven't Earned the Right to Be 'War-Weary,'" September 8, 2007, http://www.willms.com/archives/2007/09/you_havent_earn.html.

McDougall, Walter A. *Freedom Just Around the Corner: A New American History, 1585–1828*. New York: HarperCollins, 2004.

McHugh, Paul, and Glenn Treisman. "PTSD: A Problematic Diagnostic Category." *Journal of Anxiety Disorders* 21 (2007): 211–22.

McIntyre, Alisdair C. *After Virtue: A Study in Moral Theory*. Notre Dame, IN: University of Notre Dame Press, 1981.

McNally, Richard J. "Conceptual Problems with the DSM IV Criteria." In *Posttraumatic Stress Disorder: Issues and Controversies*, edited by Gerald M. Rosen, 1–14. Sussex, England: John Wiley and Sons, 2004.

McPherson, James M. *Battle Cry of Freedom: The Civil War Era*. New York: Oxford University Press, 1988.

———. *For Cause and Comrades: Why Men Fought in the Civil War*. New York: Oxford University Press, 1997.

McTiernan, David. "The Novel as 'Neutral Ground': Genre and Ideology in Cooper's *The Spy*." *Studies in American Fiction* 25, no. 1 (1997): 3–15.

Meno, Joe. *The Great Perhaps: A Novel*. New York: W. W. Norton, 2009.

Mercer, Alexander Cavalié. *Journal of the Waterloo Campaign*. London: Greenhill, 1985 (1870).

Miller, William Ian. *The Mystery of Courage*. Cambridge, MA: Harvard University Press, 2000.

Millett, Allan R., and Peter Maslowski. *For the Common Defense: A Military History of the United States of America*. 2nd ed. New York: Free Press, 1994.

Millis, Walter. *Arms and Men: A Study in American Military History*. New York: G. P. Putnam's Sons, 1956.

Mills, David. "The Dreams of Bunyan and Langland." In *The Pilgrim's Progress: Critical and Historical Views*, edited by Vincent Newey, 154–81. Totowa, NJ: Barnes and Noble, 1980.

Mitchell, Reid. *Civil War Soldiers*. New York: Viking, 1988.

Monluc, Blaise de. *The Habsburg-Valois Wars and the French Wars of Religion*. Translated by Charles Cotton (1674); edited by Ian Roy. London: Longman, 1971 (1592).

Montague, Ashley. "Natural Selection and the Origin and Evolution of Weeping in Man." *Journal of the American Medical Association* 174 (1960): 130–35.

Montaigne, Michel de. *The Complete Essays of Montaigne*. Translated by Donald Frame. Stanford, CA: Stanford University Press, 1958.

Moore, William. *The Thin Yellow Line*. New York: St. Martin's, 1975.

Moran, Charles. *The Anatomy of Courage*. 2nd ed. London: Constable, 1966.

Morford, Henry. *The Coward: A Novel of Society and the Field in 1863*. Philadelphia: T. B. Peterson, 1864.

Morris, Peter. *Baseball Fever: Early Baseball in Michigan*. Ann Arbor: University of Michigan Press, 2003.

Moser, Richard R. *The New Winter Soldiers: GI and Veteran Dissent during the Vietnam Era*. New Brunswick, NJ: Rutgers University Press, 1996.

Mothersill, Mary. "Duty." In *The Encyclopedia of Philosophy*, edited by Paul Edwards, 443. New York: Macmillan, 1967.

Murdock, Eugene Converse. *One Million Men: The Civil War Draft in the North*. Madison: State Historical Society of Wisconsin, 1971.

Murray, Williamson, and Allan R. Millett, eds. *Military Innovations in the Interwar Period*. Cambridge: Cambridge University Press, 1996.

Neagles, James C. *Summer Soldiers: A Survey and Index of Revolutionary War Courts-Martial*. Salt Lake City: Ancestry Inc., 1986.

Neely, Mark E., and Harold Holzer. *The Union Image: Popular Prints of the Civil War*. Chapel Hill: University of North Carolina Press, 2000.

Nelson, Judith Kay. *Seeing through Tears: Crying and Attachment*. New York: Routledge, 2005.

Nelson, Randy F. *The Almanac of American Letters*. Los Angeles: William Kaufman, 1981.

"Nervous Manifestations Due to the Winds of High Explosives." *Lancet* 2 (1915): 348.

Newcomb, Robert Howard. "The Sources of Benjamin Franklin's Sayings of Poor Richard." PhD diss., University of Maryland, 1957.

Nisbett, Richard, and Dov Cohen. *Culture of Honor: The Psychology of Violence in the South*. New York: Westview, 1996.

"No Coward's Death Mars U.S. in France." *New York Times*, December 28, 1944, 1.

Nussbaum, Martha C. *Hiding from Humanity: Disgust, Shame, and the Law*. Princeton, NJ: Princeton University Press, 2004.

Obama, Barack. "Nobel Prize Acceptance Speech," http://www.whitehouse
.gov/the-press-office/remarks-president-acceptance-nobel-peace-prize.

O'Brien, Tim. *Going After Cacciato: A Novel.* New York: Delacorte/S. Lawrence, 1978.

———. *The Things They Carried.* New York: Penguin, 1990.

Oggel, L. Terry. "Speaking Out about Race: 'The United States of Lyncherdom' Clemens Really Wrote." In *Prospects: An Annual of American Cultural Studies,* vol. 25, edited by Jack Salzman, 115–58. New York: Cambridge University Press, 2000.

"Order No. 227 by the People's Commissar of Defence of the USSR." Wikisource, http://www.en.wikisource.org/windex.php?title=Order_No._227_by_the_People%27s_Commissar_of_Defence_of_the_USSR&oldid=2977000.

Oren, Michael B. "Fleeing Moment: A Cultural History of Desertion." *New Republic,* June 17, 2009, http://www.tnr.com/article/fleeing-moment.

Paine, Thomas. *Paine: Political Writings.* Cambridge: Cambridge University Press, 2000.

———. *Selections: Collected Writings.* New York: Library of America, 1995.

Palmer, John M. *Baron von Steuben.* New Haven, CT: Yale University Press, 1937.

Palmer, Thomas A. "Why We Fight: A Study of Indoctrination Activities in the Armed Forces." In *The Military in America, From the Colonial Era to the Present,* new rev. ed., edited by Peter Karsten, 381–94. New York: Free Press, 1986.

Parker, Tony. *The Violence of Our Lives: Interviews with American Murderers.* New York: Henry Holt, 1995.

Petrosino, Anthony, Carolyn Turpin-Petrosino, and John Buehler. "'Scared Straight' and Other Juvenile Awareness Programs for Preventing Juvenile Delinquency: A Systematic Review of the Randomized Experimental Evidence." *Annals of the American Academy of Political and Social Science* 589 (2003): 41–62.

Phillips, Jason. *Diehard Rebels: The Confederate Culture of Invincibility.* Athens: University of Georgia Press, 2007.

Picchio Simonelli, Maria. *Lectura Dantis Americana: Inferno III.* Philadelphia: University of Pennsylvania Press, 1993.

Pike, Nathan, and Andrea Manica. "The Basis of Cowardice in Social Defenders." *Ecological Modeling* 196, nos. 3–4 (2006): 272–82.

Pilcher, George William. *Samuel Davies; Apostle of Dissent in Colonial Virginia.* Knoxville: University of Tennessee Press, 1971.

Pinker, Steven. *The Better Angels of Our Nature: Why Violence Has Declined.* New York: Viking, 2011.

Plato. *The Dialogues of Plato*. 4th ed. Translated by Benjamin Jowett. Oxford: Clarendon Press, 1964.

———. *Laches and Charmides*. Translated by Rosamond Kent Sprague. Indianapolis: Bobbs-Merrill, 1973.

———. *Plato's Symposium*. Translated by Seth Benardete. Chicago: University of Chicago Press, 2001.

Plutarch. *Plutarch's Moralia*. Vol. 3, translated by Frank Cole Babbitt. Cambridge, MA: Harvard University Press, 1931.

Polybius. *The Histories of Polybius*. Vol. 1, translated by Evelyn S. Shuckburgh. Bloomington, Indiana: Indiana University Press, 1962.

Pope, Dudley. *At Twelve Mr. Byng Was Shot*. Philadelphia: J. B. Lippincott, 1962.

Potter, David M. *The Impending Crisis, 1848–1861*. Completed and edited by Don E. Fehrenbacher. New York: Harper Torchbooks, 1976.

Powers, Kevin. *Yellow Birds*. New York: Little, Brown, 2012.

Purdum, Todd S., and Elizabeth Bumiller. "Threats and Responses: Legislation; Congress Nearing Draft Resolution on Force." *New York Times*, September 27, 2002, A18.

Purdy, Jedediah. *For Common Things: Irony, Trust, and Commitment in America Today*. New York: Alfred A. Knopf, 1999.

Putkowski, Julian. "War Pardons." October 18, 2011, http://web.archive.org/web/20110618042624/http://www.shotatdawn.info/page20.html.

Ramold, Steven J. *Baring the Iron Hand: Discipline in the Union Army*. DeKalb: Northern Illinois University Press, 2011.

Remarque, Erich Maria. *All Quiet on the Western Front*. Translated by A. W. Wheen. New York: Fawcett Crest, 1928.

Renfroe, J.J.D. *"The Battle Is God's": A Sermon Preached before Wilcox's Brigade*. Richmond, VA: n.p., 1863. Confederate Imprints Microfilm Series 4186.

Rice, John Holt. "Memoir of the Rev. Samuel Davies." *The Virginia Evangelical and Literary Magazines* 1 (1819): 112–19, 186–88, 201–17, 329–35, 353–63, 474–79, 560–67.

Rieff, Phillip. *The Triumph of the Therapeutic*. New York: Harper and Row, 1966.

Rilke, Rainer Maria. *Letters to a Young Poet*. Rev. ed. Translated by M. D. Herter Norton. New York: W. W. Norton, 1954.

Ritchie, Elspeth Cameron. "An Easier PTSD Diagnosis." *Time*, May 14, 2013, http://nation.time.com/2013/05/14/an-easier-ptsd-diagnosis/#ixzz2f5nnH8tW.

Rizzolatti, Giacomo, and Corrado Sinigaglia. *Mirrors in the Brain: How Our Minds Share Actions, Emotions, and Experience*. New York: Oxford University Press, 2008.

Robarcheck, Clayton A. "Learning to Fear: A Case Study of Emotional Conditioning." *American Ethnologist* 6, no. 3 (1979): 555–67.

Robertson, James I. *Soldiers Blue and Gray*. Columbia: University of South Carolina Press, 1988.

Robinson, Paul. *Military Honour and the Conduct of War: From Ancient Greece to Iraq*. London: Routledge, 2006.

Rogers, Alan. *Empire and Liberty: American Resistance to British Authority*. Berkeley and Los Angeles: University of California Press, 1974.

Rollman, Robert O. "Of Crimes, Courts-Martial and Punishment—A Short History of Military Justice." *JAG Law Review* 11, no. 2 (1969): 212–22.

Roosevelt, Theodore. *America at War*. New York: Charles Scribner's Sons, 1915.

———. *The Letters of Theodore Roosevelt*. Vol. 8, *The Days of Armageddon 1914–1919*, edited by Elting E. Morison. Cambridge, MA: Harvard University Press, 1954.

———. *The Rough Riders: An Autobiography*. Edited by Louis Auchincloss. New York: Library of America, 2004 (1899).

———. *The Strenuous Life: Essays and Addresses*. New York: Century, 1904.

Rosen, Gerald M., ed. *Posttraumatic Stress Disorder: Issues and Controversies*. Sussex, England: John Wiley and Sons, 2004.

Rosenberg, Bruce A. "James Fenimore Cooper's *The Spy* and the Neutral Ground." *American Transcendental Quarterly*, n.s., 6, no. 1 (1992): 5–16.

Rothfield, Lawrence. *Vital Signs: Medical Realism in Nineteenth-Century Fiction*. Princeton, NJ: Princeton University Press, 1992.

Royster, Charles. *A Revolutionary People at War: The Continental Army and American Character*. Chapel Hill: Institute of Early American History and Culture/University of North Carolina Press, 1979.

"Saddam's Message of Friendship to President Bush." Wikileaks, https://www.wikileaks.org/plusd/cables/90BAGHDAD4237_a.html.

Safire, William. "Infamy: Words of the War on Terror." *New York Times Magazine*, September 23, 2011, 32.

Samet, Elizabeth. *Soldier's Heart: Reading Literature through Peace and War at West Point*. New York: Farrar, Straus and Giroux, 2007.

———. *Willing Obedience: Citizens, Soldiers, and the Progress of Consent in America, 1776–1898*. Stanford, CA: Stanford University Press, 2004.

Saro-Wiwa, Ken. *Sozaboy: A Novel in Rotten English*. London: Longman, 1994.

Sartre, Jean-Paul. *The Devil and the Good Lord and Two Other Plays*. Translated by Kitty Black. New York: Vintage, 1962.

———. *Existentialism and Human Emotions*. Translated by Bernard Frechtman. New York: Citadel, 1985 (1957).

Sassoon, Siegfried. *The War Poems of Siegfried Sassoon*. London: Faber and Faber, 1983.

Sawyer, Charles Winthrop. *Firearms in American History*. Vol. 1, *The Colonial Period*. Boston: Author, c. 1910–20.

Scarry, Elaine. *The Body in Pain: The Making and Unmaking of the World*. New York: Oxford University Press, 1985.

Scheer, George F., and Hugh F. Rankin. *Rebels and Redcoats: The American Revolution through the Eyes of Those Who Fought and Lived It*. Cleveland: World, 1957.

Schmid, Walter T. *On Manly Courage: A Study of Plato's Laches*. Carbondale: Southern Illinois University Press, 1992.

Semmes, Harry H. *Portrait of Patton*. New York: Paperback Library, 1955.

Sewall, Richard B. *The Life of Emily Dickinson*. New York: Farrar, Straus and Giroux, 1974.

Shapiro, Joseph. "A Wounded Soldier Struggles to Adapt." *Morning Edition*, National Public Radio, November 29, 2005, http://www.npr.org/templates /story/story.php?storyId=5030571.

Sheehan, James J. *Where Have All the Soldiers Gone? The Transformation of Modern Europe*. Boston: Houghton Mifflin, 2008.

Sheehan, William, Richard J. Roberts, Steven Thurber, and Mary Ann Roberts. "Shell Shocked and Confused: A Reconsideration of Captain Myers's Case Reports of Shell-Shock in World War One." *Priory Psychiatry* 2 (2009), http://priory.com/psychiatry/ptsdshellshock.htm.

Shephard, Ben. "The Neuroses of War." Review of *From Shell Shock to Combat Stress: A Comparative History of Military Psychiatry* by Hans Binneveld and *Shell-Shock: A History of the Changing Attitudes to War Neurosis* by Anthony Babington. *Times Literary Supplement*, August 28, 1998, 8.

———. "Risk Factors and PTSD: A Historian's Perspective." In *Posttraumatic Stress Disorder: Issues and Controversies*, edited by Gerald M. Rosen, 39–61. (Sussex, England: John Wiley and Sons, 2004).

———. *A War of Nerves*. London: Jonathan Cape, 2000.

Shively, Sharon B., and Daniel P. Perl. "Traumatic Brain Injury, Shell Shock, and Posttraumatic Stress Disorder in the Military—Past, Present, and Future." *Journal of Head Trauma Rehabilitation* 27 (2012): 234–39.

"Shot at Dawn, Pardoned 90 Years On." BBC News, August 16, 2006, http:// news.bbc.co.uk/2/hi/uk_news/england/4798025.stm.

Shy, John. *A People Numerous and Armed: Reflections on the Military Struggle for American Independence*. Rev. ed. Ann Arbor: University of Michigan Press, 1990.

Silber, Nina. *The Romance of Reunion: Northerners and the South, 1865–1900*. Chapel Hill: University of North Carolina Press, 1993.

Sills, David L., ed. *International Encyclopedia of the Social Sciences*. New York: Macmillan, 1968.

Simpson, Louis. *Collected Poems*. New York: Paragon House, 1988.

Singer, Emily. "Brain Trauma in Iraq." *Technology Review*, May–June 2008, http://m.technologyreview.com/biomedicine/20571/.

Singer, J. David, and Melvin Small. *The Wages of War 1816–1965*. New York: John Wiley and Sons, 1970.

Singer, Peter. *The Expanding Circle: Ethics, Evolution, and Moral Progress*. First paperback ed. Princeton, NJ: Princeton University Press, 2011.

Singer, P. W. *Wired for War: The Robotics Revolution and Conflict in the Twenty-First Century*. New York: Penguin, 2009.

Skinner, Quentin. "Meaning and Understanding in the History of Ideas." *History and Theory* 8, no. 1 (1969): 3–53.

Sledge, Eugene B. *With the Old Breed, at Peleliu and Okinawa*. Novato, CA: Presidio, 1981.

Small, Melvin. *Antiwarriors: The Vietnam War and the Battle for America's Hearts and Minds*. Lanham, MD: Rowman and Littlefield, 2002.

Smart, Charles. *The Medical and Surgical History of the War of the Rebellion.* Part 3, vol. 1, *Medical History*. Washington, DC: Government Printing Office, 1888.

Smith, Adam. *The Theory of Moral Sentiments*. Edited by Knud Haakonssen. Cambridge: Cambridge University Press, 2002.

Snyder, Jeffrey R. "A Nation of Cowards." *Public Interest* 113 (1993): 40–55.

Sommers, Christina Hoff, and Sally Satel. *One Nation under Therapy: How the Helping Culture Is Eroding Self-Reliance*. New York: St. Martin's, 2005.

Sommerville, Diane Miller. "'A Burden Too Heavy to Bear': War Trauma, Suicide and Confederate Soldiers." *Civil War History* 59, no. 4 (2013): 453–91.

Sontag, Susan. "Talk of the Town." *New Yorker*, September 24, 2001, 28.

Southey, Robert. *Life of Nelson*. New York: Thomas Y. Crowell, 1901.

Spierenburg, Pieter. "Masculinity, Violence, and Honor: An Introduction." In *Men and Violence: Gender, Honor, and Rituals in Modern Europe and America*, edited by Pieter Spierenburg, 1–29. Columbus: Ohio State University Press, 1998.

Stafford, William. *Stories That Could Be True: New and Collected Poems.* New York: Harper and Row, 1977.

Steckel, Richard H. "Stature and the Standard of Living." *Journal of Economic Literature* 33 (1995): 1903–1940.

Stephen, James Fitzjames. *Essays by a Barrister*. London: Smith, Elder, 1862.

Stouffer, Samuel A., Arthur A. Lumsdaine, Marion Harper Lumsdaine, Robin M. Williams Jr., M. Brewster Smith, Irving L. Janis, Shirley A. Star, and Leonard S. Cottrell Jr. *The American Soldier: Combat and Its Aftermath*. Studies in Social Psychology in World War II, vol. 2. Princeton, NJ: Princeton University Press, 1949.

Stout, Harry S. *Upon the Altar of the Nation: A Moral History of the American Civil War*. New York: Viking, 2006.

Stowe, Harriet Beecher. "Introduction." In William C. Nell, *The Colored Patriots of the American Revolution*, 5–6. Boston: Robert F. Wallcut, 1855.

Strecker, Edward A. "Military Psychiatry: World War I 1917–1918." In American Psychological Association, *One Hundred Years of American Psychiatry*, 385–416. New York: Columbia University Press, 1944.

Susskind, Joshua M., Daniel H. Lee, Andrée Cusi, Roman Feiman, Wojtek Grabski, and Adam K. Anderson. "Expressing Fear Enhances Sensory Acquisition." *Nature Neuroscience* 11 (2008): 843–50.

Swett, Samuel. *History of Bunker-Hill Battle. With a Plan*. 2nd ed. Boston: Munroe and Frances, 1825.

Taylor, Charles. *Sources of the Self: The Making of the Modern Identity*. Cambridge, MA: Harvard University Press, 1989.

Theophrastus. *Characters and Observations: An Eighteenth Century Manuscript*. London: J. Murray, 1930.

Thomsen, Lotte, Willem E. Frankenhuis, McCaila Ingold-Smith, and Susan Carey. "Big and Mighty: Preverbal Infants Mentally Represent Social Dominance." *Science* 331, no. 6016 (2011): 477–80.

Thoreau, Henry David. *Walden: A Fully Annotated Edition*. Edited by Jeffrey S. Cramer. New Haven, CT: Yale University Press, 2004.

———. *The Writings of Henry David Thoreau*. Vol. 6, *Journal 1853*. Princeton, NJ: Princeton University Press, 2000.

Thucydides. *History of the Peloponnesian War: The Complete Hobbes Translation*. Chicago: University of Chicago Press, 1989.

Tillson, Albert H., Jr. "The Militia and Popular Political Culture in the Upper Valley of Virginia." *Virginia Magazine of History and Biography* 94, no. 3 (1986): 285–306.

Titus, James. *The Old Dominion at War: Society, Politics and Warfare in Late Colonial Virginia*. Columbia: University of South Carolina Press, 1991.

Tocqueville, Alexis de. *Democracy in America*. Translated by Harvey C. Mansfield and Delba Winthrop. University of Chicago Press, 2000.

Tracy, Jessica L., and David Matsumoto. "The Spontaneous Expression of Pride and Shame: Evidence for Biologically Innate Nonverbal Displays." *Proceedings of the National Academy of Science* 105, no. 33 (2008): 11655–660.

"Tribute to WWI 'Cowards.'" BBC News, June 21, 2001, http//news.bbc.co.uk/2/hi/uk_news/1399983.

Trivers, Robert. *The Folly of Fools: The Logic of Deceit and Self-Deception in Human Life*. New York: Basic Books, 2011.

Tucker, Glenn. *Hancock the Superb*. Indianapolis: Bobbs Merrill, 1960.

Tunstall, Brian. *Admiral Byng and the Battle for Minorca*. London: Philip Allan, 1928.

Twain, Mark. *Collected Tales, Sketches, Speeches, and Essays 1852–1890*. New York: Library of America, 1992.

———. *Mark Twain in Eruption: Hitherto Unpublished Pages about Men and Events*. Edited by Bernard DeVoto. New York: Grosset and Dunlap, 1940.

———. *Mark Twain's Notebook*. Edited by Albert Paine. New York: Harper and Brothers, 1935.

———. "The United States of Lyncherdom." In *Prospects: An Annual of American Cultural Studies*, vol. 25, edited by Jack Salzman, 139–50. New York: Cambridge University Press, 2000.

Twitchell, James B. *For Shame: The Loss of Common Decency in American Culture*. New York: St. Martin's, 1997.

"Two Placards of the Past Week." *Harvard Alumni Bulletin* 19, no. 21 (1917): 409.

Unger, David C. *The Emergency State: America's Pursuit of Absolute Security at All Costs*. New York: Penguin, 2012.

U.S. Department of Commerce, Bureau of the Census. *Historical Statistics of the United States: Colonial Times to 1970*. Washington, DC: Government Printing Office, 1976.

U.S. Department of State, Office of the Historian. "Document 77: Memorandum for the Record." In *Foreign Relations of the United States, 1964–1968*. Vol. 2, *Vietnam, January–June 1965*, http://history.state.gov/historicaldocuments/frus1964–68v02/d77.

U.S. Department of Veterans Affairs. "VA Simplifies Access to Health Care and Benefits for Veterans with PTSD." Press release, July 12, 2010, http://www1.va.gov/opa/pressrel/pressrelease.cfm?id=1922.

"U.S.-Dropped Leaflets Show Bin Laden in Western Clothes," CNN, January 4, 2002, http://www.cnn.com/2002/US/01/04/ret.bin.laden.leaflets/.

U.S. War Department. *Army Life*. Pamphlet 21–13. Washington, DC: Government Printing Office, 1944.

———. *Revised Regulations for the Army of the United States, 1861*. Philadelphia: J. B. Lippincott, 1861.

Van Creveld, Martin. *The Culture of War*. New York: Ballantine, 2008.

Varon, Elizabeth R. *Disunion! The Coming of the American Civil War, 1789–1859*. Chapel Hill: University of North Carolina Press, 2008.

Walker, Stephen. *Forgotten Soldiers: The Irishmen Shot at Dawn*. Dublin: Gill and Macmillan, 2007.

Wallace, James D. "Cowardice and Courage." In *Studies in Ethics*, 97–108. Oxford: Basil Blackwell, 1973.

Walsh, Chris. "'Cowardice, Weakness or Infirmity, Whichever It May Be Termed': A Shadow History of the Civil War." *Civil War History* 59, no. 4 (2013): 492–526.

Walton, Douglas N. *Courage: A Philosophical Investigation*. Berkeley and Los Angeles: University of California Press, 1986.

Ward, Harry M. *George Washington's Enforcers: Policing the Continental Army*. Carbondale: Southern Illinois University Press, 2006.

Ward, Matthew C. *Breaking the Backcountry: The Seven Years' War in Virginia and Pennsylvania*. Pittsburgh: University of Pittsburgh Press, 2003.

Warner, Joel. "The Good Soldier." *Denver Westword News*, March 20, 2008, http://www.westword.com/2008–03–20/news/the-good-soldier/.

———. *The Papers of George Washington*. Digital ed., edited by Theodore J. Crackel. Charlottesville: University of Virginia Press/Rotunda, 2008.

Watson, Ritchie Devon, Jr. *Normans and Saxons: Southern Race Mythology and the Intellectual History of the American Civil War*. Baton Rouge: Louisiana State University Press, 2008.

Webster, Noah. *An American Dictionary of the English language*. Rev. by Chauncey A. Goodrich and Noah Porter. Springfield, MA: G. and C. Merriam, 1864.

Weinstein, James. "Anti-War Sentiment and the Socialist Party, 1917–1918." In *The Causes and Consequences of World War I*, edited by John Milton Cooper, 224–49. New York: Quadrangle, 1972.

Welch, Stephen R. "Commemorating 'Heroes of a Special Kind': Deserter Monuments in Germany." *Journal of Contemporary History* 47, no. 2 (2012): 370–401.

Wessely, Simon. "The Life and Death of Private Harry Farr." *Journal of the Royal Society of Medicine* 99, no. 9 (2006): 440–43.

White, Patrick. *The Twyborn Affair: A Novel*. New York: Viking, 1980.

Wiley, Bell Irvin. *The Life of Billy the Yank: The Common Soldier of the Union*. Updated ed. Baton Rouge: Louisiana State University Press, 2008.

Wilmot, John, Earl of Rochester. *The Complete Poems of John Wilmot, the Earl of Rochester*. Edited by David M. Vieth. New Haven, CT: Yale University Press, 1968.

Williams, Kayla. *Love My Rifle More Than You: Young and Female in the U.S. Army*. New York: W. W. Norton, 2005.

Wilson, David Sloan. *Evolution for Everyone: How Darwin's Theory Can Change the Way We Think about Our Lives*. New York: Delacorte, 2007.

Wilson, E. O. *The Social Conquest of Earth*. New York: Liveright, 2012.

Winthrop, William. *Military Law and Precedents*. New York: Arno, 1979 (1920).

Wolcott, James. "From Fear to Eternity." *Vanity Fair*, March 2005, 227–28.

Wolfe, James. *Life and Letters of James Wolfe*. Edited by Beckles Wilson. London: W. Heinemann, 1909.

Woodham, Rebecca. "William Bradford Huie." *Encyclopedia of Alabama*, http://www.encyclopediaofalabama.org/face/Article.jsp?id=h-1547.

Woolf, Virginia. *Three Guineas*. New York: Harvest, 1966.

Wright, James. *Those Who Have Borne the Battle: A History of America's Wars and Those Who Fought Them*. New York: Public Affairs, 2012.

Wyatt-Brown, Bertram. *The Shaping of Southern Culture: Honor, Grace, and War 1760s–1890s*. Chapel Hill: University of North Carolina. Press, 2001.

———. *Southern Honor: Ethics and Behavior in the Old South*. Oxford: Oxford University Press, 1982.

———. *Yankee Saints and Southern Sinners*. Baton Rouge: Louisiana State University Press, 1986.

Yoelia, Moshe Hoffman, David G. Rand, and Martin A Nowak. "Powering Up with Indirect Reciprocity in a Large-Scale Field Experiment." *Proceedings of the National Academy of Science* 110 (2013): 10424–29, http://www.pnas.org/content/early/2013/06/04/1301210110.

Zobel, Hiller B. *The Boston Massacre*. New York: W. W. Norton, 1970.

Zwerdling, Daniel. "Former Soldier Helps Others Fight Army for Help." *Weekend Edition Saturday*, National Public Radio, July 7, 2007, http://www.npr.org/templates/story/story.php?storyId=11782535.

Zwingmann, Charles A. A. "'Heimweh' or 'Nostalgic Reaction': A Conceptual Analysis and Interpretation of a Medico-Psychological Phenomenon." PhD diss., Stanford University, 1959.

COLLECTIONS

Court-martial cases from the Civil War; all appear in Record Group No. 153, National Archives, Washington, DC:

Private Henry Barker, file MM437.
Private Mitchell Bernard, file MM444.
Private Samuel Clements, file LL3119.
Lieutenant Hooker DeLand, file NN2032.
Privates Benjamin Erway, file NN3420.
Private Archibald Gilchrist, file LL3020.
Private Edward Hughes, file NN3470.
Lieutenant John King, file LL294.
Lieutenant Ferdinand Ornesi, file KK5.
Lieutenant Moses Powell, file NN2032.
Private Frank A. Schmeisser, file KK347.

Private Charles Shuter, file NN3420.
Private Simon Snyder, file MM441.
Private Joseph C. Waldron, file NN2699.
Private Daniel J. Webber, file LL663.
Private Andrew Whack, file NN2699.

Pogany, Georg-Andreas. Georg-Andreas Pogany Collection (AFC/2001/001/
34120). Veterans History Project. American Folklife Center. Library of
Congress.

ILLUSTRATION CREDITS

INDEX

NOTE: Page numbers followed by *f* indicate a figure.

Beirut (Lebanon), 41
Bennett, Paul G., 147
Beowulf, 49–50
Bernard, Mitchell, 186
Bierce, Ambrose, 83, 231n46
bin Laden, Osama: on American coward-
 ice, 3, 21, 41–43; portrayal as coward
 of, 42, 43, 187
blind spots, 190–91, 247–48nn75–76
Booth, John Wilkes, 34
Bosnia War syndrome, 151
Boston Marathon bombings, 1–4, 9, 44,
 168, 187, 199n4
Boston Massacre, 27
Bowman, James, 167
Branded television show, 17, 58
branding, 139–40, 236nn16–17, 236n19
Braudy, Leo, 58, 215n45
Bristed, Charles Astor, 207n43
Brontë, Emily, 187–88
Brooks, William, 214n42
Brown, Richard Maxwell, 244n18
Brumwell, Stephen, 229n29
Brunner, Elgin Medea, 210n65
bucking and gagging, 103–4
Buddha, 51
Buid people, 46–48, 50
Bulgakov, Mikhail, 1
bullies, 9, 61–62, 168, 243n11
Bunyan, John, 221n26
Burden, Herbert, 155
Burke, Edmund, 114, 232n57
Bush, George W., 43, 97–98
Bushido ethic, 80–81
Bygott, David, 176–77
Byng, John, 105–8, 127, 228n18, 228n21

The Caine Mutiny, 66, 240n58
Callender, John, 19, 27–28, 29f, 165–66
Call of Duty video game, 130
camouflage, 90
Candide (Voltaire), 108
capital punishment, 14–15, 18–19, 104–9,
 154; during the Civil War, 33, 63–64,
 88–89, 137–39, 142; decimation
 practices of, 104–5; executioners for,
 119–26; ironic role of, 108; pardons
 issued for, 63–64, 88–89, 107, 139;

posthumous pardons and memorials
 for, 18, 155–59; during World War I,
 14–15, 203n45; during World War II,
 15, 19, 94, 104, 119–25, 126f, 225n76,
 233n72, 233n74
Capote, Truman, 170
The Captain of Company K (Kirkland),
 216n58
Captain Queeg (character, *Caine Mutiny*),
 66, 240n58
Carlton Brand (character, *The Coward*),
 17, 52–55, 57–58, 237n23
Catch-22 (Heller), 119
Céline, Louis-Ferdinand, 84
Chamberlain, Neville, 38
Chaplin, Charlie, 185
Churchill, Winston, 228n21
civil rights movement, 178, 208n42
Civil War, 30–34; attitudes towards
 cowardice in, 33–34, 51, 70–71, 77–78,
 91, 132–34, 209n43, 207n35, 207n37,
 220n3; black soldiers in, 33, 208n40,
 208n42; branding as punishment in,
 139–40, 236nn16–17, 236n19; capital
 punishment in, 33, 63–64, 88–89, 137,
 139, 142; "constitutional" defense for
 cowardice in, 141–44, 237n23, 238n29;
 duty and obedience in, 114–16; hiding
 and taking cover in, 88–90, 223n52,
 223n54; publicizing of cowardice in,
 55; rehabilitative punishments in,
 142–43; scholarly study of, 203n45;
 self-mutilation in, 69–70, 218nn82–83;
 unmitigated punishments of, 132–39;
 weaponry of, 86, 89–90. See also *The
 Coward: A Novel of Society and the
 Field in 1863*
Clark, John, 236n19
class burdens of war, 159–64
Clements, Samuel, 134–38, 235nn11–12
Cold War, 39–41, 210n56
Colonel Dax (character, *Paths of Glory*),
 120–21
Colossus: The Price of American Empire
 (Ferguson), 204n51
combat fatigue, 141
common cowardice, 173–80
the common good, 49, 212n14

fear-suppressing drugs, 92
female cowardice: labeling of, 62–63, 64,
    215n45; women in military service
    and, 64, 65–66
Ferguson, Niall, 204n51
Flanders Field monument, 157f
*The Folly of Fools: The Logic of Deceit and
    Self-Deception in Human Life* (Trivers),
    191
Forbes, John, 109–10
Foreign Policy Association, 38
forward panic, 84
Foucault, Michel, 144
The Four Feathers (Mason), 57, 203n43
Four Girls at Cottage City (Kelly-
    Hawkins), 62
Fowler, H. W., 9
fragging, 127, 234nn81–82
Franklin, Benjamin, 96, 226n80
Frederic Henry (character, *Farewell to
    Arms*), 38, 234n83
Freehling, William, 207n35
free will, 10–11; Davies's emphasis on,
    179, 230n40; duty to one's self and,
    127–30, 179–80, 234nn83–84; para-
    dox of external compulsion and,
    100–105. *See also* duty
French and Indian War, 23–27, 205n3,
    205n5; American insubordination
    in, 109–10; antirecruitment riots of,
    109; battle of Monongahela of, 27,
    84; conscription for, 108–9; recruit-
    ment challenges for, 24–27, 96,
    109–12, 226n82, 229n33, 229n35,
    230n43. *See also* Davies, Samuel
Freud, Sigmund, 67
From Here to Eternity (Jones), 147
Frost, Robert, 186
fundamentalism, 187

Gabriel, Richard, 202n30
galling aphid clone, 47–48
Gandhi, Mahatma, 51, 213n18
Gbowee, Leymah, 217n65
gender contexts, 49, 60–66; in depictions
    of men as women, 60–62, 64; in
    labeling of cowardice in women,

62–63, 64, 215n45, 216n54, 216n62;
    in women's responses to cowardice,
    57–60, 64–66, 214n39, 214n42
Gilchrist, Archibald, 238n29
Gilligan, James, 170
Give an Hour, 163
Glass, Charles, 203n45
Going After Cacciato: A Novel (O'Brien),
    234n83
Goodall, Jane, 176
Gordon, Lesley J., 203n45
The Great Perhaps (Meno), 211n3
Grendel (character, *Beowulf*), 49–50
Grossman, Dave, 71
guerrilla tactics, 87–88, 223n46
guilt, 51–52
Gulf War syndrome, 151, 153
gun control, 172–73

Haidt, Jonathan, 48
Haig, Douglas, 154
Haig, George, 154
Hamlet, 181
hand-to-hand combat, 72–74, 219nn95–96
Hardee, William J., 11
Harris, Mary B., 216n54
Harry Feversham (character, *The Four
    Feathers*), 57, 203n43
Harvard Union for Neutrality, 36
Harvey, J. Douglas, 14, 18
Hastings, Max, 14
head trauma, 151, 155
Hector (character, *The Four Feathers*), 60, 69
Heller, Joseph, 119
Hemingway, Ernest, 38, 147, 234n83
Henderson, Jackson, 208n42
Henry, Patrick, 231n49
Henry Fleming (character, *Red Badge of
    Courage*), 45, 52, 59–60; on absence of
    free will, 103; achievement of man-
    hood of, 74–76; panic and flight of,
    82–84, 86; wound of, 71–72
"The Hero" (Sassoon), 16
Heroes and Cowards: The Social Face of War
    (Costa and Kahn), 203n45
*Hero or Coward: Pressures Facing the Soldier
    in Battle* (Dinter), 203n45

on American materialism and
self-concern, 231n46; on Americans' motivation by profit, 111
trauma. *See* posttraumatic stress disorder
(PTSD)
traumatic brain injury, 151, 155
trenches, 89–90
Trivers, Robert, 191
Tsarnaev, Tamerlan, 44. *See also* Boston
Marathon bombings
Tucker, Wilford, 218n83
turning tail, 4–5, 58, 215n45
Twain, Mark, 192; on lynching, 173–74,
244n24; on moral cowardice, 178–79
Tyrtaeus, 71, 102

"The United States of Lyncherdom"
(Twain), 173–74, 244n24
unmanned weapons, 92, 98, 224–25n69,
224n71
urination, 66–68, 217n78
USS *Maine*, 34–35

Van Creveld, Martin, 79, 91
"The Veteran" (Crane), 74–75
victimhood, 167
Vietnam War, 40–41, 210n56; American
apathy towards, 178; draft-dodging
of, 125–28; medical diagnoses of
cowardice of, 150–51; mutinies and
fragging of, 127, 234nn81–82; PTSD
and, 153; sexuality as weapon in
protest against, 64–65
vigilante justice, 172–73
Voltaire, 108
volunteer military, 159–64

Waldron, Joseph C., 140
warfighting, 20, 48–76; battle inoculation
training for, 92; the common good
in, 48–49, 212n14; declining rates of
death in, 74; deficits of fear in, 92–94;
gendered contexts of, 49, 60–66;
guerrilla tactics in, 87–88, 223n46;
hand-to-hand combat in, 72–74,
219nn95–96; historical overview of,
23–44, 210n65; incontinence in,

66–68; indoctrination in, 118–26,
233n69; memory of, 74–76, 83,
219n97; the phalanx in, 101–3;
reciprocity with cowardice of,
50–52, 85, 99; self-mutilation and,
32–33, 69–70, 218nn82–83; shame
and guilt in, 50–60; in twentieth-
century wars, 116–17, 233n65;
unmanned weaponry of, 92, 98,
224n64, 224n71; wounding in,
68–74, 218n81, 219n93. *See also*
acts of cowardice in war; fear;
military contexts; names of specific
wars, e.g. Civil War; weaponry
war neurosis, 146, 166
War of 1812, 29–30
war weariness, 149–50
Washington, George, 23, 27–28; battle
of Monongahela of, 27, 84; on
cowardice, 49, 113–14; guerrilla
tactics of, 223n46
The Waste Land (Eliot), 192
weaponry: of the Civil War, 86, 89–90; of
nuclear war, 91–92; overkill with, 80,
221n15; robotic control of, 92, 98,
224n69, 224n71
Webber, Daniel J., 139–40
Whack, Andrew, 140
Where Have All the Soldiers Gone?
(Sheehan), 157–58
Whitman, Walt, 166
Wiley, Bell, 31
Williams, David H., 88, 174, 176, 223n54
Williams, Kayla, 65–66
Wilson, David Sloan, 212n11
Wilson, E. O., 49
Wilson, Woodrow, 35–36
Winthrop, William, 139
The Wizard of Oz, 4–5, 185, 187
Wolfe, James, 109
women: anti-war sex strikes by, 64–66,
217n65; on cowardice, 57–60; in
gendered depictions of male coward-
ice, 60–62, 64; labeling of cowardice
of, 62–63, 64, 215n45, 216n54, 216n62;
responses to male cowardice by,
57–60, 64–66, 214n39, 214n42